CIVIL LITIGATION

PRETRIAL CASE DEVELOPMENT AND DISCOVERY

Second Edition

■ ■ ■

Craig M. Roen
Adjunct Professor of Law
University of Minnesota Law School

Sharon Reich Paulsen
Vice President for Legal Affairs and General Counsel
University of Vermont

WEST
ACADEMIC
PUBLISHING

© 2016 LEG, Inc. d/b/a West Academic
© 2021 LEG, Inc. d/b/a West Academic
 444 Cedar Street, Suite 700
 St. Paul, MN 55101
 1-877-888-1330

West, West Academic Publishing, and West Academic are trademarks of West Publishing Corporation, used under license.

Printed in the United States of America

ISBN: 978-1-64708-475-2

To Kathy, and in memory of Peter.

— C.M.R.

To my husband.

— S.R.P.

ACKNOWLEDGMENTS

The authors gratefully acknowledge the contributions of everyone who participated in the creation of this book, and the patience of our families while we spent more time than expected on this project.

We would like to thank West Academic and particularly Louis Higgins for recognizing the importance of offering a practical guide, from a practitioner's perspective, on best practices for civil litigation.

Stacy Nordstrom provided invaluable assistance with book design and formatting. Leon Wells and Sam Andre, University of Minnesota Law School students, made sure that we relied on current law and that our citations were all in proper form. Additional thanks to Kathleen Bjornson for proofreading.

George Socha of EDRM assisted with the chapter on electronically stored information as did Michael Hannon. Connie Martin was very helpful with the chapter on litigation technology.

Finally, we both would like to thank our mentors and all of the co-counsel and opposing counsel with and against whom we have litigated, from all of whom we learned (and sometimes painfully learned) invaluable lessons.

INTRODUCTION

_____

What this book is, and is not about

The purpose of this book is to introduce you to concepts, strategies and skills necessary to become an able litigator. Though the litigation process is intended to produce fair resolutions of disputes, outcomes frequently are affected by the relative skills of counsel. Indeed, sometimes those skills determine outcomes.

This book will introduce you to a conceptual framework for thinking strategically and tactically about case development and discovery. It will also guide you through the thicket of rules that govern civil litigation. Not least, this book is intended to make you think about civil litigation in a holistic way: case development and discovery are made up of many interrelated functions, each of which, depending upon how they are executed, will support or undermine the entire enterprise.

This book is *not* a book on civil procedure. You will have studied the subject during your first year of law school. The rules of civil procedure are just part of the whole. They do not tell you how to litigate. Though we delve into many of the rules out of necessity, this is not a survey course of those rules.

Nor does this book delve into the intricacies of pleading practice, jurisdictional questions, choice of law. or remedies. Each of these subjects could (and do) fill volumes of legal texts, compendia and scholarly articles. This is a book about developing the story you wish to tell and creating a record that allows you to tell it.

Litigators are storytellers

Good litigators know that a story, well told and with a compelling narrative, is more likely to carry the day than subjecting the listener to a bland recitation of the evidence. Will the judge be persuaded to rule your way? Does the story convince *opposing counsel* that the case should be resolved in a manner favorable to your client? And barring settlement or dismissal, the key question is: Will the jury be persuaded to find in favor of your client?

Yet you can't tell the story you wish to tell without a record that supports every part of it. The litigator must *develop* the story and *develop* the evidence upon which the story will be based. Meanwhile, your opposing counsel is (or at least should be) developing a story and the record that likely differs from yours. Who has the better story? Who has developed the record necessary to fully tell the story? It doesn't just happen: it takes thought, planning and careful execution. Hence, the title of the book.

One of the many challenges all litigators face is that disputes are not black and white, even though it may seem that way to the client. Rather, there is uncertainty throughout the course of any lawsuit. As a litigator, you must become comfortable dealing with shifting facts and changing circumstances. In addition, you must be able to candidly advise the client based upon a dispassionate evaluation of the case as it develops.

Discovery practice is central to case development. It is where most litigators spend the bulk of their time. Discovery is more than just an exercise in gathering information; it is essential to developing a compelling case. Depending on how effectively it is conducted, the discovery phase of litigation can make the difference between winning and losing. This book will introduce you to strategic and tactical approaches to discovery practice geared toward:

- Developing an evidentiary record to support your case;

- Probing the adverse party's case in a thorough and efficient manner;

- Narrowing and clarifying the issues;

- Valuing the case; and, if necessary;

- Trying the case.

Ultimately, the goal is to "win" your client's case

Let's be clear: It isn't your case; it's the client's. Your job is to "win" your client's case. But what does it mean to win? Winning may come in the form of a favorable settlement, or dismissal of the case, or receiving a dispositive ruling in your client's favor, or, ultimately, convincing the finder of fact that your client should prevail. It may mean vindication for the client; it may be that justice is served.

For the lawyer, at the end of the day, winning is serving your client well. Your job is all about maximizing the chances of a successful outcome. This book is about helping you to help your client win their case. With this in mind, we begin.

A note about gender references

Throughout this book you will see references to "he" or "him," "she" or "her," or "they." None of the gender references are intended to imply a substantive difference among those references in the book.

SUMMARY OF CONTENTS

TABLE OF CONTENTS

CIVIL LITIGATION
PRETRIAL CASE DEVELOPMENT AND DISCOVERY

Second Edition

CHAPTER 1

CIVIL LITIGATION: AN OVERVIEW

■ ■ ■

A. INTRODUCTION

It is litigation counsel's job, among other things, to create a winning case within the strictures of the Rules of Civil Procedure (hereinafter "the Rules") and in a manner consistent with counsel's ethical obligations. "Winning" may mean obtaining a favorable settlement, a favorable disposition through a summary judgment motion, or a favorable trial verdict. Regardless, the job of litigation counsel is to create a persuasive case that advances the client's goals.

There are many litigation styles: aggressive or convivial, cooperative or bare-knuckled, theatrical or plodding. There is no single right way to litigate a case. But there are fundamentals and practical methods that should be used in every case in order to build a compelling narrative. Regardless of your style or personality type, the more effectively you develop your case, the more likely you are to achieve a favorable outcome for your client.

The primary focus of this book is case development and discovery practice. The two functions are interdependent: a competent litigator cannot fully develop a case without engaging in discovery,[1] nor can a litigator execute discovery in a considered manner without an overall case development plan. This book provides an overview of both, including specific methods, strategies and tactics applicable to the wide range of civil cases, from a simple auto crash to a multi-party, complex commercial dispute.

B. CASE DEVELOPMENT VS. DISCOVERY PRACTICE

It is important at the outset to understand what we mean by the terms case development and discovery practice. The two are separate, but related, processes.

Case development is the overall process of turning a client's problem into a legally cognizable and compelling case ready to be tried. It is the

---

[1] The exception to this general rule is if you are representing the defendant and are successful with a motion to dismiss under FED. R. CIV. P. 12.

process of designing and building the case, hopefully in a logical, methodical and efficient manner. It is the means by which counsel envisions what the fully realized case looks like and the plan by which she will construct it. It begins before filing the first pleading and continues to settlement, summary judgment, or trial.

In a trial skills course or a moot court program, a case file is provided to the student, including relevant law and facts. The student then advocates within the limits of the law and facts that are provided. Real cases, on the other hand, are not handed to counsel fully formed. They must be developed. The creativity and effort that counsel invests in case development will have a direct bearing on the cohesiveness and persuasiveness of the client's case.

In the event the case goes to trial, case development is what leads, ultimately, to closing argument. In order to make a compelling closing argument, what does counsel need? Fundamentally, there must be an evidentiary record that contains all of the factual support necessary to tell a persuasive story and meet the burden of proof. Case development is the planning and process by which counsel pieces together the facts and the law to create a compelling narrative for closing argument. Similarly, if the case can be decided by motion, case development is the means by which counsel constructs arguments that are case-dispositive.

Discovery practice is a necessary, but not sufficient, requirement for case development. Discovery provides for the exchange of information relating to the parties' claims and defenses. It affords the opportunity to learn about the adverse party's claims and supporting evidence, and to probe the strengths and weaknesses of the opposing party's case. Second, discovery may enable the parties to narrow issues by identifying those claims with merit and eliminating those without. As the case progresses, counsel should be able to hone in on the essential nature of the dispute and focus on those issues central to the overall case. Third, and perhaps most important, discovery practice aids case development.[2] If case development relates to developing the story to be told, discovery is an essential means

---

[2]   At least one court has taken a decidedly darker view of civil litigators and discovery practice. In Malautea v. Suzuki Motor Co., the court observed:

> The discovery rules in particular were intended to promote the search for truth that is the heart of our judicial system. However, the success with which the rules are applied toward this search for truth greatly depends on the professionalism and integrity of the attorneys involved. Therefore, it is appalling that attorneys . . . routinely twist the discovery rules into some of "the most powerful weapons in the arsenal of those who abuse the adversary system for the sole benefit of their clients." . . . An attorney's duty to a client can never outweigh his or her responsibility to see that our system of justice functions smoothly . . . [T]oo many attorneys . . . have allowed the objectives of the client to override their ancient duties as officers of the court.

987 F.2d 1536, 1546–47 (11th Cir. 1993) (internal citations omitted).

by which the evidence to tell the story is gathered and created.[3] Discovery, when properly conducted, is not like randomly casting a net into the water in hopes of catching something for dinner. Instead, to conduct effective discovery you must anticipate your needs and then use the tools of discovery to achieve your specific objectives.

C. THE ATTRIBUTES OF AN EFFECTIVE LITIGATOR

Effective case development and discovery practice can win cases. Aimless litigating and haphazard discovery practice is expensive, unproductive, and usually leads to poor outcomes. Effective litigators know that. They are meticulous and strategic about every decision. They have mastered and can use both the Rules of Civil Procedure and the Rules of Evidence to their advantage.[4]

An effective litigator must be able to:

- Gather, organize and quickly master a wide range of case-specific information in order to create a coherent narrative that not only satisfies the elements of any given cause of action or defense, but is compelling to a judge and jury;

- Fulfill two distinct roles through every step of the case: that of an objective and trusted advisor to the client, and separately, that of a zealous advocate with the skill to persuade, both orally and in writing;

- Think strategically and tactically, often in "real time";

- Assess the risks associated with going to trial;

- Value cases for settlement purposes;

- Be an active student of human behavior so as to better understand individual motivations and group dynamics;

- Roll with the punches; and

- Establish and maintain credibility and high ethical standards in every case.

---

[3] Yes, *created*. Discovery allows counsel to create evidence that did not previously exist. For example, by taking a party's deposition, the responses of the party are admissions that, if relevant, may be used at trial. Or, by having physical objects photographed during discovery, counsel may be able to create highly persuasive exhibits.

[4] Knowing what facts to gather is only part of case development. Counsel also must know how those facts will *get into evidence* at trial. This requires tailoring discovery not only to get the facts, but also to get the information that will make those facts admissible. In other words, effective litigators are mindful of the Rules of Evidence not only during trial, but also during discovery.

These attributes may seem self-evident, but in the rough-and-tumble of civil litigation, with its time and financial pressures, client demands, scheduling conflicts, interpersonal conflicts, and the ongoing effort of opposing counsel to counter everything you are trying to accomplish, it is easy to neglect the fundamentals of good litigation practice.

Too often, lawyers simply do what they have always done: launch into discovery in a rote fashion, without a clear set of objectives or a plan to achieve them.[5] A haphazard approach leaves to chance whether counsel will be able to cobble together a coherent case, or one that can even survive a dispositive motion. It virtually guarantees that opportunities will be lost and advantages foregone.

D. THE LITIGATION PROCESS

The following flowchart represents a simplified, but typical, case from the first client meeting until trial. This is for illustrative purposes only. There is no uniform litigation process; the Rules allow for a great deal of flexibility. Depending upon the type of case, its complexity, and the overall strategies and tactics counsel may choose to employ, a given case may proceed in any number of ways.

As you skim over the flowchart, consider how the case develops through the entire process. Each step in the process requires forethought and careful planning, whether it is formulating a discovery plan, doing legal research, interviewing witnesses, drafting and responding to written discovery, taking and defending depositions, attempting to enforce discovery rights, or worrying about what has been missed.

---

[5] *See* Blank v. Ronson Corp., 97 F.R.D. 744, 745 (S.D.N.Y. 1983) ("There is, in this vast expanse of paper, no indication that any lawyer (or even moderately competent paralegal) ever looked at the interrogatories or at the answers. It is, on the contrary, obvious that they have all been produced by some word-processing machine's memory of prior litigation."); Craig B. Shaffer & Ryan T. Shaffer, *Looking Past the Debate: Proposed Revisions to the Federal Rules of Civil Procedure*, 7 FED. CTS. L. REV. 178, 196 n.95 (Sept. 2013) (citing Blank v. Ronson Corp.).

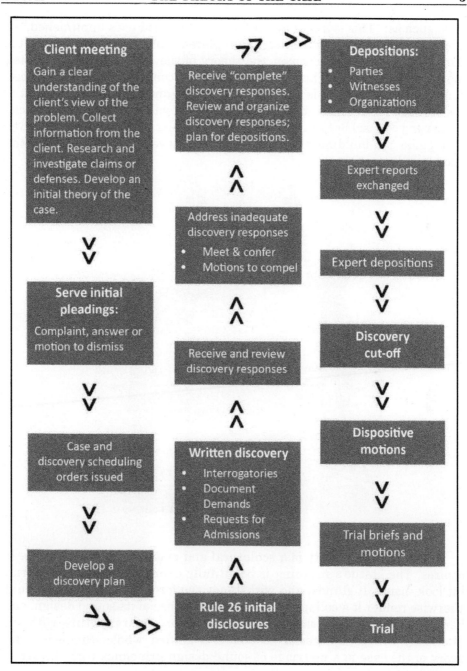

Illus. 1-1.

E. THE THEORY OF THE CASE

We refer to "the theory of the case" throughout this book. As it is commonly understood, the theory of the case contains a descriptor with a hook, such as: "This is a case about how no good deed goes unpunished," or "This is a case about how the defendant placed profits over people." That is fine, so far as it goes. However, the theory of the case is more than a tag line or even a theme. The theory of the case contains the major design elements of the case. It is akin to a blueprint, one that ensures that the case has been well constructed—that it not only will withstand the attacks of opposing counsel but also will be compelling.[6] At the same time, it serves as a guide for building the case, i.e., case development. Consider the following illustration:

Illus. 1-2.

The Statue of Liberty is a sculptural and engineering masterpiece. It inspires. The statue's meaning is beautifully expressed through its form. But look inside. It stands, and withstands the forces of nature that would otherwise render it a collapsed pile of iron, because of its sound design, one that intelligently joins the supporting interior superstructure with its artistically rendered exterior to create a unified whole. Similarly, the theory of the case is a marriage of sound design principles with the art of storytelling.

---

[6]   JAMES W. McELHANEY, TRIAL NOTEBOOK 78 (3d ed. 1994) ("The theory of the case is the basic underlying idea that explains not only the legal theory and factual background, but also ties as much of the evidence as possible into a coherent and credible whole. Whether it is simple and unadorned or subtle and sophisticated, the theory of the case is a product of the advocate. It is the basic concept around which everything else revolves.").

> **The theory of the case should include three elements:**
> 1. The law;
> 2. Evidence that satisfies the requirements of the law; and
> 3. A compelling story that conveys an imperative.

All three elements of the theory of the case are interdependent. As claims or defenses are identified, the evidence necessary to support each must be gathered through both informal and formal discovery. As evidence is gathered, that evidence helps to determine which claims and defenses are available, and to define and support the story. As the story takes shape, it guides counsel's determination of which evidence to highlight, which to downplay or disregard, and which to attempt to neutralize or explain away. As discovery progresses, counsel must constantly re-evaluate and refine the story, not only to ensure that the available evidence supports the story, but also to create a story that rings true.

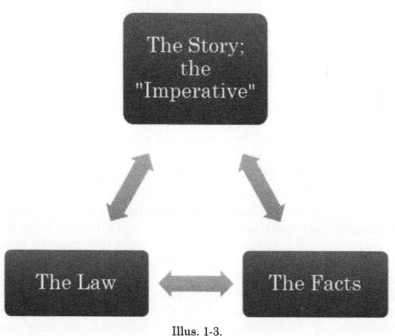

Illus. 1-3.

1. THE LAW

Researching the applicable law is a critical component of developing the theory of the case. Potential causes of action or defenses, or even potential parties, are not always self-evident. Further, counsel must make strategic and tactical decisions regarding which claims or defenses to assert, for instance, whether to take a "shotgun" or "rifle" approach in the pleadings.[7] Moreover, in more complex cases, viable causes of action or defenses may not be apparent until the facts are more fully developed. Yet, the facts may not be fully developed until after counsel serves the initial pleadings and commences discovery. This is a chicken-and-egg problem that often arises in civil cases. It means that both factual and legal research are intertwined and ongoing, and that counsel must be alert and flexible enough to modify and refine the theory of the case over the course of the litigation.

2.   THE FACTS

Each element of a given claim or defense must have sufficient evidentiary support in order to survive a dispositive motion. That evidentiary support must be of a kind that satisfies the requirements of the Rules of Evidence. That evidence may come from a variety of sources: the client, counsel's initial investigation, experts or discovery. Indeed, much of what litigators do relates to building an evidentiary record in support of the case. A challenge in constructing a case is that some relevant information is likely in the possession of the adverse party. This information may be unavailable and even unknowable until the case is formally joined and discovery is begun.

3.   THE STORY

Humans are able to make better sense of complex fact patterns when they receive those facts within the context of a coherent narrative. Stories give meaning to facts; they link cause and effect; they keep the listener engaged and interested; they are essential to the art of persuasion. Conversely, a case that lacks a narrative will present as a disassociated jumble of information.

In addition to being coherent, the story must convey an *imperative*. The imperative may speak to emotion, morals and ethics, or logic. It is the aspect of the case that conveys a sense of *fairness* that must be upheld or *injustice* that must be remedied. It is the moral of the story. The imperative is dependent on the nature of the case and the evidence. It can be informed by something as simple as the "Golden Rule," or any number of culturally shared norms. Getting this part of the theory of the case right can be a creative challenge. But getting it right is essential: the story, and its imperative, must resonate with the judge and jury.

Must the story track with what "actually happened"? Most disputes are not black and white. There are many shades of gray and varying points of view. What is true to the client may seem like fiction to the adverse

---

[7]   FED. R. CIV. P. 11 requires that counsel have a good faith basis to assert claims and defenses. Therefore, it is incumbent on counsel to determine whether factual and legal support exists for any given claim or defense before making it. Counsel who fails to meet this obligation risks imposition of sanctions.

party. Your job as counsel is to advocate for your client's truth within the parameters of your ethical obligations. Within that limitation, you are free to emphasize "good facts," neutralize "bad facts," and otherwise tell a story that is coherent, compelling, and that satisfies the requirements of the law. In other words, the litigator must tell a believable story that marries the requirements of the law to the evidence. Short of that, it is just a story, not a case.

F. THE LIABILITY CASE AND THE DAMAGES CASE

Within virtually every civil case, there are two separate but related cases: the "liability case" and the "damages case" (or, in cases where solely equitable relief is sought, the "remedy case"). As to the liability case, the question is: who did what wrong to whom? As to the damages case, the question is: what is the resulting harm and how may it be compensated? Whether you represent the plaintiff or the defendant, you will need to develop a case that answers each of these questions in a manner favorable to your client.

Consider an auto crash case. Plaintiff accuses defendant of running a red light and striking plaintiff's car. To prevail on a claim of negligence, plaintiff must establish both the liability case (the existence of a duty, a breach of that duty, and causation) and the damages case (the harm that resulted). To avoid dismissal, plaintiff must present admissible evidence to support each element of the negligence claim and a separate body of evidence to prove the nature and extent of the harm defendant's negligence caused. If the plaintiff succeeds in presenting a *prima facie* case, the defendant must present admissible evidence to rebut at least one of the elements of the liability case, and should similarly present evidence to rebut or to minimize the damages case.

Recognizing that there are actually two "cases" provides the litigator a measure of clarity in terms of: (1) overall case development, (2) developing a theory of the case, (3) developing a discovery plan, and (4) valuing the case.

Regarding case valuation, a litigator cannot fulfill the critical role of settlement advisor without having first performed an accurate assessment of the strengths and weaknesses of the client's case. Though it may seem like a digression from our subject, a short primer on case valuation will help illustrate the connection between case development and case value.

G. VALUING THE CASE: LITIGATION AS A MEANS TO ASSESS RISK

Ninety-seven percent of all civil cases are resolved before trial.[8] To best protect a client's interests, whether plaintiff or defendant, a litigator must know how to assess risk and value cases for settlement purposes.

When the age-old complaint is voiced, sometimes with a huff, that most civil cases settle only after they reach the courthouse steps, the implied criticism betrays an ignorance of what civil litigation essentially is: an ongoing process of gathering and evaluating information in order both to prepare for trial and to assess the risks associated with going to trial. *The more information counsel has, the more likely that there can be an informed valuation of the case.* Sometimes a case simply cannot be settled until all the salient facts are known.[9] Case development and discovery play a vital role in aiding counsel to assess risk, value the case, and advise the client as to the prospects of settlement.

Case valuation is inherently subjective—more art than science. There usually are multiple variables that bear upon the value of a case, many of which are almost impossible to quantify, e.g., how the parties may present to a jury, or whether the case will be tried in a "plaintiff friendly" or "defense friendly" venue. However, that does not mean that case valuation lacks method. One approach is to begin with two fundamental questions:

1. What is the strength of the liability case?

2. What is the strength of the damages case?

Answers to these questions are usually informed by evidence gathered through informal and formal discovery. However, there are times when counsel must answer these questions without the benefit of full discovery. Courts have increasingly pushed for early case resolution through court-initiated settlement conferences or mediation. This often requires the parties to assess their cases prior to discovering all the relevant facts. The further down the road the case progresses, and the more completely it is developed, the more information counsel will have to evaluate the case. The tradeoff, of course, is that the longer a case is litigated, the more expensive it becomes.

---

[8] *See Government survey shows 97 percent of civil cases settled,* PHOENIX BUS. J. (May 30, 2004, 9:00 PM), https://www.bizjournals.com/phoenix/stories/2004/05/31/newscolumn5.html. (citing U.S. Department of Justice study of state courts in the nation's 75 largest counties). The percentage of cases that terminate prior to trial is even higher in federal court. *See* Case Statistics Data Tables, Table C-4, *U.S. District Courts—Civil Cases Terminated, by Nature of Suit and Action Taken* (annual reports available for 12-month periods ending March 31), https://www.uscourts. gov/statistics-reports/caseload-statistics-data-tables?tn=C-4&pn=79&t=All&m%5Bvalue%5D%5 Bmonth%5D=&y%5Bvalue%5D%5Byear%5D=.

[9] Sometimes the salient facts go beyond what can be learned through discovery, such as who the trial judge is, and what kind of jury gets empaneled.

The following illustrates how counsel may value a case by considering the strengths of the liability case in relation to the strengths of the damages case. Assume a case in which the potential damages are $1 million. Further, assume that counsel has evaluated the case and determined there is a 50/50 chance of the plaintiff establishing liability on the part of the defendant. If both parties think that plaintiff has a roughly 50% chance of convincing a jury that defendant is at fault, and both parties think the likely damages award will be $1 million, then a simplistic valuation calculation can be made: $1 million × .5 (i.e., 50%) = $500,000. If the parties are rational actors, and there are no material factors beyond the merits of the case bearing on the decision to settle,[10] the case can be said to have an approximate value of $500,000, and a rational outcome would be for the case to settle in that range.[11]

Now assume that counsel views the case as a "case of liability," that is, the defendant is highly likely to be found liable by a jury, but counsel believes that a jury is likely to award damages in the $100,000 to $300,000 range rather than $1 million. Settlement might logically be reached in that same dollar range. Whether the case settles closer to $100,000 or $300,000 will depend on other factors, such as the added cost of going to trial, the risk of adverse publicity, the client's tolerance for risk, the negotiation skills of counsel and so forth.

It is when the parties, or more typically their counsel, do not similarly assess the liability case and/or the damages case that the likelihood of trial increases. Often, when a civil case actually gets to a trial it is because one or both sides have incorrectly valued the case. To the extent the parties similarly assess the risks, the chances of settlement increase; to the extent they diverge, the chances of trial increase. In any event, counsel must be able to advise the client using some *rational* basis to assess the liability case, the damages case, and the cost and risks associated with trial. It is the litigation process, and particularly discovery, that informs the lawyer's continuous analysis of the value of the case.

---

[10] The illustration above should be viewed as a *starting point* to valuing a case. There are other considerations that go into case valuation, including, for example, avoiding additional legal fees, ending the disruption to the lives of the litigants, and so forth. Further, there are times when other considerations trump the valuation process, such as a litigant who would rather try the case and risk a big loss than settle because of concerns about appearing to be an "easy target" in future cases, or because the litigant is sending some other message that has little to do with the merits of the particular case.

[11] We offer this simplified approach for purposes of providing an introduction to case valuation. There are volumes written on risk assessment and management, and dispute resolution theories. *See, e.g.*, Russell Korobkin, *A Positive Theory of Legal Negotiation*, 88 GEO. L.J. 1789, 1795 (2000) (providing information on Best Alternative to a Negotiated Agreement, or BATNAs); Ian Ayres, *Playing Games with the Law*, 42 STAN. L. REV. 1291 (1990) (discussing game theory).

H. THE RELATIONSHIP AMONG CASE DEVELOPMENT, THEORY OF THE CASE, DISCOVERY PRACTICE AND CLOSING ARGUMENT

Question: When the demand is $10 million and the offer is $0, what does that make you?

Answer: A trial lawyer.

Sometimes cases cannot be settled. Sometimes they go to trial. Closing argument at trial is the distillation of all that precedes it, from the initial client meeting through pretrial litigation and discovery, the trial, right up to charging the jury. Closing argument is the compelling story; *it is the theory of the case fully realized*: the law, the supporting facts, and the story with its imperative.

The body of evidence available during closing argument depends on how well you developed the case. Effective case development, in turn, requires purposeful and effective discovery practice. Aimless litigating and haphazard or rote discovery practice loses cases and compromises the opportunity for more favorable settlement terms. Effective case development and discovery practice wins cases and produces more favorable settlements.

I. ETHICAL CONSIDERATIONS: AN OVERVIEW

Lawyers are subject to rules of ethics[12] as well as, one would hope, a personal sense of right and wrong. Ethical challenges in the litigation context are common given the inherent tension between zealously advocating for the client while at the same time dealing fairly and honestly with the adverse party and opposing counsel.[13] For example, what if the client insists that counsel take an extremely aggressive litigation posture, must the lawyer comply with the client's wishes? What if counsel believes that the client's motive in pursuing litigation is to harass the adverse party?[14] What if the client wants counsel to assert "boilerplate" objections to virtually all written discovery? Is this practice ethical, or is it actually intended to thwart legitimate discovery?[15] What if the client's deposition testimony is at odds with what he told counsel under protection of the

---

[12] As we go forward, when addressing ethical issues, we will refer to the American Bar Association's Model Rules of Professional Conduct.

[13] MODEL RULES OF PROF'L CONDUCT pmbl., ¶ 9 (2020) ("Virtually all difficult ethical problems arise from conflict between a lawyer's responsibilities to clients, to the legal system and to the lawyer's own interest in remaining an ethical person while earning a satisfactory living.").

[14] *See id.* pmbl., ¶ 5; *see also id.* R. 4.4.

[15] *See id.* R. 3.4(d).

attorney/client privilege?[16] For each ethical issue that arises, you are required to exercise independent judgment,[17] and to rely upon your own conscience.[18]

Sadly, civil litigation is rife with bad behavior by litigants and their counsel. It is human nature to want to respond in kind to those who are disrespectful or who engage in gamesmanship. Resist the impulse. An adverse party's misconduct, or that of their lawyer, is not a license to lie, cheat or bully. Further, bad behavior in the litigation context has a way of coming back to bite the miscreant. Losing credibility with opposing counsel or the judge or the jury undermines the lawyer's ability to persuade, which in turn does a disservice to the client. And once credibility is lost, it is very hard to get back.

---

[16] *See id.* R. 3.3(a)(3).

[17] *Id.* R. 2.1.

[18] *Id.* pmbl., ¶ 7.

CHAPTER 2

CASE DEVELOPMENT: AN OVERVIEW

■ ■ ■

Civil litigation is very much an exercise in project management. Like other professional projects, it should follow a planned, logical progression designed to achieve clearly defined goals. The challenge is that, unlike other professional projects, civil litigation takes place in an adversarial system, with an opposing party actively attempting to prevent you from reaching your goals.

Additional challenges include the raft of arcane and often opaque rules that every litigator must follow, and judges who may or may not be inclined to indulge counsel's preferences for how the case should progress. In other words, the project that is case development (and discovery) usually takes place under challenging conditions subject to external forces sometimes beyond counsel's control.

There are two stages of case development: the informal phase and the formal phase. The first phase is largely investigatory and is conducted without the benefit of compelled discovery under the Rules. The second phase, the formal/adversarial phase, allows counsel the use of subpoenas, written discovery demands, depositions, and other discovery tools.

A. CASE DEVELOPMENT: THE INFORMAL PHASE

A new client comes to you with a problem. He may want you to file a lawsuit as a means to address the problem. Or he may have been served with a summons and complaint and needs to be defended. Either way, the dispute may arise from facts and circumstances with which you have little or no familiarity. It may involve claims and defenses you have not learned about in law school. Where to begin?[1]

1. BECOME AN EXPERT ON YOUR CLIENT'S PROBLEM

Case development begins with counsel's initial investigation. At the outset, you may not know enough about the subject matter of the case to

---

[1] Before launching into your investigation, it is important that you (1) first receive permission from the client to begin work, and (2) establish a budget for the work to be performed. This is usually accomplished by having the client sign a retainer agreement. It also is wise to follow up with a letter to the client confirming that he or she has authorized you to take specific actions on behalf of the client.

even ask the client the right questions, much less be able to identify potential causes of action or defenses. *Therefore, case development begins with you, as counsel, educating yourself on the subject matter of the dispute.* The more you know about the subject matter, the more likely you will be in a position to meaningfully evaluate the case.

Consider the following hypothetical:

A new client comes to you with the following problem. She recently started working as a sales person for a company called Très Cool Software in New York. The company develops and sells special effects software to film production companies worldwide. Yesterday, she received a letter from La-De-Dah Software Co., her previous California-based employer. The letter alleges that she is in violation of a non-compete agreement with La-De-Dah that prohibits her from working for direct competitors for two years. The letter further alleges she has improperly taken confidential information from Très Cool, also in violation of the agreement.

La-De-Dah states it will obtain a temporary restraining order prohibiting your client from contacting any existing or potential users of special effects software unless she immediately ceases all her marketing activities on behalf of Très Cool. The TRO would effectively prohibit her from doing the job she was hired for by Très Cool. As a result, Très Cool has placed her on unpaid leave.

The client tells you, contrary to the allegations in the letter, Très Cool is not a competitor of Le-De-Dah in that the former sells software for sci-fi movies, while the latter sells software for horror movies. She also tells you that she signed the agreement three months before leaving La-De-Dah and that she received no additional compensation for signing it even though the agreement, which is attached to the letter, specifically states that consideration was provided in exchange for her agreement to abide by the terms of the agreement. Finally, La-De-Dah states that its remedies will be sought in California state court, though the client now lives in New York.

Any number of legal and factual questions are occurring to you as you anticipate litigation, including:

- What is the proper jurisdiction?

- What is required to obtain a TRO? How can it be set aside?

- Is the non-compete agreement unenforceable for lack of consideration?

- Are the sci-fi and horror filmmaking markets separate?

- Has La-De-Dah interfered with the client's contractual relationship with her current employer, thus giving rise to a counter-claim?

You continue to ask questions of your client and as you do so, you are becoming increasingly indignant that Le-De-Dah would afflict her with this completely meritless and clearly malicious threat. Injustices like this one are precisely the reason you went to law school. Your mind goes to building an argument for Rule 11 sanctions against La-De-Dah and its lawyer. You are already mentally drafting your motion for dismissal of the action and for sanctions.

Hold on!

Your job is to *advise* the client of potential goals and outcomes *after* you have done your homework. Always remember that the case is the *client's* case, not *your* case. And in order to properly advise the client, you need to know what you are talking about. How does one become an expert on the client's problem? There are a number of ways, all necessary.

a.   Learn the Facts

There are many means by which to investigate the facts of a given dispute before the commencement of formal discovery. How you go about conducting an investigation is largely dependent upon the nature of the case, available resources, and counsel's imagination. Following are some of the most common.

i.   *Start with the Client*

Learning the facts begins with the client. Interview the client. However, before launching into a full-blown, exhaustive interview, it is important to develop a relationship of trust. The client needs to know that what he tells you is protected by the attorney-client privilege, that your job is not to judge the client but to represent his interests and that it is essential for him to tell you all he knows about the potential dispute—that holding back on "bad facts" will undermine your effectiveness.

Gather and review any information, documents, photographs, email, and other potentially relevant things in the client's possession.[2] A common challenge is that the client may not know what is potentially relevant, may intentionally or unintentionally color the story, and may try to hide what the client thinks are bad or embarrassing facts. So probe and cross-examine. Be (inwardly) skeptical of what you are being told. Inquire as to

---

[2]   You must ensure that the client does not intentionally or inadvertently dispose of relevant evidence. One way to protect your client (and yourself) from an accusation of failing to preserve relevant evidence is by advising the client, in writing, that it must preserve all relevant documents. Failure to do so may result in sanctions against the client *and you*. This is particularly true with regard to electronically stored information, which we will discuss further in Chapter 10.

corroborating evidence. You need *all* the information, good and bad. The last thing you want is to provide advice without knowing all the facts, or to be surprised later by information you neglected to seek and your client neglected to volunteer. Ask the hard questions and ask them early. Exhaust your client's knowledge, then verify whenever possible what the client says.

As your investigation progresses, you likely will return to the client with additional questions, additional requests for documents or other forms of evidence to which the client may have access. The client should be prepared and willing to provide to you whatever information you seek. A client who balks, stalls, or otherwise impedes your ability to investigate the client's claims or defenses is one who likely will be a problematic client down the road. Beware of the client who does not fully cooperate in the development of their own case.

ii. Use the Internet and Other Publicly Available Information

There is a mindboggling amount of information available on the internet. Company web sites, social networks, chat rooms, and any number of other sources can provide a trove of useful information about both your client and the adverse party. Google your client, the adverse party, witnesses, and products or services that might be in issue. Internet research also may lead to articles on the subject matter of the dispute, which in turn may help you to identify potential experts.

Similarly, check governmental and other public sources of information about your client, other parties or potential witnesses, and the subject matter of the dispute. For example, employment discrimination cases are often investigated by the EEOC or state equivalent agencies. Wage and labor disputes may be investigated by the NLRB. Accidents involving cars may be the subject of local or state police investigations. Accidents involving trains are investigated by the NTSB. Accidents in the work place are sometimes investigated by OSHA. Pollution-related cases may be investigated by the EPA or its state equivalent. Much of the work by these governmental investigatory agencies is available through public records and can readily be obtained by counsel.

In addition, publicly-traded companies are required to publish certain financial information, which usually can be found on their web sites and in their annual reports. Look for press releases. Some information can be obtained online for a fee through such organizations as Dunn & Bradstreet.

iii. Interview Witnesses

You do not need to wait for formal discovery in order to gather information from potential witnesses, unless those potential witnesses are represented by counsel.[3] In fact, talking with witnesses can be a vital component of the informal phase of case development and can yield information critical to early decisions regarding potential causes of action or defenses. These early interviews also provide extremely useful assessments of these potential witnesses. There are a few cautions to keep in mind, however.

Everything you discuss with a non-client witness is discoverable. Neither the attorney-client privilege nor work product doctrine protect the substance of the information exchanged, although the attorney's personal notes should be protected. So be careful about what you say—you may hear it repeated later in a deposition, or learn that it was shared with an adverse party and its counsel.

If the witness has information helpful to you, you may want to consider locking him or her in by having the witness sign an affidavit. If you do not, and if the witness subsequently has a "different recollection," there may not be much you can do about it.

Advise the witness that opposing counsel may contact them and that it is their choice whether to talk with opposing counsel (absent a subpoena). Advise the witness that opposing counsel may ask about the conversation you had with the witness. Tell the witness that anything the witness chooses to say should, of course, be truthful. And let the witness know that if you need him or her to testify at a deposition or trial, you will contact the witness before you serve him or her with a subpoena.

Finally, at all times be mindful that you should be cultivating a good relationship with the witness. Be courteous. It is more likely the witness will want to help you if you make a human connection.

iv. *Make Friends with a Librarian*

Some of the smartest, most inquisitive and creative researchers are librarians. Good research and reference librarians seem to have a detective's instincts. Many of them work in local public libraries and public university libraries.[4] Their knowledge of available sources of information can be a goldmine for litigators. And if they do not know where to find

---

[3]   If the adverse party is an organization, there are ethical limits regarding which employees you may speak with on your own. The ABA Model Rules of Professional Conduct prohibit counsel from attempting to contact management-level employees, any person whose act or omission may be imputed to the organization (such as an agent), or any person whose communication may be treated as an admission of the organization. MODEL RULES OF PROF'L CONDUCT R. 4.2 cmt. 7.

[4]   Once upon a time, lawyers spent much of their time in libraries. They are buildings filled with books. Nowadays, we have computers and the Internet. What once may have taken days rummaging through stacks of a university library system can readily be obtained online in minutes. Nonetheless, your preliminary research may lead you to places such as libraries or government offices, or cause you to realize that you need to interview people with knowledge that is not found in print or on the Internet.

certain information, they usually know some other librarian who does. Use librarians as a research tool.

There are reference libraries, medical libraries, engineering libraries, map libraries and on and on. Not everything is online (yet). Sometimes it is necessary to actually go to a library and find information that is still in its tangible form. Librarians can save you time and direct you to information that you otherwise would never find. So, make friends with a librarian.

v. Consult with an Expert

The Rules distinguish between consulting experts and testifying experts.[5] As to the former, the Rules cloak the work of consulting experts with attorney work product protection. Retaining a consulting expert early in the process of case development can be valuable and even essential. Some matters are so factually complex or obscure as to require counsel to bring in an expert who can help make sense of the circumstances.

Retaining a consulting expert early in the development of a case can lead to a number of advantages, including assistance with:

- Early evaluation of the strengths and weaknesses of the liability case (by a liability expert) and the damages case (by a damages expert);

- Gathering evidence—the expert may have sources of information not otherwise readily available;

- Inspecting, testing, examining, or otherwise analyzing physical evidence, digital information, or other evidence;

- Creating an overall case development plan and theory of the case;

- Planning specific, targeted discovery.

The downside is that experts are expensive. Depending upon the size of the case and the litigation budget authorized by the client, the cost of a consulting expert may be prohibitive. This is one of the difficult realities faced by litigation counsel and their clients: litigation is expensive. If you are not careful, the cost of developing a case can exceed the value of the case. Therefore, it is necessary for counsel to determine *before* retaining a consulting expert whether it will be a cost-effective or cost-prohibitive case expense.

How do you find a consulting expert? Talk to other lawyers. Review the pertinent literature for authorities on a given subject. It may be as simple as doing a Google search. You should also contact your local bar association, many of which maintain databases on experts. And do not

---

[5]   *See* FED. R. CIV. P. 26(b)(4).

forget about the local library or law library. A background investigation and candid review of a given expert's skills, knowledge, billing practices and so forth can save you a lot of aggravation.

However you locate consulting experts, do not be shy about interviewing several of them. Make sure you will be comfortable with the expert, that you will have a good working relationship, and that the expert will be responsive to your questions and your client's needs.[6]

vi. Retain a Private Investigator

Good private investigators can, for instance, locate hard-to-find witnesses or coax reluctant ones to cooperate. They may find a "smoking gun" document, locate background information on witnesses that can be used for impeachment, conduct sensitive surveillance, and so forth. A bad private investigator can screw up your case.

If you contemplate hiring a private investigator, get references from other lawyers who have retained the investigator. Make sure that the person within the investigation firm you wish to work with is the person who actually will be doing the work, or will be responsible for making sure the investigation is conducted according to your instructions (some very large private investigator firms tend to assign work to whoever is available, not necessarily the person who was recommended to you). Make sure your directions and goals are clear, along with your limits, and put it all in writing.

Like retaining a consulting expert, retaining a private investigator can be expensive. However, if you are charging on an hourly basis, your rates may well be higher than what your investigator charges. The question then comes down to this: can the PI conduct the investigation with the appropriate level of skill and care at less expense to your client, while freeing you to spend more time on other aspects of case preparation?

Finally, any report created by the private investigator should be protected by the attorney work product doctrine.[7] However, be aware that the *facts* learned by counsel through the private investigator's efforts, like any other facts learned during the informal phase of case development, may be discoverable.

vii. Circle Back to the Client

Once you have become an expert on the subject matter of your client's case, you likely will have accumulated a number of questions for the client that you had not thought of during the initial interview. Be sure to circle

---

[6]   *See* Chapter 9 for additional criteria for selecting testifying experts.

[7]   Costabile v. Westchester, 254 F.R.D. 160, 163 (S.D.N.Y. 2008).

back to get answers to unasked questions and to clarify any parts of the client's story that do not track with what you now know.

But be careful; this is a client management issue. The client may feel insulted or embarrassed about information you uncover that they either did not want you to know or were ignorant of themselves. So, remind the client that you are on their side and you need to learn all you can about their case. You have not been hired to pass judgment on the client but to do everything in your power to reach their goals. Never forget: the client must trust you.

b.   Learn the Law

Reading a book such as this one is a linear process. You start at the beginning and read to the end. Pre-litigation case development is not linear. So while "learn the law" comes after "learn the facts" in this chapter, in reality, learning the facts and the law go hand-in-hand, with each side informing the other, and prompting new paths of inquiry.

As a first-year law student, you learned to do legal research. You were expected to identify the issues, ferret out the applicable law, draft a balanced analysis, and then draw some conclusions. This is basic but essential work. When you represent a real client, you should conduct your legal research not only from the perspective of identifying potential causes of action or defenses, but you should view the law through the lens of the advocate. For instance, in our hypothetical, one of the legal questions that arises relates to jurisdiction. This is not a purely academic question: there are practical and tactical considerations regarding whether to leave the case where it is or seek a change of venue or removal. Is there an advantage to filing in California or New York? What are the choice of law rules used by each? Does either state's law give you a better chance of defeating the injunctive relief? In terms of inconvenience and costs to the client, which jurisdiction is preferable? Where would most of the discovery take place? How clogged are the respective courts' dockets, i.e., how long would it take to get the case to trial?

The point is this: from the perspective of a litigator, legal research is not a neutral process. As a litigator, you are researching the law, but you are assessing the law from the perspective of whether it gives you an advantage. This involves more than simply identifying viable claims and defenses: it is part and parcel of developing the case to maximize your client's chances of prevailing.

c. Compare the Requirements of the Law to the Facts You Have Gathered

Again, this is not a linear process: the facts inform what is the applicable law, which in turn may guide the gathering of additional facts as well as showing where gaps may exist.

Indeed, lawyers have an ethical obligation to ensure that claims they make on behalf of their clients are supported in both law and fact.[8] Failure to do so may lead to any number of unpleasant outcomes, including dismissal of the client's claims, harm to your reputation, and sanctions. It is best to aim carefully before you shoot.[9] There are two necessary steps: (1) carefully research potential claims or defenses; and (2) evaluate the information you have gathered *in relation* to each element of each claim or defense.

A helpful device is to *map* the elements of the claim or defense and their corroborating (or needed) evidence. Consider the following plaintiff's map based upon an auto crash:

Elements	Supporting/Missing Evidence
1. Duty	a. Judicial notice of "reasonable care" statute b. Jury instruction on reasonable care c. [Safe driving expert?] d. Defendant to admit he had duty to not text?
2. Breach	a. Defendant to admit he was texting? b. Defendant to admit he ran a red light? c. [Safe driving expert?] d. Do text records still exist? e. Subpoena girlfriend?
3. Causation	a. Witness Smith will testify she saw defendant go through red light and hit plaintiff (Problem: witness was drunk at the time and nearly a block away) b. [Accident reconstruction expert?] c. [Medical expert to testify plaintiff's injury was caused by defendant striking plaintiff?]

---

[8] *See* FED. R. CIV. P. 11.

[9] FED. R. CIV. P. 15 allows for the amendment of pleadings, including the addition of new causes of action, should evidence that becomes known during the course of discovery so warrant it. However, many attorneys in an (over)abundance of caution tend to plead every cause of action that might relate to a given dispute, then winnow them down through the course of the litigation. In our view, this practice is contrary to the requirements of Rule 11, and it has the unfortunate effect of forcing opposing counsel to engage in unnecessary and wasteful discovery.

4. Damages	Past wage loss:
	a. Pay stubs
	b. Job termination notice
	Future wage loss:
	a. Client will testify she can't find a job with her limitations
	b. [Vocational expert?]
	c. [Statistician/economist?]
	Past medical expenses:
	a. Medical bills
	b. [How do we prove they were reasonable?]
	Future medical expenses:
	a. No supporting evidence
	b. [Medical expert?]

Illus. 2-1.

The use of an evidence map[10] serves the cause of case development because it gives counsel a clear picture of the evidence in hand and the evidence still needed to support each element of each cause of action (or affirmative defense). In this way, the evidence map provides the beginnings of a discovery plan.

As the case progresses and additional evidence is gathered, you should add it to the map in order to provide a continuing overview of the case. You also should include evidence adverse to a given element of a claim or defense, under a separate heading, along with notes regarding how best to address it. This fairly simple exercise can prove to be enormously helpful to case development and discovery planning.

2.   ADVISE THE CLIENT

Litigators are advisors and advocates. Once you complete the initial investigation, it is time to meet with the client to share your findings and render advice on how (or whether) to proceed. It is essential to keep the

---

[10] We call them evidence maps. They can be called summaries, charts, spreadsheets, directories, whatever name you want to use. Law firms routinely use litigation management software to organize large amounts of information that no one could fully keep in mind. The structure of their databases is essentially a more complex, robust version of the above illustration. This type of software allows for "coding" evidence based upon objective criteria such as the dates of documents, and subjective criteria such as what claims and/or defenses a given piece of evidence may support or undermine. It allows counsel to do targeted searches and quickly identify the evidentiary strengths and weaknesses of a given claim or defense. It also assists counsel with identifying evidence responsive to discovery demands, among other uses, all of which save time, money and increase the effectiveness of counsel.

client informed of what you know. Before formal litigation is joined, you should advise the client on:

- The results of your factual investigation and legal analysis;

- The risks and benefits of proceeding with litigation;

- Your preliminary assessment of the strengths and weaknesses of the client's case;

- Your litigation plan, i.e., your theory of the case;

- Your best estimate of the costs associated with proceeding with litigation;

- A preliminary valuation of the case.

It is imperative that litigation counsel advise the client early on regarding options. There are several reasons: (1) because counsel has an ethical obligation to do so;[11] (2) because counsel must have a clear understanding of the client's goals; and (3) because counsel's failure to advise the client may result in counsel acting in a manner inconsistent with the client's desires.[12]

The challenge is that early advice presents a chicken-and-egg problem. It is difficult to confidently advise a client regarding ultimate outcomes and risks without first engaging in full-blown litigation, or at least significant formal discovery. However, the client's goal may be to avoid full-blown litigation. So you do the best you can, always being transparent and frank with the client. Advise the client that foregoing discovery in an effort at early resolution may limit your ability to fully evaluate the merits of the case. Advise the client of the trade-offs between engaging in a fully litigated case versus attempting to achieve early resolution, often with less than complete information.

Advising the client, even based upon limited information, is crucial to case development and case planning. For example, the client in our hypothetical may authorize counsel to "do anything and everything to win this case; I don't care about the cost." Conversely, the client may state, "I don't have a lot of money. I need you to try and resolve this matter quickly and inexpensively." The client's goals may have an enormous impact on your case development and litigation plan.[13]

Of course, advising the client continues throughout the course of the litigation. In Chapter 1 we discussed how litigators value cases and how, as more information becomes available, counsel's evaluation and valuation of the case may change. As the case develops, for better or for worse, it is

---

[11] MODEL RULES OF PROF'L CONDUCT R. 1.4.

[12] This is sometimes referred to as "getting ahead of the client."

[13] For instance, your client's goals may inform your decision to urge the court to order early dispute resolution or to place significant limits on the extent of discovery.

incumbent upon counsel to provide the client with updates and to seek continuing authority to act. This should be done in writing. To repeat: THIS SHOULD BE DONE IN WRITING![14]

At this point, you should be ready to either draft a demand or response letter, or a complaint, answer, or other responsive pleading. Before any document leaves your office, however, review it with the client and have the client "sign off," that is, affirm the document's accuracy to the best of the client's knowledge.[15]

B. CASE DEVELOPMENT: OVERVIEW OF FORMAL DISCOVERY

Once initial pleadings are served and the case is joined, formal discovery may begin. Formal discovery is a highly regimented, rule-bound process with numerous prescriptions and proscriptions, largely governed by Rules 16 and 26 through 37, as well as Rule 45. You must become intimately familiar with these rules as you enter the formal phase of case development.

For example, Rule 26(a) governs when and how you are required to initially disclose evidence that supports your claims or defenses. Rule 30 restricts both the number of depositions you may take and their duration. Rule 33 restricts the number of interrogatories you may serve. Rule 34 governs how you may request and produce documents. The court's scheduling order, governed by Rule 16, will dictate the time allotted to conduct discovery. Though counsel may have a view as to the amount of time necessary to complete discovery, the court may have a different opinion, and that is the only one that counts. Therefore, you must carefully plan and target discovery in order to achieve your goals within the confines of the Rules and the preferences of the court.

Even without restrictions imposed by the Rules and the court, effective discovery requires a clear sense of what counsel is trying to accomplish.

---

[14] Advising the client in writing eliminates the "he said/she said" problem if a dispute arises with the client. Though everyone likes to think that client and attorney will get along swimmingly, sometimes relationships break down. Better to have a documented history of the advice given to the client and confirmation of the authority the client has given you to act. Often these letters begin:

"This letter reflects our recent discussion in which I advised you of X. You have authorized my firm to engage in the following actions: A, B, C. . . . If anything in this letter is inconsistent with your understanding and intentions, please contact me immediately so that we may proceed according to your wishes."

[15] In addition to an initial pleading or demand/response letter, you should also send a so-called "litigation hold letter." A litigation hold letter informs the adverse party that it must preserve any evidence (usually documents but sometimes physical objects) that may be relevant to the litigation. Some may be quite simple but the more detail regarding the evidence to be preserved the more likely it is that the adverse party will (1) comply, and (2) be held responsible for failure to comply. Further, it may be that one or more parties anticipate litigation will take place in the future, so even before an initial pleading or other communication relating to the merits of the case is transmitted to the opposing party or its counsel, a hold letter may be necessary.

Discovery goals are informed by the theory of the case and counsel's identification of evidence necessary to support it. In turn, discovery acts as a feedback loop that allows counsel to continuously refine the theory of the case and the narrative that supports the client's position.

1. GOALS OF DISCOVERY

Discovery serves three basic goals: discovery of the adverse party's case; discovery for purposes of case development; and discovery in order to narrow disputed issues. These three purposes are not mutually exclusive. For example, discovery designed to probe the opposing party's claims and supporting evidence may yield evidence helpful to your client's case. Discovery intended to narrow issues may reveal that the opposing party lacks evidence to exploit a weakness in your own case. But it is useful to consider each goal separately.

a. Discovery of the Adverse Party's Case

A critical goal of discovery is to learn what the adverse party is claiming beyond what may be alleged in the pleadings, and to uncover evidence related to those claims. While Rule 26(a) requires the parties to disclose even before commencement of the formal discovery phase the evidence that supports their respective claims,[16] the Rule 26(a) initial disclosures do not obviate the need for formal discovery. Rule 26(a) requires disclosure of facts the party expects will *support its claims*.[17] Rule 26(a) does not require disclosure of *all* facts known to the opposing party. For example, there is no Rule 26(a) disclosure requirement for information that contradicts the disclosing party's supporting evidence, that reveals a gap in that evidence, or that tends to impeach the disclosing party or its supporting witnesses.

Initial disclosures are merely the first move in what can be thought of as a rather lengthy chess match. It is the job of counsel to determine how best to use discovery to probe the opposing party's claims and supporting evidence, and to uncover evidence that may undermine, discredit, or otherwise neutralize the adverse party's case. We will discuss the tools of discovery that facilitate achievement of these goals throughout much of the remainder of the book.

b. Discovery for Purposes of Case Development

As discussed above, every attorney, in cooperation with the client, can and must gather evidence and develop their case outside of the formal discovery process. But informal, non-adversarial fact-finding, as critical as it is, is never sufficient. Building the client's case, whether plaintiff or

---

[16] Initial disclosures will be covered in detail in Chapter 5.

[17] *See* FED. R. CIV. P. 26(a).

defendant, also requires formal discovery. For example, counsel may seek admissions directly related to the client's claims or defenses from the opposing party through formal requests for admissions,[18] or during the adverse party's deposition, or even during the depositions of third parties who can testify to admissions made to them by the adverse party. Counsel may subpoena and depose a non-party in order to obtain helpful documents and to establish their admissibility.[19] Counsel may inspect and photograph property[20] in order to create exhibits. The point is that discovery is not the passive reception of information; it is a purposeful process of actively gathering evidence in support of your case (and to undermine the opposing party's case), including evidence in the possession of others whom you can reach only through use of the formal discovery rules.

c.   Discovery for the Purpose of Narrowing Issues

It is common for a complaint to contain multiple causes of action arising from the same set of allegations. It is equally common for the answer to contain a plethora of affirmative defenses, as well as counterclaims. Whether litigators engage in this form of pleading practice in an (over)abundance of caution, or whether they have a tendency to shoot first and aim later, the fact remains that many cases begin with something of a shotgun approach. Targeted discovery may help eliminate or narrow issues prior to trial.

Narrowing issues early in the formal discovery process reduces costs and may facilitate early settlement. It also is advantageous from the perspective of your relationship with the court. Litigators who continue to press unmeritorious claims, particularly in the face of discovery that reveals the lack of evidentiary support for those claims, not only risk raising the ire of the judge, they tend to undermine their own credibility. For any lawyer, that is a bad result.

d.   Discovery to Obtain *Admissible* Evidence

An additional dimension to discovery has to do with the Rules of Evidence. There is an important distinction between evidence in the context of discovery versus evidence in the context of trial or dispositive motion practice. As to the latter, counsel must be able to satisfy the Rules of Evidence in order for the evidence to be made part of the record; in order for it to become part of the record, evidence must be *admissible*.[21]

---

[18] *See id.* 36.

[19] *See id.* 45.

[20] *See id.* 34.

[21] Consider the requirements of FED. R. CIV. P. 56, which governs motions for summary judgment. Rule 56(c)(2) requires that the court consider evidence that is admissible at trial. To the extent either party relies on evidence not otherwise admissible at trial, opposing counsel may

Therefore, your discovery practice must not only seek facts related to claims and defenses, it must be tailored to get the information necessary to ensure the admissibility of those facts, documents or other information. In other words, discovery goes beyond gathering information: it also involves developing a record of *admissible* evidence.[22]

2. IMPROPER DISCOVERY GOALS

Abusive discovery tactics are, unfortunately, used by some lawyers. They can take many forms. However, the Rules of Civil Procedure as well as the Rules of Professional Conduct explicitly forbid abusive or otherwise improper discovery. Specific examples and remedies available to counsel are addressed in Chapter 13. However, it is worth pointing out at this juncture a few practices that the rules specifically proscribe.

Counsel may not engage in discovery tactics for any improper purpose, such as to harass, cause unnecessary delay, or needlessly increase the cost of litigation.[23] Counsel may not use discovery to annoy, embarrass, oppress, or place an undue burden or expense on the opposing party.[24] The variations of abusive discovery are nearly infinite, but to give the reader a sense of them, here are two examples. In a commercial contract dispute, counsel attempts to conduct discovery into the opposing party's extra-marital affairs. Clearly the discovery sought has nothing to do with the merits of the case and is intended to embarrass the opposing party. Similarly, in a minor auto accident case, counsel for defendant serves hundreds of requests for admissions and seeks all of the plaintiff's medical records from the date of her birth. The improper goal, of course, is to impose an undue burden on the adverse party.

Similarly, it is improper to fail to cooperate in discovery. Passive-aggressive discovery tactics abound. Failing to come to a reasonable agreement on dates for depositions is one example. Failing to timely

---

object to that evidence and the court should not rely upon it when ruling. The advisory committee's notes to the 2010 amendment specifically state:

> Subdivision (c)(2) provides that a party may object that material cited to support or dispute a fact cannot be presented in a form that would be admissible in evidence. The objection functions much as an objection at trial, adjusted for the pretrial setting. The burden is on the proponent to show that the material is admissible as presented or to explain the admissible form that is anticipated.

FED. R. CIV. P. 56 advisory committee's note to 2010 amendment.

[22] For example, assume counsel wishes to offer at trial certain records obtained from a business. Are they admissible? It depends. They may be party admissions (if obtained from an opposing party) and are offered under FED. R. EVID. 801(d)(2). Or, they may fall within the Rule 803(6) exception to the rule against hearsay if it is a business record of a non-party. Either way, the records must be shown to be authentic pursuant to FED. R. EVID. 901 or 902. In other words, just getting a pile of useful documents does not mean they are *admissible*. The Rules of Evidence require more. Counsel must know those requirements in order to conduct thorough and complete discovery.

[23] FED. R. CIV. P. 26(g).

[24] *Id.* 26(c)(1).

provide substantive, non-evasive discovery responses is another typical example of the failure to cooperate in discovery.

Discovery abuse also implicates the Rules of Professional Conduct.[25] Although it is rare, lawyers who engage in egregious discovery misconduct may find themselves the subject of disciplinary action by their state bars.[26]

3.   THE DISCOVERY "TOOLKIT"

The Rules of Civil Procedure provide a powerful toolkit designed to allow the parties to uncover relevant information. The ultimate goal is to shine enough light on the dispute that the parties achieve a just result, whether through settlement, motions, or trial.

- **Initial disclosures:**[27] Required pre-discovery disclosure of witnesses, documents, and other evidence that support the party's claims and defenses.

- **Interrogatories:**[28] Formal questions put to the adverse party that must be answered under oath.

- **Document demands:**[29] Compels the production of documents in the possession of the adverse party, including electronically-stored information.

- **Inspection demands:**[30] Requires the adverse party to allow inspection of tangible things or entry upon land.

- **Requests for admissions:**[31] Compels the adverse party to admit or deny the truth of alleged facts or contentions.

- **Depositions:**[32] Allows for the recorded examination, under oath, of any person, including the adverse party (use a subpoena[33] to compel the attendance of non-parties).

---

[25]   MODEL RULES OF PROF'L CONDUCT pmbl., ¶ 5. ("A lawyer should use the law's procedures only for legitimate purposes and not to harass or intimidate others."). Rule 3.4 is even more to the point: "A lawyer shall not: . . . make a frivolous discovery request or fail to make reasonably diligent effort to comply with a legally proper discovery request by an opposing party." *Id.* R. 3.4. Similarly, "a lawyer shall not use means that have no substantial purpose other than to embarrass, delay, or burden a third person, or use methods of obtaining evidence that violate the legal rights of such a person." *Id.* R. 4.4.

[26]   Clare v. Coleman (Parent) Holdings, Inc., 928 So. 2d 1246, 1248 (Fla. Dist. Ct. App. 2006) ("Florida law allows for the revocation of an attorney's *pro hac vice* status when the misconduct 'adversely impacts the administration of justice.' "); Cincinnati Bar Assn. v. Marsick, 692 N.E.2d 991, 992–93 (Ohio 1998) (attorney suspended from the practice of law for six months for suppressing evidence when responding to interrogatories).

[27]   FED. R. CIV. P. 26(a).

[28]   *Id.* 33.

[29]   *Id.* 34.

[30]   *Id.* 34.

[31]   *Id.* 36.

[32]   *Id.* 30.

[33]   *Id.* 45.

- **Physical and mental examinations:**[34] Allows for the physical and/or mental examination of an adverse party whose physical and/or mental condition is at issue.

- **Subpoenas:**[35] Compels non-parties to produce documents, allow inspections or appear for a deposition.

- **Judicial enforcement of discovery:**[36] Upon motion, the court may compel discovery when the adverse party (or non-party witnesses) fails to cooperate.

We discuss the breadth of these tools, their limitations, and strategies for their use in the coming chapters.

C. CASE DEVELOPMENT FLOWCHART REVISITED

The formal discovery phase of the case development process, as careful and deliberate as you may be, never goes completely as planned. Contradictory information will come to light; witnesses may change their stories; you may find some gray where your client saw only black and white. Bad things happen. They almost always do during the course of litigation. So you adjust. You may even need to modify your theory of the case.

It is helpful to keep in mind the flowchart introduced in Chapter 1 and designed to illustrate the steps you may go through as you continue to develop the case. One way to look at it is as a linear progression through the litigation process. Another way to view it is as an information feedback loop. As you continue to gather evidence through the course of discovery, that evidence will inform your theory of the case, which you should continue to adjust accordingly as you also continue to adjust your discovery plan based on information received or not received throughout formal discovery.

---

[34] *Id.* 35.

[35] *Id.* 45.

[36] *Id.* 37.

CASE DEVELOPMENT FLOWCHART

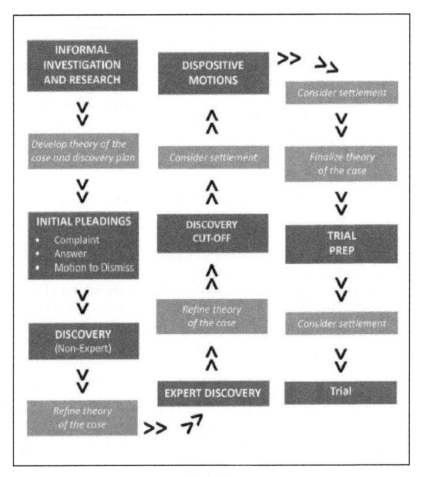

Illus. 2-2.

The important take-away is that case development is continuous. It begins with the initial client meeting and continues until trial and sometimes even through trial. Throughout this process you should repeatedly re-evaluate the theory of the case as the universe of known evidence expands.

That is not to imply that case development is an omnivorous process, incorporating all evidence gathered along the way, like a giant rolling snowball that picks up everything in its path. To the contrary, case development is also an exercise in selectivity. Some evidence may not be useful, or may not fit the narrative. Certain facts that initially seemed important may become irrelevant as the theory of the case evolves. As in any construction project, there are bound to be materials that must be discarded. Let them go, adjust, and re-adjust some more.

That is the life of a litigator.

CHAPTER 3

MANAGEMENT OF THE LITIGATION: THE CRITICAL PATH METHOD

■ ■ ■

Litigation is a complicated, multi-dimensional process. Success requires more than knowledge of the rules and tools of litigation, more than an ability to tell a compelling story. Success requires planning and management. The theory of the case answers the question: *What is the story we wish to tell?* The case development process answers the question: *What is our overall approach to fully developing the theory of the case?* Case planning and management answers the question: *How do we effectively manage the case development process?*

In other words, case management and planning is about execution. It dictates who will do what and in which order.[1] In order to execute your litigation plan effectively and efficiently, it helps to look at the lawsuit from the vantage point of a project manager. Our approach is borrowed from a well-established project management tool: the Critical Path Method.

A. THE CRITICAL PATH METHOD

To manage a lawsuit, you must determine the tasks necessary to build the case and determine *the order in which to proceed*. Though there are various ways to manage the litigation process, the Critical Path Method ("CPM") is the best tool we have encountered, especially for complex litigation.

The CPM was created during the 1950s in order to facilitate the efficient management of large-scale, complex projects.[2] Think: designing and building nuclear submarines. As a litigator, your task is not quite as complex, but it is helpful to apply the same management principles.

---

[1]   Your case management plan also helps inform your effort to obtain a favorable scheduling order, which means you need to create it *before* you meet with opposing counsel to negotiate the Rule 26(f) plan. In other words, you need to have a clear idea of the discovery you need and how long it will take before you attempt to negotiate a Rule 26(f) joint discovery plan.

There is something of a "chicken and egg" problem with regard to the Rule 26(f) discovery plan versus counsel's litigation/discovery plan. Each tends to inform the other. For instance, the court-set trial date (which may or may not be the same date recommended by counsel) can impact your discovery plan. Conversely, the time you estimate it will take to complete discovery will guide your proposals *vis a vis* the Rule 26(f) joint discovery plan and its attendant deadlines.

[2]   *See* James E. Kelley & Morgan R. Walker, *Critical-Path Planning and Scheduling*, 1959 PROC. OF THE E. JOINT COMPUTER CONF. 160.

CPM begins with the question: what is the ultimate goal? The ultimate litigation goal, at least for planning purposes, is to make the case trial-ready. At its most basic, CPM involves constructing a logical model of the project in order to achieve the specific goal. The model requires that you do the following:

1. List all anticipated tasks necessary to complete the project;

2. Estimate the time necessary to complete each task (and the total time required to achieve all necessary tasks);

3. Note the dependencies among the tasks, meaning which tasks depend for their completion upon other tasks being performed first;

4. Assign the person or group responsible for completing each task.

We will go through them one by one.

1. IDENTIFY THE "TASKS"

Discovery tasks include, for example, preparing various forms of written discovery, issuing witness subpoenas, taking party and non-party depositions, conducting inspections or examinations of things, and arranging medical examinations. Invariably, there also will be the tasks of enforcing discovery rights: so-called "meet and confer" letters to draft and motions to compel to brief and argue. The tasks to be performed are guided by the discovery goals, which in turn are guided by the theory of the case. A basic list of tasks might include:

1. Prepare and serve initial disclosures;

2. Prepare and serve written discovery demands, including

   - Interrogatories

   - Document demands

   - Requests for admissions;

3. Prepare and serve responses to discovery;

4. Prepare the client for his deposition and defend the deposition;

5. Identify and retain experts;

6. Prepare for and take depositions, such as

   - Adverse parties

   - Key witnesses

   - Experts;

7. Subpoena non-party documents and witnesses.

In most cases, the universe of tasks will be more extensive and detailed. In complex cases, the list of tasks easily can reach into the hundreds. Further, tasks not directly related to discovery, but which "eat up the clock" also must be factored in, such as non-dispositive and dispositive motions, preparation of trial documents, and so forth.

2. DETERMINE THE TIME NEEDED TO COMPLETE EACH TASK AND AN OVERALL TIMELINE

At the inception of litigation, you should identify every task you can think of necessary to achieve your ultimate litigation goal. You then must determine a timeline in which to fit all the identified tasks in a logical order. In an ideal world, you would be free to dictate the date of the trial, conduct discovery in a timeframe of your own choosing, and prepare for post-discovery motions and trial at your own pace. However, parties cannot always agree to a trial date and the court often *imposes* a trial date of *its* choosing, including deadlines for completing discovery and for submitting trial documents such as trial briefs, jury instructions, special verdict forms, and motions in limine.[3] All task deadlines are dependent upon the court-imposed discovery cut-off and trial date. Therefore, you must peg your timeline and all tasks it contains to these court-determined deadlines or you will find yourself scrambling and not properly prepared.

The time allotted for discovery will have an impact on how and at what pace discovery proceeds. For example, assume a one-year period to complete discovery in a case involving three parties, each allowed to take up to 10 depositions and each intending to engage in at least one round of written discovery before depositions begin. Under the Rules, parties have 30 days to respond to written discovery. And then, when the responses are received, counsel must take time to review them. Invariably, there will be disputes regarding the adequacy of the written responses, so more time will be needed to enforce discovery rights. The motion practice to compel discovery can take anywhere from several weeks to several months. This means that four to six months may pass before any party is prepared to schedule depositions. That leaves little time to complete the first round of depositions, a second round of written discovery (and its attendant disputes and motions to compel), a second round of depositions, and then the completion of expert depositions, which typically take place toward the close of discovery. What initially seemed like plenty of time suddenly seems wholly inadequate.

Another challenge is that it frequently is difficult to predict the time necessary to complete tasks on your litigation plan. For example, opposing counsel may need an extension of time to respond to discovery. Witnesses

---

[3] *See* FED. R. CIV. P. 16(b)(3), which grants broad authority to the court to control the pretrial schedule.

may not be available when you want them for depositions. The process of scheduling and then arguing motions can take anywhere from a few weeks to several months, depending on local rules and the court's caseload—and then you need to wait for the court to rule. You must make allowances for all of these variables when you create and manage your overall timeline.

With all this in mind, you must negotiate a Rule 26(f) discovery plan with opposing counsel which, in turn, the court will consider before it issues a Rule 16 pretrial order setting forth a number of deadlines and cutoffs, including:

1. Deadline for initial disclosures;

2. Deadline for joinder of additional parties;

3. Deadline for amendments to pleadings;

4. Deadline for exchange of expert reports;

5. Discovery cutoff;

6. Non-dispositive motion (discovery motion) cutoff;

7. Dispositive motion cutoff;

8. Deadline for trial documents;

9. Trial date.

It is enough to make anyone's head spin. This is why you should create a timeline that includes all anticipated litigation tasks, factoring in flexibility for the inevitable, unpredictable hiccups along the way.

3. DETERMINE THE SEQUENCE OF YOUR TASKS

It is not enough to simply list all litigation tasks. You also must logically sequence the tasks and identify dependencies among them. Though there are a number of obvious sequences, e.g., gathering all evidence needed by experts before producing a final expert report, sequencing of tasks is highly case specific.

In a commercial dispute, for example, it often makes sense to obtain all possibly relevant documents before beginning any depositions. That could mean serving a set of document demands on the opposing party and subpoenas *duces tecum* on one or more non-parties before scheduling depositions. Or, in a product liability case, the logical first step may be to conduct an inspection of the product, photograph it and conduct forensic tests before serving written discovery or taking depositions. In some cases, it may be necessary to take a deposition as a first step, especially if there is the possibility that the party or witness may become unavailable.[4]

---

[4]   *See* FED. R. CIV. P. 27 and 32.

When there are multiple issues in a case, different sources for documents, and many depositions to be taken, it is easy to get the sequencing wrong. It is frustrating, for example, to take a witness's deposition, only to find out later that certain newly-produced documents would have made the deposition more effective.

Therefore, you should carefully map out your discovery plan in order to proceed logically and to fit all tasks into a defined period of time. This may involve proceeding on several discovery tracks simultaneously. For instance, you may need to serve several forms of written discovery on multiple parties simultaneously, and schedule selected depositions while additional rounds of written discovery are pending that are designed to obtain information relating to additional rounds of depositions. This level of complexity means you will need to plan each track of discovery taking into account the dependencies among the various tasks. Similarly, you must make sure that the completion of each discovery track occurs in an order that does not create bottlenecks or undue delays.

The bottom line is this: you must carefully think through a discovery plan tailored to the needs of the case. It is better to have a plan that may need to be revised from time to time than to have no plan at all.

4. ASSIGN TASKS

Litigation practice often involves the work of more than one person. There may be a team of lawyers working on a case. There likely will be support staff such as paralegals and secretaries. There may be outside consultants and investigators. Therefore, each task should be assigned to a specific individual or group in order to ensure that each person working on the case knows his responsibilities and can be held accountable to complete his tasks in a timely manner. In other words, everyone must work off the same plan and must see how their tasks relate to the others.

The Critical Path Method is as simple or as complicated as the litigation requires. A straightforward auto crash case may not require a great deal of CPM planning. Conversely, a class action lawsuit or multi-district litigation may involve hundreds of tasks to be executed on parallel tracks and involving dozens of team members across several phases of discovery. Either way, a CPM approach to case management, and particularly discovery management, vastly improves the efficiency and effectiveness of the litigation process.

B. DOCUMENTING THE CRITICAL PATH METHOD

CPMs can take many forms. Some are written as intricate flowcharts containing complex symbols and multi-color codes. Some are expressed as a ladder progression. There is no one right way of documenting a CPM. However, lawyers tend to be more comfortable communicating with words, so a CPM document using words seems apt so long as it is understandable and not so cumbersome as to become unworkable.

At a minimum, a litigation CPM document should contain the following elements:

1.   Clearly identified, individual tasks;
2.   Due dates for each task, as well as court-imposed deadlines;
3.   Individuals or groups assigned for each task;
4.   A field to indicate the status of each task;
5.   A revised date notation to indicate when the CPM document was last updated.

Following is a simplified example of a CPM document for case management. It is essentially a "to do" list, but organized in a manner that allows anyone working on the case to readily understand the overall plan, including the work flow, deadlines, and individual responsibilities. It contains a considered and logical progression of discovery tasks with due dates designed to ensure effective execution of the discovery plan. Further, each task is assigned to a specific team member. This instills accountability into the process. Notice also that the example reflects the status of each task as of the document's revised date. The CPM document should be routinely updated to record the progress of the case, and every time it is updated, the revised date in the upper right hand corner should be changed.

Smith v. Jones, et al., Case No. 123456

Client = Smith   Updated: 2/15/20

DUE	TASK DESCRIPTION	ASSIGNED	STATUS
8/15/19	Research causes of action; Memo to all	RAK	DONE
9/1/19	Draft complaint	RAK	DONE
9/15/19	Serve S & C	JAC	DONE
9/30/19	Draft 1st rogs, doc demands, RFAs	RAK	DONE
10/30/19	R26(f) meeting	CMR	DONE
11/21/19	File R26(f) report	RAK	DONE
11/30/19	Serve R26(a) initial disclosures	CMR	DONE
11/30/19	Serve 1st rogs, doc demands	JAC	DONE

12/30/19	P's 1st rog responses and doc demands due		15-DAY EXTENSION GRANTED (DUE 1/14/20)
1/7/20	**SCHEDULING HEARING**	CMR	DONE
1/13/20	Finalize responses to Ds' 1st rogs and doc demands	CMR/RAK	DONE
1/14/20	Serve P's responses to Ds' 1st rogs and doc demands	JAC	DONE
1/31/20	Retain liability expert Retain damages expert	CMR	DONE—ALICE DOE [Need to locate damages expert]
2/25/20	P's initial depo prep	CMR	
3/28/20	Prepare depo outlines	CMR	
3/28/20	Subpoenas and depo notices to: J Jones ABC Co. XYZ Co.	JAC	
5/31/20	Complete depos of: J Jones ABC Co. XYZ Co.	CMR	
7/15/20	Serve RFAs	RAK	
8/15/20	Serve supplemental discovery responses	RAK	
8/30/20	**DISCOVERY CUTOFF**		
10/31/20	**NON-DISPOSITIVE MOTION CUTOFF**		
12/31/20	**LAST DAY FOR SJ MOTIONS**		
2/15/21	**TRIAL DOCUMENTS DUE**	RAK	
3/2/21	**TRIAL**	CMR	

Illus. 3-1.

There is no one right way of managing a lawsuit. However, there is a wrong way. Failing to plan and failing to actively manage the case is the wrong way.

C. MANAGING THE BUDGET

Effective litigation management requires more than tracking and managing discrete tasks; it also requires managing the budget. Though the vicissitudes of civil litigation often make it difficult to predict how much a case will cost to prosecute or defend (not to mention the unknown of whether the case will settle early, late, or not at all), clients large and small usually demand that their counsel estimate the cost of proceeding. If you do not accurately predict the time and cost required for your case, you and/ or your client easily can end up losing money, even if you win a favorable verdict or settlement. Your client may be unable or unwilling to pay for attorney time and expenses in excess of the amount budgeted.

You can use your CPM document as an aid in estimating costs, keeping in mind the need to budget for unexpected twists and turns as the case progresses. By using the CPM to estimate the cost of litigation, you are in a better position to advise the client on the wisdom of going forward with a given case, as well as estimating the costs of varying approaches. You also can use it to determine, as the case progresses, whether you are proceeding within budget. In short, your CPM document can help you keep the client informed about progress on the merits and progress from a dollars and cents perspective.

CHAPTER 4

THE SCOPE AND LIMITS OF DISCOVERY

■ ■ ■

Case development and discovery are inextricably bound to the Rules of Civil Procedure. Once a case is in suit, the Rules control what counsel may and may not do in a host of ways, but particularly with regard to the gathering of evidence. This chapter examines Rule 26 as it relates to the scope and limits of discovery.[1]

Rule 26 is the seminal rule of discovery. It sets forth the parameters for what information is discoverable, generally allowing broad and liberal discovery,[2] but also limiting discovery—and in some instances prohibiting it altogether. In order to effectively plan and conduct discovery, a clear and thorough understanding of Rule 26 is essential.[3]

Rule 26 is not a model of clarity. The Rule is lengthy, it digresses, and it is something of a labyrinth. It often must be read in conjunction with other rules. It has been repeatedly amended in efforts to curb improper or abusive discovery tactics and to take account of evolving discovery-related challenges. Therefore, rather than address each of its disparate elements as if they form a coherent whole, this chapter focuses on the broadest aspect of the Rule: what is discoverable.

A. RULE 26(b)(1): THE SCOPE OF DISCOVERY

Rule 26(b)(1) defines the general scope of allowable discovery:

Parties may obtain discovery regarding any nonprivileged matter that is relevant to any party's claim or defense and proportional to the needs of the case, considering the importance of the issues at stake in the action, the amount in controversy, the parties' relative access to relevant information, the parties' resources, the importance of the discovery in resolving the issues, and whether

---

[1] Later chapters examine other sections of Rule 26, such as those that address the joint discovery plan, initial disclosures, discovery of electronically stored information ("ESI"), discovery of experts, and protective orders.

[2] As the Supreme Court has noted, the "broad and liberal" treatment accorded the discovery rules is designed to facilitate "mutual knowledge of all the relevant facts gathered by both parties" and to permit inquiry "into the facts underlying [the] opponent's case." Hickman v. Taylor, 329 U.S. 495, 507 (1947).

[3] There are additional limits on the scope of discovery that are not contained in Rule 26. They are addressed in Section B, *infra*, as well as in subsequent chapters that address specific forms of discovery.

the burden or expense of the proposed discovery outweighs its likely benefit.

It is important to understand the potential scope and breadth of this rule. Discovery of information relevant to matters raised in the pleadings automatically falls within the permissible scope of discovery provided the information sought is not privileged and is proportional to the needs of the case. The proportionality language is meant to help combat the problem of over-discovery[4] while remaining mindful that discovery appropriately extends beyond information that may potentially be admissible under the Rules of Evidence.[5] Proportionality as it relates to any particular case tends to become clearer as the case progresses,[6] and may require judicial involvement.[7] Importantly, proportionality is not limited to considerations of case values. It may also relate, for example, to the case's complexity, if the dispute involves claims relating to the public vindication of a party, or is a matter of great public concern.[8]

At bottom, with regard to the scope of discovery, the court will want answers to two basic questions:

1.   What does the requested information have to do with the particular issues in the case?

2.   Is the discovery narrowly tailored to obtain the desired information?

If you have developed a coherent theory of the case, you will be better able to state the specific reasons for your discovery requests, i.e., how the sought-after information relates to a specific claim or defense, and how they are proportional to the needs of your case.

B. LIMITS ON THE SCOPE OF DISCOVERY

The Rule 26 grants the parties much latitude, allowing discovery of relevant information[9] even if that information is not admissible under the Rules of Evidence.[10] There are, however, limits. Rule 26 gives the court

---

[4]   FED. R. CIV. P. 26 advisory committee's note to 1983 amendment; *id.* 26 advisory committee's note to 2015 amendment.

[5]   Rule 26 is explicit about this: "Information within this scope of discovery need not be admissible in evidence to be discoverable." *Id.* 26(b)(1); *see also id.* 26 advisory committee's note to 2015 amendment.

[6]   "The parties may begin discovery without a full appreciation of the factors that bear on proportionality." *Id.* 26 advisory committee's note to 2015 amendment.

[7]   "The present amendment again reflects the need for continuing and close judicial involvement." *Id.*

[8]   *Id.*

[9]   The relevance standard in Rule 26(b)(1) is not the same as relevance defined by the Federal Rules of Evidence. As to the latter, relevance is an *admissibility* standard, whereas relevance in the context of discovery is broader. Therefore, objections to discovery based upon the Rules of Evidence are misplaced.

[10]   *See* FED. R. CIV. P. 26(b)(1); *see also id.* 26 advisory committee's note to 2015 amendment.

substantial discretion to tailor the bounds of discovery to the particular nature and needs of an individual case,[11] and the advisory committee notes make clear that courts are expected to actively manage and control the discovery process.[12]

1. "FISHING EXPEDITIONS" ARE PROHIBITED

The discovery rules do not allow fishing expeditions; "some threshold showing of relevance must be made before parties are required to open wide the doors of discovery."[13] While relevance in discovery is broader than that required for admissibility at trial, the object of inquiry must have some evidentiary value before a court will compel disclosure of otherwise inadmissible material.[14] Put another way, discovery is meant to allow the parties to flesh out allegations for which they initially have at least a *modicum* of support.[15] It is never enough to claim that discovery should go forward on the bare hope that it might yield helpful information. As a matter of sound practice, when drafting discovery, you should have a *specific purpose* for the information you seek.

At risk of being redundant, the theory of the case informs the reasons for the discovery and provides focus: it provides the response to the claim that "counsel is merely engaging in a fishing expedition."

2. "PROPORTIONALITY" AS A LIMIT ON DISCOVERY

The proportionality limitation on the scope of discovery that is embedded in Rule 26(b) explicitly limits discovery to that which is "proportional to the needs of the case."[16] Proportionality takes into account

---

[11] *See, e.g.,*

Rule 26(b)(1): "*Unless otherwise limited by court order*, the scope of discovery is as follows . . . ." (emphasis added).

Rule 26(b)(2)(A): "By order, the court may alter the limits in these rules on the number of depositions and interrogatories or on the length of depositions under Rule 30."

Rule 26(b)(2)(C): "On motion or on its own, the court must limit the frequency or extent of discovery otherwise allowed by these rules or by local rule . . . .";

see also Rule 16(c)(2)(F):"At any pretrial conference, the court may consider and take appropriate action on the following matters: . . . . (F) *controlling and scheduling discovery* . . . ." (emphasis added).

[12] "The present amendment again reflects the need for continuing and close judicial involvement in the cases that do not yield readily to the ideal of effective party management. It is expected that discovery will be effectively managed by the parties in many cases. But there will be important occasions for judicial management, both when the parties are legitimately unable to resolve important differences and when the parties fall short of effective, cooperative management on their own." FED R. CIV. P. 26 advisory committee note to 2015 amendment.

[13] Hofer v. Mack Trucks, Inc., 981 F.2d 377, 380 (8th Cir. 1992).

[14] Martinez v. Cornell Corrections of Texas, 229 F.R.D. 215 (D.N.M. 2005).

[15] Here is another reason to do your homework *before* formal discovery begins. To the extent you have developed a body of evidence and thought through how it relates to anticipated discovery, the more likely you will be able to convince the judge that the discovery you seek is relevant to a claim or defense, even if not otherwise admissible.

[16] FED. R. CIV. P. 26(b)(1).

"the importance of the issues at stake in the action, the amount in controversy, the parties' relative access to relevant information, the parties' resources, the importance of the discovery in resolving the issues, and whether the burden or expense of the proposed discovery outweighs its likely benefit."[17] The effect is to give the court broad authority to manage and maintain control over the discovery process, even to the extent that it may limit discovery otherwise allowed by the rules.[18]

The proportionality concept was introduced in 1983 as a means " 'to deal with the problem of over-discovery.' "[19] The intent was " 'to guard against redundant or disproportionate discovery . . . [and] to encourage judges to be more aggressive in identifying and discouraging discovery over-use.' "[20] Under the proportionality rule, a party may seek protection against otherwise allowable discovery if it is unwarranted by the size of the case. To illustrate, assume a dispute arising from the private sale of a boat. The agreed price is $20,000. After the sale, the buyer claims that the seller misrepresented the age of the motor, and that the boat is actually worth only $10,000. Rule 30 allows each party up to ten depositions without leave of court.[21] The defendant schedules ten depositions, most of which do not involve material witnesses. Depositions are expensive and time consuming. Given the relatively modest amount in dispute, and the limited issues in the case, a court may well find that defendant's discovery is unwarranted, particularly when one or two depositions, along with well-tailored interrogatories, would do. In such a case, the court may limit discovery in order to make it proportional to the amount in dispute and the complexity (or lack thereof) of the issues.[22]

Conversely, in a case involving many material witnesses, multiple sources of documents, numerous experts, and complex legal issues, the court may "manage up" the presumptive number of interrogatories and

---

[17] *Id.*

[18] The Rule 26 grant of authority to the court to limit discovery is complementary to the court's Rule 16 authority to manage pretrial procedures, including the discovery schedule.

[19] FED. R. CIV. P. 26 advisory committee's note to 1983 amendment.

[20] *Id.* 26 advisory committee's note to 2015 amendment. The 1993 amendment retained the proportionality concept, but separated it into a different paragraph. The 2015 amendments saw a return of proportionality to the section of the rules that defines the appropriate scope of discovery:

The present amendment restores the proportionality factors to their original place in defining the scope of discovery. This change reinforces the Rule 26(g) obligation of the parties to consider these factors in making discovery requests, responses, or objections. Restoring the proportionality calculation to Rule 26(b)(1) does not change the existing responsibilities of the court and the parties to consider proportionality, and the change does not place on the party seeking discovery the burden of addressing all proportionality considerations.

Id.

[21] *Id.* 30(a)(2)(A)(i).

[22] The money at stake is not, however, the only consideration in a proportionality determination. A case may involve little money but "seek[ ] to vindicate vitally important personal or public values." FED. R. CIV. P. 26 advisory committee's note to 2015 amendment.

depositions in order to allow for a full vetting of the evidence.[23] In complex litigation, it is not unusual for courts to increase the permissible number of interrogatories and depositions, particularly if the parties are in agreement.[24]

3. PRESUMPTIVE LIMITS (OR LACK THEREOF) ON PARTICULAR KINDS OF DISCOVERY

In addition to the Rule 26 limitations, depositions and interrogatories have specific presumptive limits generally applicable to all cases:

- **Oral depositions.** Rule 30 limits the number of depositions each party may take to ten, whether taken orally or by written question. Each deposition is limited to a single day, not to exceed seven hours.[25]

- **Depositions by written questions.** Rule 31 follows the same limitations on depositions as Rule 30.

- **Interrogatories.** Rule 33 limits the number of interrogatories to 25, including discreet subparts.[26]

- **Document demands.** Rule 34 does not contain a numerical limit on the number of demands.

- **Requests for admissions.** Rule 36 does not contain a numerical limit on the number of requests for admissions.

4. PRIVILEGED COMMUNICATIONS, ATTORNEY WORK PRODUCT, AND CONFIDENTIAL INFORMATION

There are three categories of information that generally receive protection from discovery: privileged communications, attorney work product, and otherwise confidential information.[27]

---

[23] FED. R. CIV. P. 26(b)(2)(A) specifically states: "By order, the court may alter the limits in these rules on the number of depositions and interrogatories or on the length of depositions under Rule 30." This is typically done upon a showing that the additional discovery is warranted, given the complexity and overall size of the case.

[24] *See, e.g.,* Thykkuttathil v. Keese, 294 F.R.D. 601, 603 (W.D. Wash. 2013) (deposition limit expanded due to complexity of case); Am. Civil Liberties Union v. Gonzales, 237 F.R.D. 120, 125 (E.D. Pa. 2006) (interrogatory limit expanded); Archer Daniels Midland Co. v. Aon Risk Servs., Inc. of Minnesota, 187 F.R.D. 578, 586 (D. Minn. 1999) (recognizing the permissibility of seeking extra depositions or interrogatories, but noting that, in doing so, the requesting party "must make a particularized showing of why the discovery is necessary").

[25] FED. R. CIV. P. 30(a)(2) allows, with leave of court, an upward departure from this presumptive limit.

[26] FED. R. CIV. P. 33(a)(1) states: "Leave to serve additional interrogatories may be granted to the extent consistent with Rule 26(b)(1) and (2)." Thus, again, the court may allow an upward departure from this presumptive limit.

[27] Chapter 12 addresses these protections.

a. Privileged Communications

Rule 26(b)(1) explicitly limits discovery to "nonprivileged" information.[28] The Rules do not, however, define what is privileged. Although privilege is commonly raised in relation to attorney-client communications, it may include many types of communications, depending upon the jurisdiction in which the case is pending. In civil cases, state law governs the existence and parameters of privileges.[29] Therefore, in order to determine whether proffered discovery seeks privileged information protected from disclosure, counsel must look to the law of the state that will provide the rule for decision.[30] Commonly recognized privileges include the attorney-client privilege, doctor-patient privilege, therapist-patient privilege, marital privilege, and priest-penitent privilege.

b. Trial Preparation Materials, the Attorney Work Product Doctrine, and Non-Testifying Experts

There are categories of material and information prepared by or for attorneys in the course of litigation or in anticipation of litigation that also fall outside the scope of generally-allowable discovery.

i.   Trial Preparation Materials and the Attorney Work Product Doctrine

Protection of trial preparation materials, and the broader protection for attorney work product, is not based upon privilege. These protections are based upon the premise that counsel's mental impressions, thoughts, and strategies, as a matter of policy, generally remain confidential. Work product may include materials prepared during litigation or in anticipation of litigation,[31] material prepared by a lawyer or for a lawyer,[32] and material that is tangible or intangible, written or unwritten.[33]

---

[28] FED. R. EVID. 502 provides for the protection of attorney/client communications and attorney work product. Basically, it provides that disclosure of otherwise protected information will not be construed as a waiver if the disclosure is inadvertent. Counsel should request that the court include by incorporation Rule 502 in its pretrial order.

[29] *See id.* 501.

[30] *Id.* Under choice of law rules, that may or may not be the state where the action is pending. *See In re* Yasmin and Yaz (Drospirenone) Mktg, Sales Practices & Products Liab. Litig., No. 3:09–MD–02100–DRH, 2011 WL 1375011, at *4 (S.D. Ill. Apr. 12, 2011).

[31] FED. R. CIV. P. 26(b)(3)(A); *see also* Hickman v. Taylor, 329 U.S. 495, 510–11 (1947).

[32] United States v. Nobles, 422 U.S. 225, 238–39 (1975) ("[T]he doctrine is an intensely practical one, grounded in the realities of litigation in our adversary system. One of those realities is that attorneys often must rely on the assistance of investigators and other agents in the compilation of materials in preparation for trial. It is therefore necessary that the doctrine protect material prepared by agents for the attorney as well as those prepared by the attorney himself."); *see also* FED. R. CIV. P. 26(b)(3)(A).

[33] Although Rule 26(b)(3)(A) refers specifically to protecting "documents and tangible things," Black's Law Dictionary defines work product to include "[t]angible material *or its intangible equivalent, in unwritten or oral form*, that was either prepared by or for a lawyer or prepared for litigation, either planned or in progress." *Work Product*, BLACK'S LAW DICTIONARY (11th ed. 2019)

There are two types of work product—fact work product and opinion work product.[34] Typically, documents reflecting factual information gathered for litigation purposes are considered fact work product and receive only qualified immunity from discovery.[35] Pursuant to Rule 26(b)(3), these documents are discoverable if there is a showing of substantial need for the information and an inability otherwise to obtain the information without "undue hardship."[36] Opinion work product, however, includes the lawyer's legal strategy, evaluation of the case, inferences, and other subjective thoughts.[37] This type of information receives almost absolute protection from disclosure.[38]

ii. Non-Testifying Experts

There are two categories of experts: experts employed to testify at trial, and non-testifying experts hired to serve as consultants to counsel. Communication with and the opinions of non-testifying experts generally are not subject to discovery.[39] Rule 26(b)(4)(D) sets out the limitation:

Expert Employed Only for Trial Preparation.

Ordinarily, a party may not, by interrogatories or deposition, discover facts known or opinions held by an expert who has been retained or specially employed by another party in anticipation of litigation or to prepare for trial and who is not expected to be called as a witness at trial.

The protection, while strong, is not absolute.[40] If a party shows exceptional circumstances, for example, a need for information reviewed or tested by

---

(emphasis added). Courts similarly recognize the work product protection as extending beyond "tangible things." *See, e.g.,* United States v. Deloitte LLP, 610 F.3d 129, 136 (D.C. Cir. 2010) ("Rule 26(b)(3) addresses only 'documents and tangible things,' but *Hickman*'s definition of work product extends to 'intangible' things.") (citations omitted).

[34] Leventhal v. Lohmann, 721 So. 2d 1249, 1250 (Fla. Dist. Ct. App. 1998) ("There are two types of work product, fact work product, which is information gathered in anticipation of litigation, and opinion work product, which consists of counsel's opinions, conclusions and theories.").

[35] *See* FED. R. CIV. P. 26(b)(3)(A) advisory committee's note to 1970 amendment; *see also* Coogan v. Cornet Transp. Co., 199 F.R.D. 166, 168 (D. Md. 2001).

[36] FED. R. CIV. P. 26(b)(3)(A)(ii).

[37] Lockheed Martin Corp. v. L-3 Commc'ns Corp., No. 6:05–CV–1580 ORL31KRS, 2007 WL 2209250, at *9–10 (M.D. Fla. July 29, 2007).

[38] *In re* Green Grand Jury Proceedings, 492 F.3d 976, 980 (8th Cir. 2007) ("Opinion work product . . . enjoys a nearly absolute immunity and can be discovered only in very rare and extraordinary circumstances"). For more information regarding work product protection, see Craig M. Roen & Catherine O'Conner, *Don't Forget to Remember Everything: The Trouble with Rule 30(b)(6) Depositions,* 45 U. TOL. L. REV. 29 (2013).

[39] Chapter 9 addresses expert discovery in more detail.

[40] *See* FED. R. CIV. P. 26(b)(4)(D)(ii).

the consulting expert but which now is no longer available, the court may open the door to discovery.[41]

An important purpose of the rule protecting communication with consultants is to grant counsel the ability to consult candidly with non-testifying experts in order to better understand the subject matter of the case and more accurately evaluate the client's position. The rule also addresses the concern that experts may be unwilling to consult if doing so carries a risk the expert will need to turn over materials and/or testify, and serves to promote the interest in having each side—develop its own case at its own expense.[42] The disclosure rules regarding testifying versus consulting experts become more complicated when an attorney subsequently decides to use as a testifying expert someone initially hired as a consulting expert.[43]

c.   Otherwise Confidential Information

The Rules of Civil Procedure do not specifically protect confidential information from disclosure during discovery. However, Rule 26(c)(1) states that a court may issue a protective order instructing that "a trade secret or other confidential research, development, or commercial information not be revealed or be revealed only in a specified way."[44]

Information commonly considered confidential and therefore worthy of protection from discovery includes:

- Trade secrets;[45]

- Other business data or information that has economic value due to its non-public nature (i.e., proprietary information);[46]

- Information that may be protected from disclosure pursuant to agreements (including settlement agreements);[47]

---

[41] *See* Yeda Research & Dev. Co v. Abbott GmbH & Co. KG, 292 F.R.D. 97, 107–108 (D.D.C. 2013).

[42] *See* Bank Brussels Lambert v. Chase Manhattan Bank, N.A., 175 F.R.D. 34, 45 (S.D.N.Y. 1997) (citing Rubel v. Eli Lilly and Co., 160 F.R.D. 458, 460 (S.D.N.Y. 1995)). The work and opinions of non-testifying experts hired by counsel to assist with trial preparation is another form of work product: "[t]angible material or its intangible equivalent, in unwritten or oral form, that was either prepared by *or for* a lawyer or prepared for litigation" constitutes work product. *Work Product*, BLACK'S LAW DICTIONARY (11th ed. 2019) (emphasis added).

[43] *See, e.g.*, McCormick v. Halliburton Energy Servs., Inc., No. CIV–11–1272–M, 2015 WL 2345310 (W.D. Okla. May 14, 2015); Yeda Research & Dev. Co., 292 F.R.D. at 112–114.

[44] FED. R. CIV. P. 26(c)(1)(G).

[45] *See In re* Remington Arms Co., 952 F.2d 1029, 1032 (8th Cir. 1991) (discussing the balancing a court must do when determining whether or not to protect trade secrets from discovery).

[46] *See* Rice v. United States, 39 Fed.Cl. 747, 749–50 (1997) (discussing the analysis for determining when protection of proprietary information is appropriate).

[47] *See* Malone v. Ameren UE, 646 F.3d 512, 516 (8th Cir. 2011) (determining that the district court did not abuse its discretion in disallowing discovery of a confidential settlement agreement).

- Information precluded from disclosure by court order in another case;[48]

- Information precluded from disclosure pursuant to statute.[49]

5. DISCOVERY CONDUCTED FOR IMPROPER PURPOSES

Rule 26(c)(1) allows litigants to seek protective orders[50] from improper or overbroad discovery:

> The court may, for good cause, issue an order to protect a party or person from annoyance, embarrassment, oppression, or undue burden or expense . . . .[51]

This limitation on improper discovery is echoed in Rule 30, which governs oral depositions:

> At any time during a deposition, the deponent or a party may move to terminate or limit it on the ground that it is being conducted in bad faith or in a manner that unreasonably annoys, embarrasses, or oppresses the deponent or party.[52]

In other words, discovery is limited to *legitimate* purposes. Using discovery to abuse an adverse party is never legitimate. And, as Chapter 13 explains, such conduct is sanctionable.

In the following chapters, we will begin to shift focus from more general concepts to specific tools, strategies, and tactics for obtaining evidence in support of your case.

---

[48] *See* Ohio-Sealy Mattress Mfg. Co. v. Duncan, 95 F.R.D. 99 (N.D. Ill. 1982) (deciding to preclude discovery of material already protected in a concurrent case).

[49] Examples potentially include medical records and other information deemed private under state or federal records laws. A party may waive such statutory protections if the otherwise protected information is relevant to a claim or defense. Under such circumstances, the typical response is for the court to enter a protective order that requires disclosure for purposes of the litigation but subject to strict limitations and protections.

[50] Motion practice, including motions for protective orders, will be addressed in greater detail in Chapter 13.

[51] FED. R. CIV. P. 26(c)(1).

[52] *Id.* 30(d)(3)(A).

CHAPTER 5

THE RULE 26(f) REPORT AND DISCOVERY PLAN AND RULE 26(a) INITIAL DISCLOSURES

■ ■ ■

We now enter the thicket of Rule 26 requirements.[1] It is unavoidable. Nobody loves this part of litigation, but getting this part of the case right is essential to properly advocating for your client. Conversely, getting this part of the case wrong is like tripping over your shoelaces at the sound of the gun.

We begin with Rule 26(f) because that is where, sequentially, the Rule 26 process starts. Rule 26(f) relates to pretrial scheduling and how discovery shall proceed. Under Rule 26(f) the parties must "meet and confer" and then produce a joint report regarding the result of their efforts to cooperatively come up with a discovery plan. We then turn to Rule 26(a), which governs required initial disclosures.

The Rule 26(f) meet and confer must take place before the Rule 16 pretrial conference,[2] that is, before counsel appear before the court to discuss a scheduling order. However, before you meet with opposing counsel for the Rule 26(f) meet and confer, it is essential to first develop your own litigation plan. The reason should be obvious: you must first have an understanding of your own discovery objectives, and the time necessary to achieve them, before you can negotiate a joint scheduling and discovery plan. In other words, if you have not thought through your own plan (remember the Critical Path Method discussion in Chapter 3), you will lack the necessary information to negotiate a joint plan with opposing counsel, or to persuade the court of the reasonableness of your recommendations should the parties fail to reach an agreement.

---

[1] Bear in mind that the rules vary widely across the states as to discovery plan requirements; some state rules are substantially different from the federal rules.

[2] FED. R. CIV. P. 26(f)(1).

A. RULE 26(f) REPORT AND PROPOSED SCHEDULING ORDER

The Rule 26(f) report is something of an omnibus document jointly prepared by counsel.[3] It is intended to inform the court about the legal issues in dispute, any stipulations between the parties, and a proposed discovery schedule. The meet and confer process is intended to spur counsel to explore areas of agreement, clarify areas of disagreement, and otherwise work cooperatively toward the goal of developing a manageable pretrial schedule and discovery plan.[4] The parties submit the Rule 26(f) report to the court, sometimes with competing recommendations. To the extent the parties fail to agree on all terms of a plan to manage the litigation, the court will resolve the differences at a Rule 16 conference. Following the Rule 16 conference, the court will issue a pretrial order that sets forth, among other things, a discovery schedule.[5]

1. CONTENTS OF A RULE 26(f) REPORT

Rule 26(f) contains a number of specifics about which counsel must meet and confer, but the Rule does not provide an exhaustive list of all discovery issues that may arise, nor does it provide clear directives as to how to present the required information to the court. Therefore, rather than parse the language of Rule 26(f) here, we instead provide a summary of the information that a Rule 26(f) report normally would contain.

Rule 26(f) Report Requirements	Contents	Comment
Description of the case	Each party's summary of the case. Joint statement of stipulated facts, demand for jury trial and/or expedited trial.	Typically, this is a bare bones statement of each party's view of the case.
Pleadings	Identify pleadings that have been served and filed.	Deadlines for amendments to the pleadings are dealt with separately.

---

[3]   See exemplar form of a Rule 26(f) report in the Appendix.

[4]   FED. R. CIV. P. 29 allows the parties to enter into stipulations regarding discovery without leave of court so long as the stipulations do not interfere with the time set for completing discovery, motions or the trial date.

[5]   *Id.* 16(b).

Fact discovery	Deadlines for completion of fact discovery and any upward or downward departures from presumptive discovery limits.	You should have your discovery plan prepared before attempting to negotiate these deadlines and limits.
Expert witness discovery	Identification of anticipated trial experts, as well as deadlines for reports and depositions.	You should develop early in the litigation an understanding of the type of experts who will be necessary.
Other discovery issues	• Protective orders • Discovery of ESI • Privilege claims • Fed. R. Evid. 502 non-waiver of privilege agreement	Deal with these issues upfront or you will face avoidable disputes and delays during the discovery process.
Proposed motion schedule	• Amending pleadings • Non-dispositive motions, such as motions to compel • Dispositive motions	Motion deadlines should follow discovery deadlines.
Final pretrial conference and trial ready dates	Self-explanatory.	The final pretrial should post-date all discovery cutoffs and motion dates.
Other issues	• Insurance information • Settlement conferences and ADR • Stipulation for trial by magistrate judge	The subject matter of the case or the issues presented may make it prudent or necessary to address additional topics.

Illus. 5-1.

THE RULE 26(F) REPORT AND DISCOVERY PLAN

2. HELPFUL TIPS REGARDING
THE RULE 26(f) REPORT

Developing a litigation plan (see Chapter 3) informs your discovery needs, which in turn helps you prepare to negotiate the terms contained in the Rule 26(f) report, such as the amount of time necessary to complete discovery. However, there are additional considerations you must take into account.[6] We cannot address them all in this book, but following are a number of issues that commonly arise, or are otherwise worth noting.

a. Assume There Will Be Discovery Disputes and Plan Accordingly

Invariably, discovery disputes arise. The interrogatory responses were due in 30 days, but opposing counsel "forgot" to send them out and promises to get them to you "as soon as I can." They don't come. Depositions are scheduled, canceled, rescheduled, re-canceled. Once interrogatory responses are finally received, they turn out to be woefully inadequate. All of this is common. In fact, much of what litigators do is argue over discovery.

Therefore, as you plan discovery, you should anticipate and plan for motions to compel. The problem, of course, is that discovery disputes can cause delays, and delays can create havoc with counsel's overall discovery plan. There are two ways to minimize this problem.

First, the entire case should not grind to a halt while discovery motions are prepared or pending. Discovery that is not dependent on the disputed discovery should continue to go forward. Second, you can help minimize the time required for discovery motions by putting short timelines on the meet and confer process.[7] Remember, the Rules require counsel to meet and confer before filing discovery motions. The purpose of the meet and confer requirement is to encourage informal resolution of discovery disputes. The problem is that recalcitrant counsel may attempt to drag out the meet and confer process in an effort to run the clock on discovery. So when you are negotiating a discovery timeline as you prepare your Rule 26(f) report, you might want to attempt to get opposing counsel to agree to a short timeframe for engaging in any discovery-related meet and confer.[8] Absent a stipulation from opposing counsel, ask the court to impose a short time limit on the meet and confer process. Even if the court declines to set

---

[6] Hopefully, the reader has begun to gain an appreciation for why litigation and discovery planning needs to begin *before* the case is joined and *before* counsel meets to draft the Rule 26(f) report: there are a lot of moving parts.

[7] This may be easier said than done. Counsel does not dictate the court's schedule. Usually, counsel contacts the court administrator (or the judge's clerk) to ask for a date. If the dispute is particularly time sensitive, depending on your judge, it may be appropriate to send a letter to the court asking for an expedited hearing.

[8] *See* FED. R. CIV. P. 37(a)(1).

specific time limits for completing the meet and confer process, simply by raising the issue the judge will get the message counsel is conveying and likely will be more sensitive to any gamesmanship the adverse party may engage in down the line.

b.   Consider Seeking Upward or Downward Departures from Presumptive Discovery Limits Depending on the Size, Complexity or Overall Value of the Case

i.   *Beware the Presumptive Limits on Discovery*

Interrogatories are presumptively limited to no more than 25 per party.[9] Depositions are presumptively limited to no more than ten, each to be completed in a single day and not to exceed seven hours.[10] Rule 26, however, allows the parties to stipulate to departures from any presumptive discovery limits or for the court to alter or impose limits, either by motion or of its own accord.[11] Generally, the court will take an equitable and practical approach to setting discovery limits, so you must be prepared to persuade the court regarding the necessity of an upward or downward departure.

Regarding upward departures, you should ask yourself: is the case so complex as to merit additional discovery beyond the presumptive limits? It is not unusual that even in a moderately simple case—for example, a straightforward employment dispute, 25 interrogatories may be insufficient to address all the issues. Similarly, it is not uncommon for the court to expand the deposition limit.

In the alternative, if the case is quite simple, or one in which the amount in dispute is relatively small, counsel may wish to limit the expense of litigation by limiting the scope of allowable discovery through a downward departure from the presumptive limits. Recall that Rule 26 specifically authorizes the court to limit discovery in proportion to "the needs of the case, considering the importance of the issues at stake in the action, the amount in controversy, the parties' relative access to relevant information, the parties' resources, the importance of the discovery in resolving the issues, and whether the burden or expense of the proposed discovery outweighs its likely benefit."[12]

---

[9]   *Id.* 33(a)(1).

[10]   *Id.* 30(a)(2)(A)(i), (d)(1).

[11]   *Id.*; *see also id.* 26(b)(1), (b)(2).

[12]   *Id.* 26(b)(1).

ii. Beware the Problems That Arise with Discovery Limits in Multi-Party Litigation

Particular problems relating to discovery limits arise in multi-party litigation. Assume a case where there are multiple defendants with disparate issues and defenses. Some courts have imposed the presumptive limits not per party, but per *side*.[13] Such mechanical application of the presumptive limits can result in an unfair restriction on a given party's access to discovery when there are multiple parties on one side of the case. Conversely, mechanical application of the presumptive limits on each party rather than each side may unfairly burden the single party litigating against multiple parties.

When there is an imbalance between the number of plaintiffs and the number of defendants, or when a third-party defendant or intervenor must conduct discovery into both the plaintiff's case and the defendant's case, you should be prepared to argue for relative parity *vis a vis* discovery limits, or aggregate discovery limits on similarly situated parties so that neither side has an unfair advantage.[14]

c. All Non-Dispositive and Dispositive Motion Cut-Off Dates Should Post-Date the Discovery Deadline

Both non-dispositive and dispositive motion cut-off dates should come later in time than the discovery deadline. Perhaps the best way to illustrate this is by presenting two examples.

Assume a discovery cut-off date of December 31. Assume the non-dispositive motion cut-off (including motions to compel) is the same date. If you receive inadequate discovery responses from the opposing party on December 31, you have lost your opportunity to bring a motion to compel due to the non-dispositive motion deadline. Although the court may grant leave to file a motion beyond the cut-off date, it is not wise to put yourself in this position.

Similarly, assume a discovery cut-off date of December 31 and a dispositive motion cut-off date of January 30. If the discovery received by December 31 is inadequate and requires a motion to compel, by the time you resolve the discovery problem, you may be on top of, or past, your summary judgment deadline. Further, if depositions continue through the end of the discovery period, by the time the reporter prepares the transcript and the deponent reads and signs it, you might have difficulty meeting the

---

[13] *See, e.g.*, Thykkuttathil v. Keese, 294 F.R.D. 597, 599 (W.D. Wash. 2013).

[14] For more on this topic, see FEDERAL JUDICIAL CENTER, MANUAL FOR COMPLEX LITIGATION § 11.422 (4th ed. 2004).

dispositive motion deadline.[15] Therefore, as a practical matter, you should seek a dispositive motion cut-off date at least 60 days after the discovery cut-off date, and perhaps longer in particularly complex cases.

d. Electronically Stored Information ("ESI")[16]

Effective management of the electronically stored information ("ESI") discovery process requires special preparation in advance of the Rule 26(f) meet and confer. For example, how can you confidently meet the Rule 34 requirement that document demands be stated with reasonable particularity unless you have a detailed understanding of how the opposing party defines its ESI, or how it stores, manages, retains, and disposes of its ESI? Given the import and complexity of ESI discovery, we recommend that you bring an ESI checklist[17] to the meet & confer and insist that each topic relevant to the case be fully addressed.

What is good for the goose is good for the gander, though. It is essential to understand your own client's ESI before the meet and confer process. You must, for example, have a firm grasp of what ESI your client has, including knowledge of where it resides, who administers it, who has access to it, what the retention policies are, and whether the retention policies are followed. By investigating your own client's ESI, you will be in a better position to engage in a meaningful meet and confer process, and you also will be better positioned to ferret out helpful documents, become aware of problematic documents, and be ready to timely respond to opposing counsel's discovery of your client's ESI. Moreover, courts expect counsel to have this level of familiarity with their client's ESI—and expect counsel to have it *before* the Rule 26(f) conference:

> For the Rule 26(f) conference to be effective, attorneys must be familiar with their clients' information systems. This familiarity usually requires understanding what information is available; how it may be altered or made unavailable by routine computer operations; and what is entailed in identifying, preserving, collecting, reviewing, and producing it. Attorneys need to identify those persons who are most knowledgeable about the client's computer systems and meet with them well in advance of the Rule 26(f) conference; it may also be useful to have those persons present at the conference. Some courts put such requirements in

---

[15] Even if you were able to obtain the deposition transcript that same day, a deponent who elects to "read and sign" may take up to an additional 30 days before the court reporter can certify the transcript. *See* FED. R. CIV. P. 30(e)–(f).

[16] Go to Chapter 10 for a detailed discussion of ESI discovery, production, and management.

[17] The United States District Court for the Northern District of California promulgated such a checklist. *See* Appendix.

local rules, guidelines, or protocols; other courts use case-management orders to tell the attorneys what to expect.[18]

At a minimum, you should be prepared to address and get agreement at the Rule 26(f) meet and confer regarding ESI issues that commonly arise. Agreements should include the following:

1. Any production of ESI shall include unique identifiers for each page;

2. Any ESI production shall be made in a readily searchable format;

3. The locations from which each tranche of ESI originated shall be specifically identified;

4. All ESI that may relate to the dispute shall be preserved in a verifiable manner, i.e., ensuring that ESI is not inadvertently spoliated; and

5. Any privileged or otherwise confidential information inadvertently disclosed shall retain its protected status and shall be returned or deleted.

ESI and Rule 26: A View from the Bench

"All too often, attorneys view their obligation to 'meet and confer' under Rule 26(f) as a perfunctory exercise. When ESI is involved in a case, judges should insist that a meaningful Rule 26(f) conference take place and that a meaningful discovery plan be submitted for use in the Rule 16 conference with the court."[19]

---

e. **Protective Orders for Documents That Are Privileged, Proprietary, or Otherwise Confidential, Including a Rule 502 Order**

There are times when there may be a legitimate need for discovery of information that is privileged or otherwise confidential. Or the litigation itself may be about privileged or confidential information. For example, in a trade secrets dispute, the information that is allegedly a trade secret (and therefore presumably confidential) must be safeguarded throughout the litigation so that it is not publicly disclosed. Similarly, patient records in a medical malpractice case, and employees' private data in an employment case will require protection.

---

[18] BARBARA J. ROTHSTEIN ET AL., FED. JUDICIAL CTR., MANAGING DISCOVERY OF ELECTRONIC INFORMATION: A POCKET GUIDE FOR JUDGES 8–9 (2d ed. 2012), *available at* http://esiattorneys. com/app-site-content/uploads/2013/05/2nd-edition-Judges-pocket-guide.pdf.

[19] Rothstein, *supra* note 18, at 6.

Although the parties may need and be entitled to access to these types of sensitive information, they often do not want others—such as competitors, the media, or the general public—to obtain access.[20] Protective orders address this problem. Though there are many different types, and some are *sui generis*, in many jurisdictions there are standard form protective orders found on the courts' web sites.[21]

Protective Order Components

- Identify documents subject to protection
- Describe how documents will be safeguarded
- Describe how inadvertently disclosed documents should be handled
- Describe procedure for disposal of documents at the conclusion of the case

---

While a protective order can issue at any time during discovery, it is preferable to discuss and resolve protective order issues at the Rule 26(f) meet and confer and then ask the court to issue the protective order at the inception of discovery. Otherwise you risk wasting valuable discovery time when you receive the following response to a document request: "Documents responsive to this request are confidential, proprietary, or otherwise privileged and therefore will not be produced unless and until an appropriate protective order has been issued."

It happens from time to time that privileged or otherwise confidential documents are inadvertently disclosed. Inadvertent production should not result in waiver of whatever protection attaches to the information. Protective orders typically include language that preserves those protections and provides for a means to either return the documents or destroy them.[22]

Finally, make sure the court's order incorporates Federal Rule of Evidence 502. Such an order is authorized by 502(d). There should be no disputes over the inadvertent disclosure of protected information. It should not constitute a waiver of any privileged or otherwise protected

---

[20] *See* Masonite Corp. v. Cnty. of Mendocino Air Quality Mgmt. Dist., 49 Cal. Rptr. 2d 639, 650 (1996) (ruling that information not designated as a trade secret in reports became public records upon disclosure).

[21] See, for example, the District of Minnesota's standard form protective order in the Appendix.

[22] The protective order should include language similar to that found in FED. R. EVID. 502(d), which states that inadvertent disclosure of protected information does not constitute a waiver of whatever protection attaches. FED. R. EVID. 502(d). FED R. CIV. P. 16(b)(3)(B)(iv) now specifically includes language that permits the court to incorporate the protections of Rule 502(d) into the scheduling order as does FED. R. EVID. 502(d).

information. Rule 502 sets forth the specific procedures for curing inadvertent disclosures; counsel should simply agree to follow the rule.

f.   In Document-Intensive Cases, Agree on Protocols for Document Productions, Including Unique Identifiers on All Documents

In document-intensive cases, where thousands, or perhaps millions, of pages are produced by multiple parties over an extended period of time, it is easy to make a disorganized mess of the record you are attempting to build. To prevent confusion and to simplify matters for everyone, it is prudent to come to agreement on document production and labeling protocols at the Rule 26(f) meet and confer:

1.   All documents produced (and even those withheld but identified on privilege logs) shall be Bates numbered or otherwise uniquely identified;[23]

2.   Each party that produces documents shall add a prefix to the Bates numbers (or other numbering system) that unambiguously identifies the producing party;[24]

3.   A master set of deposition exhibits shall be created: once a document is used in one deposition it shall retain the same deposition exhibit number in all subsequent depositions.[25]

Usually, counsel will agree to these types of ministerial matters, but if you are dealing with a difficult adversary, be prepared to raise these issues at the Rule 16 hearing.

g.   Generally, Expert Discovery Should Take Place After the Completion of "Fact" Discovery[26]

Thus far, we have discussed a singular discovery cut-off. In fact, you should advocate for two: a "fact" discovery (i.e., non-expert witness discovery) cut-off, followed by a period of expert discovery that has a separate discovery cut-off. Here's why.

Your discovery plan probably includes gathering evidence necessary to your expert's analysis and opinions.[27] You may not be able to gather all the

---

[23] Bates numbering is nothing more than sequential numbering of documents. This can be done both electronically and on hard copy.

[24] For example, if the La-De-Dah Software Corp. produces documents, the first page of the first document may be identified as: LA0000001. Every subsequent page would then be identified sequentially.

[25] Be careful. Multiple iterations of a document may appear quite similar but should be separately numbered.

[26] The form Rule 26(f) report we use as an exemplar (*see* Appendix), distinguishes between "fact" discovery and "expert" discovery, so we adopt that distinction here.

[27] An expert opinion must be based upon, among other things, "sufficient facts or data." FED. R. EVID. 702. Oftentimes, the "facts and data" must be obtained through discovery.

facts or data she will need until the completion of fact discovery. Therefore, you should try to get agreement from the opposing counsel that neither side's expert reports shall be due, nor expert depositions taken, until after the end of fact discovery. Such an agreement should not be difficult to get as it is in the parties' mutual interest to conduct discovery in this fashion.

There is another reason to "bifurcate" discovery between fact and expert discovery: cost. Experts can be expensive. Although it is not ideal, sometimes a client is unwilling to pay for experts unless and until it is absolutely necessary. Perhaps the client is hoping that the case will settle before incurring the expense of experts. Bifurcating discovery enables you, if necessary, to delay retention of an expert.

h.   Cost Sharing Agreements

Ordinarily, each party bears its own costs associated with developing its respective cases. Sometimes, however, there is discovery that all parties have a common interest in pursuing. For example, all parties may have an interest in obtaining documents from a third-party, or all parties may have an interest in inspecting, testing, or otherwise documenting physical spaces or objects. Further, all parties may wish to depose a witness who desires to have his expenses paid for in relation to his deposition (such as travel costs or reimbursement for lost wages).

One way to mitigate costs is to share them with other parties. If it is apparent there will be shared interests in conducting certain discovery, it is a good idea to enter into a cost sharing agreement. You can do this by stipulation or by requesting the court to include it in the pretrial scheduling order.[28]

i.   Phased Discovery

Phased discovery is ostensibly intended to save time and money. The idea is straightforward: if there are discreet case-dispositive issues, then before engaging in full-blown discovery, the parties should limit discovery to the case-dispositive issues. If the case is disposed of on a discreet issue, then time and money has not been wasted on conducting discovery into the other issues in the case.

For example, in order to bring a Family Medical Leave Act case against an employer, there must be a showing that the company employs 50 or more employees. Plaintiff alleges that the employer meets the threshold; defendant employer claims otherwise. Depending on the outcome of this issue, the claim is actionable or it is not. Therefore, the defense may seek phased discovery in which the first phase is limited to whether the employer meets the statutory threshold. At the end of that phase, defense

---

[28]   For more on this topic, see MANUAL FOR COMPLEX LITIGATION, *supra* note 14, at § 11.422.

counsel may seek summary judgment and thereby conclude the litigation without the need for additional discovery.

j.   In Cases Where the Parties Are in Different States or Countries, Try to Get Agreement as to Where Depositions Shall Take Place

If witnesses are in far-flung locations or if the parties themselves are located in separate jurisdictions, it is helpful to seek agreement during the Rule 26(f) meet and confer process as to where witnesses will be deposed. Generally, it is more cost effective to bring the witnesses to where counsel are located than the other way around. If counsel are from different jurisdictions, it becomes particularly prudent to negotiate deposition locations during the Rule 26(f) meet and confer.[29] Generally speaking, plaintiffs are subject to deposition in the jurisdiction where their action is pending,[30] defendants are subject to deposition in the jurisdiction where they live,[31] and corporate defendants may be deposed where the corporation has its principle place of business.[32] Third-party witnesses may be deposed in the community where they live.[33] Any witness may agree to be deposed in an alternative location.

k.   Requests for Discovery Referees in Complex or Particularly Contentious Cases

There are cases that are so complicated, or that contain the seeds of so many discovery disputes, or that are so acrimonious that the appointment of a discovery referee is warranted. Rule 53 permits the court to appoint special masters to facilitate litigation. Special masters typically are attorneys with extensive experience with litigation matters. They are deputized by the court and may be appointed to oversee or rule on a number of matters, including discovery disputes.

Discovery referees (or special masters as they are sometimes called) must be paid for by a party, or by cost sharing among the parties. They can be expensive but helpful in quickly resolving discovery disputes. In the right kind of case, use of discovery referees may actually help the parties to save money, as well as time and a great deal of aggravation, by tamping down aggressive behavior and quickly getting to the heart of the matter.

---

[29] *See* FED R. CIV. P. 29 ("[T]he parties may stipulate that . . . a deposition may be taken before any person, *at any time or place*, on any notice, and in the manner specified.") (emphasis added).

[30] Culhane v. MSC Cruises (USA), Inc., 290 F.R.D. 565, 566 (S.D. Fla. 2013).

[31] Buzzeo v. Bd. of Educ., Hempstead, 178 F.R.D. 390, 392 (E.D.N.Y. 1998).

[32] Paleteria La Michoacana, Inc. v. Productos Lacteos Tocumbo S.A. de C.V., 292 F.R.D. 19, 22 (D.D.C. 2013).

[33] *See* Prudential Ins. Co. of Am. v. Nelson, 11 F. Supp. 2d 572, 579 (D.N.J. 1998) (finding a non-party witness with residency in Florida to be subject to procedure in Florida).

B. RULE 26(a) INITIAL DISCLOSURES

Parties have 14 days from the date of the Rule 26(f) conference to make their initial disclosures.[34] Initial disclosures are required absent any request from the opposing party,[35] and must include the following information:[36]

- The identities of supporting witnesses, along with the subjects of the information they possess;

- Supporting documents;

- A computation of damages, along with supporting evidence;

- Insurance information in the event coverage is available to pay any claims.

The purpose of Rule 26(a) disclosures is to streamline the discovery process.[37] However, there is no obligation at this stage to disclose (1) the identity of witnesses or documents that are adverse to your case, or (2) evidence that is solely for the purpose of impeachment. Further, foundational evidence generally is not disclosed at this stage of the litigation. Thus, although Rule 26(a) initial disclosures are helpful and informative, they are no substitute for actively engaging in discovery. Indeed, Rule 26(a) disclosures likely only scratch the surface of the information the parties need to mine.[38]

1. DISCLOSURE OF SUPPORTING WITNESSES

Depending upon counsel's litigation style and the litigation tactics counsel chooses to employ, witness disclosures range from general to specific. For example, a bare-bones witness disclosure might read:

> "Melvin G. Witness, 123 Disclosure Ln., Vagueland. Mr. Witness has knowledge regarding the defendant's negligence in this case."

Is this sufficient disclosure? Probably.[39]

At the other end of the spectrum, the witness disclosure may be extremely detailed. It might include not only the name, location, and

---

[34] 26(a)(1)(C).

[35] *Id.* 26(a)(1)(A).

[36] *Id.* 26(a)(1)(A)(i)–(iv).

[37] *Id.* 26(a) advisory committee's note to 1993 amendment.

[38] *See* Appendix for a Rule 26(a) initial disclosure template.

[39] Bush v. Gulf Coast Elec. Co-op., No. 5:13–CV–369–RS–GRJ, 2015 WL 3422336, at *3 (N.D. Fla. May 27, 2015) ("Making a general disclosure of a witness in an initial disclosure is both common and appropriate."); Tift v. Ball, No. C07–0276RSM, 2007 WL 3047228, at *1 (W.D. Wash. Oct. 18, 2007) ("It is not necessary to provide a detailed narrative of all the facts known to each witness; a brief description of the general topics of each witness' knowledge will suffice."). *But see* Beane v. Util. Trailer Mfg. Co., No. 2:10 CV 781, 2013 WL 1344763, at *2 (W.D. La. Feb. 25, 2013) (finding a very short disclosure with no accompanying exhibits, facts, or data to be insufficient).

general subject to which the witness is expected to testify, but it may set forth chapter and verse of what the witness allegedly knows and is prepared to testify to. Why would counsel go to the trouble of "over-disclosure" if it is not required by the Rule? One answer is that it may apprise opposing counsel of the overwhelming strength of the case as an attempt to prompt an early settlement.

2. DISCLOSURE OF SUPPORTING DOCUMENTS

Initial document disclosures should describe with particularity the documents in support of the case, or otherwise counsel should simply produce the documents. In cases where the documents are voluminous, it is sufficient and generally preferable to first identify the documents and offer to make them available to the opposing party for inspection and copying. On the other hand, if the documents are relatively few, there really is no reason to not simply copy and produce them.

3. DISCLOSURE OF DAMAGES CALCULATIONS

Rule 26(a) also requires the parties to make initial disclosure of their claimed damages. This requirement typically only applies to plaintiffs, but if the defendant has asserted a counter-claim, it too may be required to provide damages information.

The initial damages disclosure must identify the categories of damages claimed, the dollar computation for each category of damages, and the documents and other evidence supporting the claimed damages.[40] It is no excuse to have not yet conducted a sufficient investigation.[41] At the same time, courts recognize that calculations may change as additional information becomes available. In that case, the disclosing party is required to formally supplement its initial disclosures,[42] which sometimes happens several times over the course of discovery.[43] Disclosures that are insufficient subject a party to potential exclusion of insufficiently identified categories or amounts of damages,[44] and subject the party and counsel as well to fees and costs attached to a motion to compel.[45]

---

[40] FED. R. CIV. P. 26(a)(1)(A)(iii).

[41] Id. 26(a)(1)(E).

[42] Id. 26(e)(1).

[43] E.g., Aetna Inc. v. Blue Cross Blue Shield of Michigan, No. 11–CV–15346, 2012 WL 4355545, at *2 (E.D. Mich. Sept. 24, 2012) ("The Court will order Plaintiff to supplement its response to Plaintiff's initial disclosures to provide up-to-date calculations for each category of damages claimed and produce the documents or other evidentiary material on which each calculation is based."); Williams v. Sprint/United Mgmt. Co., 235 F.R.D. 494, 507 (D. Kan. 2006) (denying motion to compel interrogatory due to the adequacy of the plaintiff's fifth supplemental disclosure).

[44] FED. R. CIV. P. 37(c)(1).

[45] See id. 37(a)(5). Under Rule 37(a)(5), if a motion to compel disclosures is granted or if the disclosures are not submitted until after the motion to compel is filed, "the court must" award reasonable expenses and fees to the moving party unless the motion to compel was filed prior to a

The bottom line is this: make the Rule 26(a) initial disclosure of all damage categories and calculations, including all supporting documents and evidence, that can be reasonably determined at the time the disclosure is due. Also identify those damages that are subject to expert opinion (and therefore will be disclosed in greater detail through the expert's report), or are otherwise to be determined by the jury as general damages (e.g., claims for pain and suffering).[46] As each element of the overall damages claim becomes known (such as through expert opinion), you must supplement your damages disclosures.[47]

When considering a party's Rule 26(a) initial disclosure obligations, it should be obvious why pre-discovery case development is essential, but we will state the obvious nonetheless. The rules require initial disclosures very early in the life of the case. If you have not done an adequate job of pre-discovery case development, you likely will have failed to identify the reasonably discoverable universe of witnesses and documents that support the case. This will signal to opposing counsel that you have not properly investigated and prepared the case, which is valuable information indeed.

There is another, and equally compelling, reason to make timely and complete disclosures: Rule 37(c). The rule prohibits parties from offering evidence in a motion or trial that the party failed to disclose as required by Rule 26(a). Counsel who has "hidden the ball," attempted to sandbag the opposing party by failing to disclose its supporting evidence, or otherwise has simply been negligent in developing her case in a timely manner, runs the substantial risk of being denied the use of undisclosed evidence—even if the evidence is crucial to surviving a summary judgment motion or prevailing at trial.[48] Better to over-disclose than under-disclose.

There is another form of gamesmanship that is sometimes employed at this stage of discovery: hiding evidence by using the "needle in a haystack" tactic. For example, a party may identify 100 potentially

---

good faith attempt to resolve the disclosure dispute, the nondisclosure was substantially justified, or other circumstances make an award of fees and costs unjust. FED. R. CIV. P. 37(a)(5)(A) (emphasis added); *see also* Isom v. Midwest Division-OPRMC, No. 13–2602–RDR, 2014 WL 3541842, at *4 (D. Kan. July 17, 2014).

[46] Some jurisdictions require identification of a specified damages amount even for general damages meant to be determined by a jury. *E.g.*, Sandoval v. Am. Bldg. Maint. Indus., Inc., 267 F.R.D. 257, 282 (D. Minn. 2007); Dixon v. Bankhead, No. 4:00CV344–WS, 2000 WL 33175440 at *1 (N.D.Fla. Dec. 20, 2000). *But see* Williams v. Trader Publishing, Co., 218 F.3d 481, 486 n. 3 (5th Cir. 2000) ("Since compensatory damages for emotional distress are necessarily vague and are generally considered a fact issue for the jury, they may not be amenable to the kind of calculation disclosure contemplated by Rule 26(a)(1)(C)."); Scheel v. Harris, No. CIV.A. 3:11–17–DCR, 2012 WL 3879279, at *7 (E.D. Ky. Sept. 6, 2012) (" '[B]ecause emotional suffering is personal and difficult to quantify and because compensatory damages are typically considered a fact issue for the jury, emotional distress damages are not subject to the kind of calculation' required for initial disclosure purposes.").

[47] FED. R. CIV. P. 37(c).

[48] Hill v. U.S. Dep't of Homeland Sec., 570 F. App'x 667, 670 (9th Cir. 2014); Lee Valley Tools, Ltd. v. Indus. Blade Co., 288 F.R.D. 254, 260 (W.D.N.Y. 2013) ("A failure to disclose under Rule 37 encompasses . . . the untimely production of documents and information required to be produced.").

supportive witnesses, and make available for review 1 million supposedly supporting documents as part of its initial disclosures. The game, of course, is to try to force opposing counsel to go hunting for the truly relevant evidence, thus causing confusion and running up costs. This is a form of discovery abuse[49] and one that may run afoul of counsel's ethical responsibilities.[50]

Once the parties have made their initial disclosures, presumably in good faith, you may deploy the slings and arrows of formal discovery against your adversary. Onward.

---

[49] Preferred Care Partners Holding Corp. v. Humana, Inc., No. 08–20424–CIV–UNGARO, 2009 WL 982460, at *18 (S.D. Fla. Apr. 9, 2009) (sanctioning defendant Humana for the untimely production of over 10,000 pages of documents); S.E.C. v. Collins & Aikman Corp., 256 F.R.D. 403, 411 (S.D.N.Y. 2009) ("A page-by-page manual review of ten million pages of records is strikingly expensive in both monetary and human terms and constitutes 'undue hardship' by any definition.").

[50] MODEL RULES OF PROF'L CONDUCT R. 3.4, 8.4 (2020).

CHAPTER 6

OVERVIEW OF FORMAL DISCOVERY

■ ■ ■

The discovery rules provide litigators with a broad complement of fact-finding tools. Lawyers can use them to compel both parties and non-parties to answer questions and provide information. However, these tools should be used judiciously. You should not cast your discovery net aimlessly into the sea hoping to catch something of use. Discovery is a tactical pursuit for evidence that serves specific purposes: to build an evidentiary record that supports the theory of the case; to explore the strengths and weaknesses of the opposing party's case; and to advance the process of narrowing issues. In order to meet these goals it is best to identify objectives in advance and proceed according to a carefully considered but always flexible plan.

In this chapter we will provide an overview of the tools of discovery, define some important terms, and introduce the concept of discovery strategy.

A. DISCOVERY TOOLS: FORMS OF DISCOVERY

Following is a brief introduction to the tools of discovery; we provide more detailed information in subsequent chapters.

1. INTERROGATORIES: RULE 33

Interrogatories are formal written questions directed to the opposing party. The responding party must answer in writing, under oath, within 30 days.[1]

Interrogatories may be broad or narrow, depending on your purpose, on the information you already have, and on the nature of the claims or defenses about which you are seeking information. For example, an interrogatory may broadly ask the opposing party to "Identify all evidence that supports your claim that defendant negligently operated his vehicle on July 1, 2015, thus allegedly causing an automobile accident." In other situations it may be more effective to serve a narrowly-tailored interrogatory: "State with particularity the precise words you claim defendant uttered on July 1, 2015, which allegedly slandered plaintiff. Include in your response the identity of each and every person who heard

---

[1]   FED. R. CIV. P. 33(b).

the allegedly slanderous words, including each such person's name and address."

Rule 33 presumptively limits the number of interrogatories each party may serve on any other party to 25, including discreet sub-parts.[2] Therefore, you need to use them judiciously and craft them with precision.

2. REQUESTS FOR PRODUCTION: RULE 34

Rule 34 addresses requests for documents, electronically stored information (ESI), and tangible things. You also can use Rule 34 to inspect, test and photograph physical objects and land. By far the most common use of Rule 34 is to obtain documents and ESI.

Rule 34 requests must be specific. You do not need to identify the particular document you seek—you often do not yet know what specific documents exist. But you "must describe with reasonable particularity" the documents or categories of documents you want.[3] It is not proper, for instance, to request "All documents, from any source or location, that in any way relate to this lawsuit."

There are no presumptive limits to the number of Rule 34 requests you may propound, so if some documents that are produced lead you to realize that other relevant documents or categories of documents may exist, you are free to send additional document requests. However, some courts limit the number of Rule 34 requests per their pretrial orders.

3. REQUESTS FOR ADMISSIONS: RULE 36

A request for admission is a contention or assertion of fact that an adverse party is asked to adopt as true. A request for admission is not written in the form of a question: you are asking the receiving party to agree with a statement. There are no presumptive limits to the number of admission requests a party may serve. You may direct requests for admission to:

(A) facts, the application of law to fact, or opinions about either; and

(B) the genuineness of any described documents.[4]

This is a powerful but often overlooked tool. It can be an effective means of eliminating apparent disputes over facts or positions taken by the parties. This type of discovery is also useful for probing adequate foundation for the admissibility of documents.

---

[2] *Id.* 33(a)(1).

[3] *Id.* 34(b)(1).

[4] *Id.* 36(a)(1).

When served with a request for admission, the responding party must unequivocally admit, deny, or "when good faith requires that a party qualify an answer or deny only a part of a matter, the answer must specify the part admitted and qualify or deny the rest."[5] If a party cannot admit or deny the request, it must "state in detail" why it cannot.[6] If the party to whom you have directed your requests for admissions fails to respond within 30 days, the requested matters are deemed admitted.[7]

Like cross-examination, requests for admissions are most effective when leading and narrowly tailored. For example:

"Admit that defendant was not wearing his prescription eyeglasses at the time of the accident that is the subject of this lawsuit."

or

"Admit that this lawsuit is not barred by the 6-year statute of limitation as set forth in Minn. Stat. § 541.05."

Broad requests and requests that seek admission of an ultimate legal issue, e.g., "Admit that Widget X is a trade secret," will likely not be effective. It is helpful to consider an analogy to baseball. Use requests for admission to hit a series of singles. If you aim for the fence, you are likely to fall short.

4. DEPOSITIONS: RULE 30

Rule 30, which governs depositions by oral examination, is the most frequently used deposition rule, and the one we focus upon in this overview.[8]

While written discovery requests and responses are drafted, reviewed, and edited in the quiet of counsel's office, depositions require immediate, unedited, unfiltered responses under oath. This makes depositions a particularly useful discovery device. Depositions enable you to gain a wealth of information,[9] and also afford you the opportunity to size up the witness. Does he make an attractive witness? Is he believable? Is he

---

[5] *Id.* 36(a)(4).

[6] *Id.* 36(a)(4).

[7] *Id.* 36(a)(3).

[8] The deposition rules are as follows:

Rule 27: Depositions to Perpetuate Testimony.

Rule 28: Persons Before Whom Depositions May Be Taken.

Rule 30: Deposition By Oral Examination.

Rule 31: Depositions By Written Questions.

Rule 32: Using Depositions in Court Proceedings.

[9] Deposition witnesses must respond to all questions, unless the questioning calls for privileged information or is made for an improper purpose, such as to harass or embarrass the witness. FED. R. CIV. P. 30(c)(2).

sympathetic? Is he combative, or might a line of questioning cause him to become overtly hostile? Is he selective with what he remembers?

The key to taking an effective deposition is preparation. Part of that preparation includes gathering and carefully organizing as much information as possible that you anticipate may relate to the subjects that will be addressed during the deposition. The more you know about the subject matter of the deposition, the more likely you will be able to elicit valuable testimony and the less likely you will be fooled by misleading testimony. This is why it is generally better to conduct written discovery before taking deposition testimony.

5.   PHYSICAL AND MENTAL EXAMINATIONS: RULE 35

Whenever there are claims of physical or emotional harm, Rule 35 comes into play. Rule 35 provides that a court may order a party whose mental or physical condition is in controversy to submit to an examination by a qualified expert. As a matter of practice, however, if a party makes a claim for damages arising from physical or emotional harm, counsel generally agree to such examination without the need for a court order.

What is sometimes disputed, though, is the scope or nature of the examination. How far back may the adverse party's expert inquire regarding the party's health history? May the expert inquire into a party's nasty divorce proceedings in a subsequent case when emotional harm is alleged? May the examination include an invasive procedure such as a biopsy? All these issues, by their very nature, tend to be case specific. The only general rule is that the examination should be limited to the information that is necessary for the expert to draw valid conclusions. We will explore this concept further in Chapter 11.

6.   SUBPOENAS: RULE 45

If you want a non-party witness or organization to appear at a deposition, to produce documents, or to allow inspection of property or tangible objects, you must serve it with a subpoena.[10] Subpoenas are court orders and thus are issued by the court and backed by the court's authority to enforce the subpoena. A recipient who fails to comply with the requirements of a subpoena may be held in contempt of court. However, you do not want to frighten or antagonize a witness if you can avoid it. It is by far better to work cooperatively with the subject of a subpoena in order to maintain good will. Therefore, it is generally good practice to contact the witness beforehand and let him know that a subpoena is coming. It also is good practice to coordinate with the recipient and opposing counsel when

---

[10]   Even with a cooperative witness who would comply with your discovery absent a subpoena, it generally is best to serve the witness with a subpoena to ensure compliance.

scheduling a time and place for the witness to appear or make available the property or tangible objects to be inspected.[11]

7. STIPULATIONS: RULE 29

Rule 29 authorizes the parties to stipulate to any number of discovery procedures, so long as the stipulation does not affect the court's scheduling order. Unless all civility has broken down, counsel generally should try to coordinate when and where depositions and document productions will take place. For instance, they may negotiate and stipulate the order in which depositions will go forward. There are any number of discovery activities that go more smoothly when counsel work cooperatively.

B. TERMINOLOGY: FACTS, EVIDENCE, CONTENTIONS AND FOUNDATION

As is true in most areas of the law, it is important to define words and terms. Therefore, before discussing formal discovery further, we begin by focusing on the meaning of a few key terms.

1. WHAT IS A FACT (AND IS THE ABSENCE OF A FACT A FACT)?

Black's Law Dictionary defines a fact as "something that actually exists."[12] But in the context of a lawsuit, "facts" often are hotly contested: what may be a fact to one party is a fabrication to another. Generally, an *alleged* fact is not a *fact* unless the parties stipulate to it, or a court takes judicial notice of it,[13] or the fact finder ultimately accepts it as a fact. In the context of litigation, when lawyers talk about "facts" they generally are talking about allegations—an assertion that remains to be proven.[14]

For example, assume a defamation lawsuit. Plaintiff claims that defendant falsely stated that plaintiff took a dive in a prizefight in exchange for a bribe. Defendant responds that the allegedly defamatory statement is not actionable because the statement is true. So far, these are just a series of unsubstantiated allegations. During discovery, defendant deposes a witness who testifies, "I paid plaintiff to take a dive." Does the testimony mean the event "truly happened"? No. The deposition testimony

---

[11] Of course, if the witness refuses to talk with you or your investigator, or makes it clear that he has no intention of cooperating, there is no risk in losing good will. Further, it is better not to alert a hostile witness that a subpoena is coming as he may try to evade it. But it is still a matter of courtesy to coordinate with opposing counsel.

[12] Fact, BLACK'S LAW DICTIONARY (11th ed. 2019).

[13] *See* FED. R. EVID. 201.

[14] In the context of summary judgment, however, the court will treat an unopposed assertion of fact as an established fact.

provides *evidence* of the existence of the fact, but it does not by itself convert the allegation into an established fact.

Can the absence of a fact be a fact? Yes. Establishing through discovery the absence of a fact (or, more precisely, the absence of evidence that tends to prove a fact) is an important discovery goal that can be issue-dispositive or even case-dispositive. As you craft your discovery requests and responses, remember that in summary judgment you can win individual issues or even the entire case if you can show the absence of admissible evidence to support the opposing party's claims or defenses.[15]

How might you prove the absence of a fact? In short, by using discovery to seek all evidence that supports the opposing party's claims or defenses, keeping in mind all elements necessary to the proof of those claims and defenses. If the opposing party fails to produce admissible evidence necessary to support a claim or defense, you have proven the absence of a fact.

2. WHAT IS EVIDENCE?

Evidence ≠ fact. Evidence is something (testimony, documents and other tangible objects, and even demonstrations of events) that *tends to prove or disprove the existence of an alleged fact.*[16] Put another way, it is something that a finder of fact may consider in deciding a case. When one party asks another in discovery, "What facts support your claim of X?" what the party really is asking is "What *evidence* supports your claim that X is a fact?"

"Evidence," however, is not necessarily the same as "admissible evidence." Admissible evidence is evidence that satisfies the Rules of Evidence and may be considered by a finder of fact.[17] An important goal during discovery is to develop all of the admissible evidence you need to support your claims or defenses. This means you not only need the evidence itself, you need the information that makes the evidence admissible. For example, you may have a great document that helps prove one of your claims, but unless you also can lay a *foundation* for the document, it will not be admissible evidence.

The difference between evidence and admissible evidence is important to keep in mind as you design and execute your discovery plan. You should design your discovery not only to gather evidence, but also to establish that the evidence is based upon sufficient foundation (or if you intend to challenge the opposing party's evidence, to establish that foundation is lacking).

---

15   *See* FED. R. CIV. P. 56(c)(1).

16   BLACK'S LAW DICTIONARY, *supra* note 12 (emphasis added).

17   *Id.* ("Evidence that is relevant and is of such a character that the court should receive it.").

3. WHAT IS A CONTENTION?

A contention is an opinion or belief.[18] Contentions are neither facts nor evidence; they are *inferences* drawn from facts or evidence. Essentially, they are allegations. Nonetheless, they are discoverable, generally through interrogatories.[19] A contention interrogatory seeks information regarding a party's opinions or contentions. Contention interrogatories serve to clarify issues and narrow the scope of the dispute.[20] Such an interrogatory may ask a party to identify its contentions, and to identify the bases for its contentions. It is improper to ask for legal analysis, but asking a party to articulate its position and explain the factual, evidentiary, or legal basis for a specified contention is permissible.[21]

For example, the plaintiff may allege in his complaint that the defendant maliciously defamed the plaintiff. Through the use of an interrogatory, the defendant may ask, "Identify all evidence that you contend support your claim that defendant maliciously defamed the plaintiff." Though such a question may appear to impermissibly seek the opposing counsel's work product,[22] numerous courts have found that discovery into the evidentiary basis of a party's contentions is permissible.[23]

4. WHAT IS FOUNDATION?

You will not find the word "foundation" in the Rules of Civil Procedure or in the Rules of Evidence.[24] However, to get evidence admitted "into evidence" at trial, you need to provide sufficient foundation. This means you must show, for example, that your document is authentic, your witness

---

[18] Contention, MERRIAM-WEBSTER, http://www.merriam-webster.com (search for "contention").

[19] "An interrogatory is not objectionable merely because it asks for an opinion or contention that relates to fact or the application of law to fact, but the court may order that the interrogatory need not be answered until designated discovery is complete, or until a pretrial conference or some other time." FED. R. CIV. P. 33(a)(2).

[20] *See, e.g., In re* Methyl Tertiary Butyl Ether Products Liability Litigation, 117 F.Supp.3d 276, 293–94 (S.D.N.Y. 2015); *In re* eBay Seller Antitrust Litigation, No. C 07–1882 JF (RS), 2008 WL 5212170, at *1–2 (N.D. Cal. Dec. 11, 2008).

[21] *See, e.g.,* Gilmore v. City of Minneapolis, Civil No. 13–1019 (JRT/FLN), 2014 WL 4722488, at *5–6 (D. Minn. Sept. 22, 2014); *see also* JOHN KIMPFLEN ET AL., FEDERAL PROCEDURE § 26:525 (L. Ed. 2015); 8B ALAN WRIGHT ET AL., FEDERAL PRACTICE AND PROCEDURE § 2167 (3d ed. 2015).

[22] The claim that such an interrogatory impermissibly seeks work product would be based upon the assertion that categorizing the evidence that supports a given claim is fundamentally part and parcel of the attorney's analysis, and therefore would be protected by the work product doctrine.

[23] For a discussion regarding contention interrogatories and the work product privilege, see 8B ALAN WRIGHT ET AL., FEDERAL PRACTICE AND PROCEDURE § 2026 (3d ed. 2015).

[24] Many rules of evidence actually are foundational rules, and you will find the word "foundation" used throughout the explanatory notes to the rules, but you will not find it in the rules themselves.

is competent to give the testimony you want to elicit, and your expert has necessary credentials.

A case may turn on foundational issues. If you cannot properly lay foundation for your proffered evidence, then it will not be admitted at trial or considered for summary judgment. Therefore, it is irrelevant for purposes of deciding the case. It is as if the evidence does not exist.

Keep this in mind during discovery. The foundational information you need in order to get your evidence admitted may be in the hands of the opposing party or an independent witness.[25] On the other side of the coin, if you can prove through discovery that the opposing party's proffered evidence lacks foundation, you may be able to prevent that evidence from being admitted. Depending on the importance of the evidence to the opposing party's case, this can set you up for settlement or for a dispositive motion.

C. PLANNING DISCOVERY, STEP ONE: REVIEW WHAT YOU KNOW

Before launching formal discovery, first review what you know and map out what you need. This includes your own informal investigation, the pleadings, and the parties' Rule 26(a) initial disclosures. Add all available evidence to your evidence map. Once you have done that, return to your discovery plan and the Critical Path Method document you have created and make necessary adjustments.

All this should be done *before* drafting discovery demands or noticing depositions. Once it is done, continuously review it. Look for emerging patterns of evidence, inconsistencies, contradictions, and gaps. Consider whether you need discovery to establish foundation for evidence that supports your case. Circle back to your theory of the case and evaluate whether it remains valid or needs to be modified. Begin to make a list of questions you have (which will become interrogatories and deposition outlines), documents you want (which will become document requests), physical things you want to inspect, photograph, test (which will become a request to inspect). Do not worry about wordsmithing at this point: the goal is to let your curiosity and imagination take hold. Then, and only then, begin the process of formal discovery.

---

[25] Oftentimes, counsel will stipulate that documents produced through the course of discovery are authentic. Be careful. First, that a document is "authentic" does not automatically make it admissible. Second, if you have possession of documents that are responsive to document requests posed to you but that you do not know to be "authentic" for purposes of the evidentiary rules, you should carefully consider whether you want to enter into such a blanket stipulation.

D. PLANNING DISCOVERY, STEP TWO: CONSIDER YOUR OVERALL DISCOVERY STRATEGY AND SEQUENCING

Chapter 2 introduced the three primary goals of discovery: (1) case development; (2) discovery of the opposing party's case; and (3) issue narrowing. Discovery for the purpose of case development is to discover and create admissible evidence helpful to your case. Discovery into the opposing party's case is intended to probe its strengths and weaknesses and draw out information that undermines its case. Discovery for the purpose of narrowing issues is intended to identify claims and contentions that lack evidentiary support and therefore should be dismissed, either voluntarily or by way of motion.

The client's goals for the case as a whole also affect discovery strategy. Before devising a discovery plan you should consider whether early settlement is a priority, whether there is a significant chance of prevailing at the summary judgment stage, or whether you expect that the case may either make it to trial or not settle until the eve of trial.

Different overall goals affect the approach to discovery. For example, if early settlement is a goal, you may want to start with some limited discovery aimed at quickly revealing the strengths of your case or the weaknesses of the opposing party's case. If you believe you can prevail on summary judgment, focus on exactly what you need for that purpose. If your goal is to get to trial (that is, your client has no intention of settling), your approach to discovery may be more comprehensive.[26] In addition to the client's goals, several other important variables will affect your discovery plan, including the size of the case, its complexity, available client resources (that is, the litigation budget), limits on time and scope of discovery set by the court, and the extent and complexity of discoverable documents. There is no "one-size-fits-all" discovery strategy, but following are some frequently applicable guidelines.

1. GENERALLY, BEGIN WITH BROAD DISCOVERY, THEN NARROW

As a general rule, it is best to start with broad discovery. One of the dangers of seeking specific information without regard to its broader context is that you may miss the forest for the trees or miss opportunities to follow promising leads. Starting instead with a first round of broad discovery may provide insights and clues into the most promising avenues of more focused discovery, and may reveal avenues for discovery that you

---

[26] Regardless of your goal, you need to be prepared to try the case if it cannot be resolved. Therefore, your discovery plan should account for this possibility by building in sufficient time to ramp up discovery if it becomes apparent the case is likely to go to trial.

did not even know existed. To paraphrase former Secretary of Defense Donald Rumsfeld:

> There are known knowns. These are things we know that we know. There are known unknowns. That is to say, there are things that we know we don't know. But there are also unknown unknowns. These are things we don't know we don't know.[27]

In the context of case development and discovery, the *known knowns* are the result of the pre-discovery investigation. The *known unknowns* are the gaps in the record you know need developing. And then there are the *unknown unknowns*. Broad discovery can reveal all sorts of unexpected and unanticipated things. An example may help.

> Plaintiff's hand is crushed by a retracting crane arm. Plaintiff sues defendant crane manufacturer, claiming defendant failed to warn of the risk. Defendant serves interrogatories and document demands on plaintiff generally asking about the nature of plaintiff's employer's business and plaintiff's job responsibilities. Plaintiff responds with a general description, stating that he is a crane operator who provides subcontracting services to XYZ Company. Defense counsel subpoenas XYZ Company's records in order to better understand the nature of the work performed. Turns out, those records specifically identify who was on the job that day, which leads to a witness, who then testifies that moments before plaintiff's hand was crushed, he said to the witness, "Keep your hands clear of the crane when it retracts—it can crush your hands."

Sometimes you just get lucky. But in that case defense counsel made her own luck by initially conducting broad discovery that led to unknown, but promising areas of inquiry.

Once you have a wide perspective on the case, you are in a better position to then make informed decisions about where to focus.

2. GENERALLY, WRITTEN DISCOVERY BEFORE DEPOSITIONS

As a general rule, it is better to conduct an initial round of written discovery before taking depositions.[28] With few exceptions, you get one chance to depose a witness,[29] so it is important to make the most of each deposition. By first serving interrogatories, requests for production, and requests for admissions, you can learn things that will affect the way you

---

[27] Donald Rumsfeld, Sec'y of Def., Department of Defense News Briefing (Feb. 12, 2002).

[28] Yes, there are exceptions. There are always exceptions. For example, it may be that the deposition of a records custodian is necessary in order to identify categories of documents that counsel would subsequently request pursuant to Rule 34.

[29] *See* FED. R. CIV. P. 30(a)(2)(A)(ii).

conduct your depositions. This has several advantages. First, it enables you to be more efficient with your time during each deposition, which is important since depositions have time limits. Second, information learned from written discovery may reveal useful areas of inquiry that you otherwise may have missed. Similarly, having the written discovery responses ahead of time gives you an opportunity to further explore the responses, fill in gaps, or identify contradictions and inconsistencies.

Moreover, documents are immutable. As such, they act as anchors, or points of reference, to which any manner of questioning can be tethered. For example, in a case involving a claim of wrongful termination, a performance review may be used as an exhibit during the deposition of the person who terminated the employee. If it is a glowing or even just satisfactory review, imagine the questions you might ask the witness about the company's "official" position that the employee was incompetent. Similarly, if it is a poor review, the deposition provides an opportunity to test the reviewer by asking for specific examples of poor performance, and to box in the opposing party so they have no opportunity to provide additional support for the termination during trial. If you schedule depositions before obtaining the opposing party's documents you may miss entire lines of questioning.

3. MULTIPLE ROUNDS OF DISCOVERY

Multiple rounds of discovery are common, particularly in larger cases where counsel has anticipated this need and negotiated discovery deadlines that afford the time to do so. It may be that a first round of written discovery, followed by a first round of depositions, reveals new areas for exploration, or the need to engage in more focused discovery in areas covered in only a general way during the first round.

Often, however, discovery cannot be divided into neat segments where there is a clear end to "Round 1," followed by a clear beginning of "Round 2." For some issues, a single round of discovery may suffice. For other issues, multiple rounds may be required, each moving along according to the vicissitudes of the discovery process.

4. EXPERT DISCOVERY AFTER THE COMPLETION OF "FACT DISCOVERY"

Many cases involve the use of experts. In those cases, it is typical to conduct expert discovery after fact discovery (a misnomer for non-expert discovery) is completed. The Rule 26(f) report and the court's scheduling order should take this into account. The reason that expert discovery should come at the end of the formal discovery process is that oftentimes expert opinions are dependent to some extent upon information that is gathered through the formal discovery process. Therefore, counsel should stipulate that expert reports will be exchanged after the completion of fact discovery, with expert depositions conducted after the exchange of reports.

5. ALLOW TIME FOR DELAYS AND DISCOVERY DISPUTES

Discovery seldom goes completely as expected. Initial discovery responses may be inadequate, requiring motions to compel; it may be difficult to schedule witnesses for depositions; obtaining and assessing electronically stored information (ESI) may be problematic. Therefore, it is important to build into your discovery plan sufficient time to deal with inevitable delays.

Remember, the opposing party is allowed 30 days to respond to written discovery. If that discovery is inadequate (and you should assume it will be), you need to factor in additional time for the meet and confer process, as well as the notice requirements for a motion to compel. Then add time for the court to rule. If you intend to conduct multiple rounds of written discovery, assume you will go through the same process with each round.

Give yourself plenty of time to conduct depositions. There are at least three schedules that will need to be coordinated: yours, the opposing counsel's and the witness's. If your case involves the taking of more than a couple of depositions, getting all of them scheduled and completed can take several months.

If your case involves experts, you will need to factor in time for the experts to complete their reports after the completion of fact discovery. Remember, you may not be the expert's only client and the report may take a substantial amount of time to prepare.

Therefore, as you plan, assume several months of expected and unexpected delays. Failing to do so may result in the discovery clock running out before you can complete your work. This puts you in the awkward position of seeking from the court additional time to conduct discovery as well as a trial continuance. Though courts tend to grant continuances for good cause, and convivial opposing counsel may stipulate to a continuance, you are placed in a vulnerable position. If the court denies your request for additional time, you may be unable to obtain the best possible litigation outcome for your client.

CHAPTER 7

WRITTEN DISCOVERY

■ ■ ■

> "Edna, we need to serve our standard written discovery. Also, get me a tee time for after lunch; I feel like getting in a round of golf."
>
> —Edwin Hack, attorney who has been losing cases quickly and slowly for over a generation

This chapter addresses the most common forms of written discovery: interrogatories (Rule 33); document requests (Rule 34); and requests for admission ("RFAs") (Rule 36). Each form of discovery requires a formal written request, and each formal written request requires a formal written response within 30 days.[1]

No discovery is "standard" or "the usual." Discovery requires planning and precision: you should tailor all discovery requests to the particular claims and facts of the case you are litigating. Having said that, there is nothing wrong with relying on exemplar written discovery in order to save time and incorporate language that is well-established and routinely used.[2]

Responding to discovery requires similar care. Without sufficient preparation you risk under-disclosure, over-disclosure, or disclosure of inaccurate information. To minimize these risks you must investigate and fully inform yourself of the available evidence, carefully read and interpret each request, prepare specific objections when warranted, and then draft precise, substantive responses.

A. WRITTEN DISCOVERY: GENERAL CONSIDERATIONS

The tools of written discovery are flexible and powerful. Written discovery allows counsel to cast a broad net or to make focused requests that allow the capture of information that otherwise may not be available to your client. It also allows counsel to craft requests that can *create* evidence that supports your case. Carefully crafted written discovery that

---

[1] FED. R. CIV. P. 33(b)(2) (interrogatories), 34(b)(2)(A) (document demands), 36(a)(3) (requests for admissions).

[2] Westlaw Next contains useful litigation materials, including exemplar written discovery, in the sections entitled "Practical Law" and "Forms." *See also* Appendix for exemplar written discovery demands.

is completed prior to depositions can make those depositions substantially more productive and efficient. When done well, written discovery requires the opposing party to commit to positions and to show its hand in terms of what it knows about the matters in dispute. Because responses qualify as party admissions, if relevant, they are admissible at trial and can also be used in support of dispositive motions.[3] And although you can take an individual's deposition only once, you can serve multiple rounds of written discovery, which is particularly useful as the case develops.

For all of its advantages, written discovery also has some limitations. It is the adverse attorney, not the party, who construes the discovery requests and usually drafts the responses to them. This means that responses often include a plethora of objections, and substantive responses are carefully wordsmithed. The written discovery process is slow: a month to respond, often followed by a meet and confer process regarding inadequate responses, many times followed by a motion to compel, which is sometimes followed by "amended" or "supplemented" responses, which may or may not be adequate, and may or may not start the dispute resolution process all over again.

1. DRAFTING WRITTEN DISCOVERY

Well-written discovery is precise, unambiguous, and written in plain English. Easier said than done, but well worth the effort. The goal is to minimize the ability of opposing counsel to object to or interpret the discovery in a manner you did not intend.

Following are several suggestions for drafting effective written discovery.

a. Use Definitions

Always include definitions of potentially ambiguous words and phrases. These definitions should precede interrogatories and requests. This alleviates the need to repeat definitions in each discovery request and it makes the set of requests shorter and more coherent. Definitions allow the drafter to minimize confusion and thus limit the ability of opposing counsel to construe requests in ways the drafter did not intend. Definitions also are useful for clarifying the scope of the information being sought. Though definitions may be objected to, those objections often are not well taken.[4]

---

[3] FED. R. EVID. 801(d)(2).

[4] Prefacing interrogatories with reasonable definitions is not prohibited by the Federal Rules of Civil Procedure because such a procedure might be helpful in avoiding unnecessary repetition. However, the use of unreasonable definitions may render interrogatories unreasonably burdensome. *See* 7 JAMES WILLIAM MOORE ET AL., MOORE'S FEDERAL PRACTICE § 33.31(2) (3d ed. 2001).

Consider the following interrogatory:

"Identify all persons with knowledge relating to Plaintiff's claim that Defendant breached the contract."

Seems pretty straight forward, right? But, what is a "person"? Does it include only natural persons? Or is it intended to include creatures of law that are considered persons, such as corporations? And does the term "all persons" include only the parties with knowledge of the drafting or substantive terms of the contract, or does it include, for example, the secretaries who typed up various drafts of the document, or persons who may have received copies, but have no substantive knowledge of the drafting or terms, or those who can authenticate or dispute the authenticity of the signatures? With regard to the word "contract," which contract? What if defendant has claimed that there are competing iterations, or that no contract was ever formed due to mutual mistake?

Defining terms will go a long way toward depriving opposing counsel the opportunity to obfuscate or otherwise fail to provide a substantive response. As a matter of practice, it is useful to either CAPITALIZE or use **boldface** type to denote defined terms so as to alert opposing counsel that a given term is defined.[5]

b. Quote or Refer to Specific Causes of Action or Affirmative Defenses When Requesting Related Information

When possible, you should quote directly the language contained in the adverse party's pleadings. Quoting from pleadings deprives the opposing party the ability to claim that the language is unclear or ambiguous. Quoting from pleadings is particularly useful for contention interrogatories. For example:

IDENTIFY all PERSONS, DOCUMENTS, COMMUNICATIONS, or any other facts and evidence that you contend support your claim at paragraph 25 of your Answer that "Plaintiff's claims are barred by the doctrine of unclean hands."

c. Do Not Limit Requests to Information That Supports the Adverse Party's Claims

While you certainly want to use discovery to uncover all information that supports the adverse party's claims, keep in mind that the adverse party may also have information that helps *your* client. If your discovery seeks only information that *supports* the adverse party's claims, you risk

---

[5] *See* Appendix for a list of commonly defined terms.

missing critical information. Therefore, ask for *all* information, not simply supporting information. For example:

> IDENTIFY all PERSONS, DOCUMENTS, COMMUNICATIONS or any other facts and evidence that RELATE to your claim at paragraph 25 of your Answer that "Plaintiff's claims are barred by the doctrine of unclean hands."

Although convenient, be cautious when using the word "relate." Opposing counsel may argue that all things are related to some extent, and therefore the request is overly broad.[6] There are two ways to ward off a sustainable objection. First, define "relate" in such a way as to frame the scope of the request.[7] Second, describe with as much precision as possible the substance of what you are seeking.[8]

d. Make Sure the Discovery Relates to an Issue in the Case

In almost every discovery dispute where the responding party claims that the discovery sought is "overly broad, unduly burdensome, or is not reasonably calculated to lead to the discovery of admissible evidence" (a common and outdated litany of objections),[9] the court's likely first question will be, "Counsel, *why* do you need this information?"

Therefore, you should draft each written discovery request with that question in mind. Your discovery plan (see Chapters 2 and 3) should answer this question, and should be your constant guide during the discovery process.

The next challenge is to draft the discovery in a manner that does not inadvertently call for information that goes beyond the intended scope. For example, assume you represent the defendant in a case involving a claim of a back injury to an 80-year-old retired plaintiff. Your expert advises that he will need "all of the plaintiff's medical records" before examining the plaintiff. Does "all" really mean *all*, from birth until the present date? Not likely. Realistically, what the expert needs are medical records relating to the plaintiff's prior history of back injuries and perhaps other chronic or

---

[6] *See, e.g.,* United States v. Clay, Civ. Action No. 05–382–JMH, 2009 WL 365820, at *7–9 (E.D. Ky. Feb. 9, 2009); Moss v. Blue Cross & Blue Shield of Kansas, Inc., 241 F.R.D. 683, 696 (D. Kan. 2007) (defendant objects to plaintiff's interrogatories for all related information as overly broad, unduly burdensome, and not reasonably calculated to lead to the discovery of admissible evidence).

[7] For a common definition of the word "relate," *see* Appendix.

[8] Sonnino v. Univ. of Kansas Hosp. Auth., 221 F.R.D. 661, 667–668 (D. Kan. 2004) ("[A] request or interrogatory may be overly broad or unduly burdensome on its face if it uses an omnibus term as 'relating to' or 'concerning.' . . . When, however, the omnibus phrase modified a specific type of document or specific event, rather than a large category or all documents or events, the request is not deemed overly broad on its face.").

[9] Rule 26(b)(1) was amended in 2015 so as to limit discovery to that which is relevant to any claim or defense and is proportional to the needs of the case.

acute injuries if the expert can articulate *how* these records are relevant to his evaluation of the plaintiff.

When framing the scope of a given request, consider the following:

- Is there a relevant timeframe relating to the issue or matter being inquired into?

  Example: "Identify all persons employed by the defendant between January 1, 2016 to December 31, 2020."

- Is there a category of relevant individuals?

  Example: "Identify all persons who have made a claim of gender-related discrimination at any time against the defendant."

- Is there a relevant geographical limitation?

  Example: "What was the Plaintiff's gross sales in its Northern sales region for the year 2018?"

- Can the request be limited to specific allegations?

  Example: "Identify all facts and evidence that support your claim that the Plaintiff took reasonable steps to safeguard its alleged trade secrets."

- Can documents be described with some precision?

  Example: "Produce all documents in defendant's possession, custody or control that contain the name WidgetCo."[10]

As is typical with issues relating to the scope of discovery, there is no one-size-fits-all rule: the scope of allowable discovery is dependent upon: (1) the subject matter of the dispute; and (2) the extent to which the propounding party is able to convince the court that it comports with Rule 26(b)(1) (relevant to claims and proportional to the needs of the case).

2. DRAFTING RESPONSES TO WRITTEN DISCOVERY

When responding to written discovery, begin here: a lawyer may not offer false evidence,[11] conceal material with potential evidentiary value,[12] falsify evidence,[13] or fail to make a reasonably diligent effort to comply with a legally proper discovery request.[14] These are ethical mandates, not to be

---

[10] Of course, the word "document" would be defined, and would include a detailed definition of electronically stored information, or ESI.

[11] MODEL RULES OF PROF'L CONDUCT R. 3.3(a)(3).

[12] *Id.* R. 3.4(a).

[13] *Id.* R. 3.4(b).

[14] *Id.* R. 3.4(d).

taken lightly. As an officer of the court, counsel has a duty to be candid with the tribunal and to conduct herself fairly in relation to opposing counsel.

The Rules treat evasive or incomplete discovery as a failure to respond for purposes of motions to compel.[15] And courts should not take discovery abuses lightly (though some are more permissive than others). Engaging in gamesmanship when responding to discovery can result in sanctions.[16] If that is not enough to get counsel's attention, courts also are known to exclude evidence that should have been disclosed during discovery, regardless of its importance to the case.[17]

a. Claiming Privilege, Work Product or Other Protections

One of the most important functions of litigation counsel is to vet any information that may need to be disclosed. Once you gather all information potentially responsive to discovery requests, you must determine whether any of it is protected from disclosure by a privilege, the attorney work product doctrine, court order, or other protection.

Withholding documents based upon a claimed privilege requires preparation of a privilege log.[18] Rule 26(b)(5) requires parties to specifically state the basis for withholding privileged or otherwise protected materials and to "describe the nature of the documents, communications, or tangible things not produced or disclosed—and do so in a manner that, without revealing information itself privileged or protected, will enable other parties to assess the claim."

b. Objections Generally

Objections must be timely served, or else they are waived, absent a showing of good cause.[19] If you are unable to timely complete discovery

---

[15] FED. R. CIV. P. 37(a)(4).

[16] *See* Sentis Group., Inc. v. Shell Oil Co., 559 F.3d 888, 908 (8th Cir. 2009) (appeal from dismissal of claims due to discovery gamesmanship); *see also* Comstock v. UPS Ground Freight, Inc., 775 F.3d 990, 993 (8th Cir. 2014) (affirming sanctions for discovery abuses); Davenport v. Charter Commc'ns, LLC, 302 F.R.D. 520, 527 (E.D. Mo. 2014).

[17] *See* FED. R. CIV. P. 37(c)(1); *see also* Musser v. Gentiva Health Services, 356 F.3d 751, 758 (7th Cir. 2004) (failure of plaintiff to identify particular witnesses as experts justified exclusion of their testimony as experts, resulting in dismissal of plaintiff's case); Osunde v. Lewis, 281 F.R.D. 250, 264 (D. Md. 2012) (failure to timely supplement expert disclosures justified excluding testimony, resulting in dismissal of wrongful death claim); Semi-Tech Litig. LLC v. Bankers Trust Co., 219 F.R.D. 324, 325 (S.D.N.Y. 2004) (holding that the LLC's disclosure of experts on eve of discovery period's expiration was untimely).

[18] *See* Appendix for an exemplar privilege log.

[19] *See* FED. R. CIV. P. 33(b)(4) regarding waiver of objections to interrogatories. With regard to document demands, even though Rule 34 does not contain the same waiver language as Rule 33, some courts hold that objections to document demands are waived if not timely made. *See, e.g.,* Caudle v. District of Columbia, 263 F.R.D. 29, 32 (D.D.C. 2009).

responses, it is imperative to either get an extension of time in which to answer, or otherwise timely serve objections.

Oftentimes, responding counsel will preface every response with boilerplate objections, raising the same objections to every request. Do not do this. There are two good reasons not to cut and paste boilerplate objections: (1) the rules require that counsel set forth specific objections;[20] and (2) the practice usually leads to costly and time-wasting discovery disputes. Moreover, courts have consistently held that an objection to a discovery request cannot be merely conclusory. For example, the "overly broad and burdensome" objection, without specifying the basis of the objection, is not valid.[21] Therefore, "general objections" set forth in a preamble to responses, and "boilerplate objections" that fail to specify the bases of those objections, are inappropriate. Objections should be specific and well-founded. Objections to definitions and/or instructions may be made in the preamble section of your discovery responses.

These are some of the most common objections:

- Overly broad (now outdated; relevance is the standard)

- Unduly burdensome (also outdated; not proportional to the needs of the case is the standard))

- Not relevant to a claim or defense

- Not reasonably calculated to lead to the discovery of admissible evidence (again, the standard is relevance)

- Vague, ambiguous, or unintelligible

- Argumentative (requires the adoption of a disputed allegation, fact, or assumption)

- Violates the attorney-client privilege; doctor-patient privilege; or some other privilege or protection (e.g., trade secrets)

- Calls for disclosure of attorney's mental impressions (work product)

- The information sought is equally available to the parties[22]

---

[20] *See, e.g.,* FED. R. CIV. P. 33(b)(4) (for interrogatories). In fact, Rule 33(b)(5) requires counsel to sign responses in relation to objections. The signature requirement is to be read with Rule 26(g), which not only requires counsel's signature, but also provides for sanctions for improper responses or objections.

[21] *See* Mead Corp. v. Riverwood Natural Res. Corp., 145 F.R.D. 512, 515 (D. Minn. 1992).

[22] Some courts find this objection to be improper. *See, e.g.,* St. Paul Reinsurance Co. v. Commercial Fin. Corp, 198 F.R.D. 508, 517 (N.D. Iowa 2000) (an objection on the ground that the information sought is equally available to the propounding party "is insufficient to resist a discovery request") (citations omitted). Other courts find the objection valid under some circumstances. *See, e.g.,* Hoffman v. United Telecommunications, Inc., 117 F.R.D. 436, 438 (D. Kan. 1987) ("Plaintiff-intervenor claims that because the data is equally available to both parties,

- Prematurely calls for contentions and the bases upon which they are made[23]
- Prematurely calls for expert opinion
- Exceeds the limits of allowed discovery
- Promulgated to harass or embarrass

c.   Substantive Responses

Litigants have an affirmative duty to respond to discovery requests truthfully, in full, without evasion.[24] Further, as additional information becomes known to the parties, they have an affirmative duty to supplement discovery responses in order to correct erroneous or incomplete information.[25]

As a general matter, Rule 26(g) requires counsel to make reasonable efforts to ensure that discovery responses are complete.[26] As a practical matter, this means that all written discovery responses should be based upon a thorough investigation that usually is conducted or directed by counsel. Responses need not be limited to information within the personal knowledge of the party. In fact, responses should not be so limited unless the request itself is. Moreover, whether or not requested, you *must* disclose all information that supports your client's claims[27] or else you may not use that information for motions or at trial.[28]

On the other hand, a party is not obligated to shoot itself in the foot. If, for example, a party is served with a contention interrogatory asking for all facts or evidence *supporting* one of its claims, the responding party has no obligation to disclose information that *undermines* that claim. Likewise, if a discovery request is vague or ambiguous, counsel is not required to read it as broadly as it can be read and may, in fact, choose to clarify the scope of the request in the response, then provide only that information that falls within that scope. For example, assume the following interrogatory:

"Identify all information related to this lawsuit."

This interrogatory would likely be met with a number of objections, not the least of which is that it is vague and calls for a response that is indefinite as to time and scope. What constitutes "information"? This is not

---

defendant should do its own research. There is case law supporting this view."); Brunswick Corp. v. Chrysler Corp., 43 F.R.D. 208, 209 (E.D. Wis. 1967).

[23]   Although Rule 33(a) specifically allows contention interrogatories, the Rule also gives the court authority to issue an order delaying the response until discovery is complete. FED. R. CIV. P. 33(a)(2); *see also* McCarthy v. Paine Weber Group, Inc., 168 F.R.D. 448, 450 (D. Conn., 1996).

[24]   FED. R. CIV. P. 37(a)(4).

[25]   *Id.* 26(e), 37(c).

[26]   *Id.* 26(g); Bernal v. All Am. Inv. Realty, Inc., 479 F. Supp. 2d 1291, 1333 (S.D. Fla. 2007).

[27]   FED. R. CIV. P. 26(a)(1).

[28]   *Id.* 37(c).

sophistry—it is a legitimate issue. Does it include unsubstantiated allegations? Which evidence is counsel to consider "information"? For its response, a party may include a preamble such as:

> Because the use of the word "information" is ambiguous, [Party] will assume the interrogatory calls for evidence that [Party] has determined to be factually based and reliable. Based upon that understanding, [Party] states as follows: [Substantive response follows setting forth "information" that pertains to the responding party's claims].

So long as the response includes the appropriate objection, and the responding party makes clear what it believes the request calls for, there is nothing improper in responding to ambiguous or vague discovery requests in a manner most advantageous to the responding party.

Because discovery responses are statements of the parties, they may be treated as party admissions.[29] As such, they may be used as evidence at trial or for purposes of summary judgment. Sloppy, incomplete or unsupported responses can come back to haunt the responding party, for example, as a prior inconsistent statement. Therefore, it is essential that counsel carefully draft responses, stating no more than is necessary. Further, it is essential that counsel review with the client the responses in order to ensure accuracy. It is not enough to send a copy to the client with the instruction to sign and return the document. The client will have to live with the responses for the life of the case (and in some instances, long after), so making sure the responses are accurate is essential.

d.   Signature of Counsel and Party

Discovery responses must be signed by the responding party and its counsel, certifying that to the best of counsel's knowledge, the responses are complete and correct and objections are not interposed for an improper purpose.[30] This is no small matter. If the court determines that "a certification violates [Rule 26(g)] without substantial justification, the court, on motion or on its own, must impose an appropriate sanction on the signer, the party on whose behalf the signer was acting, or both. The sanction may include an order to pay the reasonable expenses, including attorney's fees, caused by the violation."[31] In addition, you may lose credibility with the court, something you obviously want to avoid.

e.   Obligation to Supplement Responses

If additional information comes to light after you have served written discovery responses, you have an affirmative duty to supplement those

---

[29] FED. R. EVID. 801(d)(2).

[30] FED. R. CIV. P. 26(g).

[31] *Id.* 26(g)(3).

responses.[32] Counsel should include the additional information in a discovery response denoted as a supplement to whichever previous response is being supplemented. Put another way, the supplemented response should *not* be denoted as a "corrected" response, or "amended" response. For purposes of the optics of how the document may be characterized, it is best to give it a name that does not imply inconsistency or error.

f.   Non-Responses

Be on the lookout for non-responses as they pose a number of tactical considerations. Non-responses come in all shapes and sizes, but at bottom they usually mean the same thing: "We don't know," or "We currently are aware of no evidence responsive to this request." Here are a couple of examples of non-responses:

> "Discovery is continuing. This interrogatory will be supplemented at a later date."

> "Upon information and belief, [Party] asserts that . . ."[33]

There are two ways to deal with non-responses. One is to bring a motion to compel (after you meet and confer with opposing counsel). The other is to do nothing for the time being. In general, the path you choose may depend on whether the discovery sought relates to evidence that ostensibly supports the opposing party's claims, or whether it is designed to bolster your case.

If your discovery request seeks information supportive of the opposing party's claims, consider doing nothing for the time being. Pursuant to Rule 37(c), if a litigant fails to disclose evidence in support of its claims during discovery, then that evidence should be barred for purposes of motions or trial. Therefore, should opposing counsel stonewall, or otherwise fail to identify whatever evidence she may have in support of a given claim or contention, then when the proper time comes, you are well-situated to move the court to exclude or otherwise disregard the evidence if opposing counsel attempts to sandbag you with it. We will discuss this tactic in greater detail in Chapter 15.

If, however, you believe the information you seek may support your claims, then you will need to move forward with the process of compelling disclosure. If you have a coherent discovery strategy, you will be in the position to persuade the court as to why the information should be disclosed. And if the opposing party claims it has no such evidence, it should be required to so state, in writing, and the response should be

---

[32]   *Id.* 26(e).

[33]   "Upon information and belief" is, essentially, a misleading phrase. Translation: "We hope there is evidence to support this claim, but we are in possession of none at this time."

affirmed by the opposing party.[34] If it later turns out that there was, in fact, evidence responsive to your requests, and it was not disclosed because the opposing party simply did not want you to get it, then you will be well-situated to make your motion for appropriate sanctions.[35]

B. INTERROGATORIES

Rule 33 presumptively limits the number of interrogatories that may be served on a party to 25, including discrete subparts.[36] Note that interrogatories may not be directed to non-parties. Rule 33 does not set forth specific requirements as to the form of interrogatories, but it does explicitly limit the scope of each interrogatory to the permissible scope of discovery defined in Rule 26(b), i.e., any non-privileged matter that is relevant and proportional to the needs of the case.

Interrogatories are generally most useful for discovery of the adverse party's case. They are ideal for getting the "who, what, when, where, why and how" for each of the opposing party's allegations. Conversely, interrogatories are not particularly effective for obtaining damaging admissions or for creating evidence to support your own client's case because the responses, while signed by the opposing party, are drafted and carefully wordsmithed by the party's attorney so as to limit the disclosure of damaging evidence.

Interrogatories can be thought of as open-ended questions. The challenge is in making them as open-ended as possible while at the same time being specific regarding the information you seek.

Rule 33 allows parties to inquire into facts and evidence, but it also explicitly allows contention interrogatories: interrogatories that call upon the adverse party to set forth specific claims it is making, as well as the evidentiary and legal bases for those claims.[37] Contention interrogatories serve two purposes: (1) to learn more about the opposing party's position on various issues, and (2) to help narrow issues. Given the broad nature of

---

[34] *See* FED. R. CIV. P. 26(g).

[35] *See id.* 37(c)(1).

[36] What constitutes a "discrete subpart" often is not clear. The general rule is, "interrogatory subparts are to be construed as one interrogatory . . . if they are logically or factually subsumed within and necessarily related to the primary question." Kendall v. GES Exposition Services, Inc., 174 F.R.D. 684, 685 (D. Nev. 1997) (quoting Ginn v. Gemini, Inc., 137 F.R.D. 320, 322 (D. Nev. 1991)).

[37] "[T]he phrase 'contention interrogatory' is used imprecisely to refer to many different kinds of questions. Some people would classify as a contention interrogatory any question that asks another party to indicate what it contends. . . . Another kind of question . . . asks an opposing party to state all the facts on which it bases some specified contention. Yet another form of this category of interrogatory asks an opponent to state all the evidence on which it bases some specified contention. Some contention interrogatories ask the responding party to take a position, and then to explain or defend that position, with respect to how the law applies to facts. A variation on this theme involves interrogatories that ask parties to spell out the legal basis for, or theory behind, some specified contention." *In re* Convergent Tech. Sec. Litig., 108 F.R.D. 328, 332 (N.D. Cal. 1985).

contention interrogatories, courts may allow a party to delay responding to a contention interrogatory until discovery nears completion.[38] Although attorneys regularly object to contention interrogatories on the basis that they run afoul of the attorney work product doctrine, this generally is not a valid objection.[39]

1. DRAFTING INTERROGATORIES

Each case requires carefully tailored interrogatories. This means there are few shortcuts. However, we can offer some helpful ideas.[40] First, it may be useful to begin with an interrogatory about the interrogatories. Consider the following:

> IDENTIFY each and every PERSON who contributed in any way to responding to these interrogatories. For each PERSON YOU identified, include in YOUR response the specific interrogatories to which each such PERSON contributed.[41]

This is a particularly useful interrogatory because it identifies potential witnesses, and the subject matter for which they have information. Though opposing counsel may object that the interrogatory invades the attorney-client privilege, it does not. It seeks only factual information: who contributed what information to the responses, not what counsel may have discussed with her client.[42] There also should be a companion document request seeking all documents the identified witnesses referred to or relied upon when contributing to each interrogatory answer.

---

[38] *See, e.g.*, Kartman v. State Farm Mut. Auto. Ins. Co., 247 F.R.D. 561, 566 (S.D. Ind. 2007) ("[T]he Court has discretion to delay a response to a contention interrogatory."); *In re* Convergent Technologies Sec. Litig., 108 F.R.D. 328, 345 (N.D. Cal. 1985) ("[T]he court concludes that defendants have failed to make a showing sufficient to justify an order compelling plaintiffs, at this time, to answer the contention interrogatories as they relate to allegations of control by defendants Harris and Meise."). The advisory committee notes also are clear: "Since interrogatories involving mixed questions of law and fact may create disputes between the parties which are best resolved after much or all of the other discovery has been completed, the court is expressly authorized to defer an answer." FED. R. CIV. P. 33(b) advisory committee's note to 1970 amendment. *But see* Pouncil v. Branch Law Firm, 277 F.R.D. 642, 650 (D. Kan. 2011) (denying request to delay response to contention interrogatories).

[39] *See, e.g.*, Spandaro v. City of Miramar, No. 11–61607–CIV, 2012 WL 3042988, at *3 (S.D. Fla. July 25, 2012) and cases cited therein ("Numerous courts have rejected the proposition that interrogatories which seek material or principal facts that support a party's allegations violate the work product doctrine."). Be careful, however, when wording contention interrogatories so you do not appear to be seeking opposing counsel's strategy or analysis. *See, e.g.*, Kodak Graphic Commc'ns Canada Co. v. E.I. du Pont de Nemours & Co., No. 08–CV–6553T, 2012 WL 413994, at *7 (W.D.N.Y. Feb. 8, 2012) (attorney work product objection sustained).

[40] *See* Appendix for a number of exemplar interrogatories.

[41] The capitalized words are words you will have defined in your preamble. *See* Appendix for a listing of commonly defined terms.

[42] Upjohn v. United States, 449 U.S. 383, 395 (1981) (attorney-client privilege does not protect underlying facts from disclosure).

Moving beyond the meta-interrogatory, drafting interrogatories well incorporates everything we have discussed thus far:

- A clear understanding of your objectives;

- A clear understanding of how the interrogatories fit into your overall discovery plan;

- The ability to write precisely, unambiguously, and in plain English;

- Use of defined terms;

- Reference to the adverse party's own allegations when appropriate;

- The ability to frame the scope of the interrogatory as broadly as possible, while at the same time asking for specificity.

With regard to wordsmithing, there are a number of rules of thumb:

- Use proper nouns and defined relative pronouns only, even if it means the phrasing may be somewhat stilted;

- Use specific dates when defining scope, rather than terms like "last year," or "during the time of employment";

- Use adjectives and descriptive clauses to broaden or narrow interrogatories, such as:

  o "Any and all facts and evidence"

  o "Including but not limited to"

  o "Each and every"

  o "Excluding any information protected by . . ."

  o "Relating and/or referring to."

An example may be instructive. Consider a simple breach of contract case in which the plaintiff claims the defendant failed to deliver 10,000 widgets. Defendant claims a *force majeure* event excuses performance. Plaintiff serves interrogatories that contain the following defined terms:

YOU and YOUR shall mean defendant WidgetCo.

CONTRACT shall mean the contract entered into between YOU and Plaintiff on February 8, 2020.

IDENTIFY as it relates to persons shall mean each person's name, address, title and relationship to YOU.

IDENTIFY as it relates to documents shall mean a description of the DOCUMENT, including any dates that may appear on the DOCUMENT, and who created the DOCUMENT.

PERSON shall mean natural persons as well as any organization such as partnerships and corporations.

INTERROGATORY NO. 2:

IDENTIFY any and all facts and evidence, beginning February 8, 2020, through the present, that relate to YOUR claim contained in Paragraph 11 of YOUR Answer that "WidgetCo is excused from performance due to a *force majeure* event." Include in YOUR response any term or terms of the CONTRACT that support your claim.

The interrogatory, though relatively short, calls for a broad disclosure of information, including specific information about witnesses and documents. The "any and all facts and evidence" clause goes beyond information that supports the defendant's claim. If defendant has raised additional affirmative defenses, similarly worded interrogatories for each affirmative defense may be warranted.

2. RESPONDING TO INTERROGATORIES

Counsel has an ethical obligation to respond to discovery truthfully and fully. What constitutes a "full" response is subject to interpretation. As a general rule of thumb, if the information to be disclosed helps your case, then consider a more detailed response in order to avoid a later accusation that you failed to adequately disclose information that you intend to rely on for purposes of motions or trial.

Conversely, to the extent the interrogatory calls for information that hurts your case, you generally should tailor your response as narrowly as possible, providing only the information called for in the interrogatory. Sometimes, however, it may be advantageous to provide a fuller than necessary response, something that might be called a "poison pill response." Such a response may provide a broader context to explain bad facts, or to call into question the veracity of those bad facts. Consider again the breach of contract/*force majeure* example. Assume the contract contains no *force majeure* clause. Defendant may respond:

RESPONSE TO INTERROGATORY NO. 2:

Both the Plaintiff's and Defendant's businesses are located in the state of Oklahoma, and more specifically, in what is known as "tornado alley." Companies doing business in "tornado alley" assume that there is a risk of business interruption due to tornadoes. In fact, Plaintiff Joe Jones, who signed the contract, was and is aware that dealings among businesses in "tornado alley" include the assumption that commerce may be interrupted by tornado damage, as Plaintiff is well aware since his own business was struck by a tornado in 2012, preventing it from operating for almost one year. Two months after the contract was signed, and with both parties aware of the risks of business interruption due to tornadoes, Defendant's manufacturing facility was struck by an F-4 tornado as rated by the National Weather Bureau. The entire facility was destroyed, causing numerous injuries to Defendant's employees and the loss of all business income. Documents evidencing the F-4 tornado, including National Weather Bureau records and photographs of Defendant's destroyed facility are provided with this response.

Though the defendant more or less answers the interrogatory, the response also places the absence of a *force majeure* contract clause in a broader context, one that not only raises a "course of dealings" argument, but also articulates the defendant's plight. Plaintiff will likely object to the response, but it is unlikely that a judge would require the defendant to strip out the "contextualizing" facts. As such, this is not an interrogatory response the opposing party would want to use as an exhibit at trial.

Another way to look at the "poison pill response" is as an opportunity to articulate your theory of the case. Doing so helps party witnesses who may be deposed by allowing them to refer to the party's discovery responses, and to rely on those responses when testifying. Additionally, by laying out a narrative that essentially articulates the party's theory of the case, it allows responding counsel to refer the adverse party to a seminal response that incorporates all responsive information. In other words, this approach allows counsel to frame a coherent response in a favorable manner, then refer the reader to that response when answering additional interrogatories.

Finally, Rule 33(d) gives the responding party the option to refer the opposing party to documents if the documents are sufficient to answer the question posed, and the responding party makes the documents available for inspection. This approach, in contrast to the "poison pill response," provides no narrative—it simply presents documents without comment. To use this approach, the documents cited must fully contain the information sought. So, with regard to a contention interrogatory that asks the responding party if it is making certain contentions, and if so, what evidence it has to support those contentions, it is likely not sufficient to simply refer the adverse party to documents without identifying which contentions are supported by which documents.

C. DOCUMENT REQUESTS

Rule 34 governs document requests. Like any other form of discovery, the scope of document requests is limited by Rule 26(b)(relevant to a claim or defense, and proportional to the needs of the case). Document requests must describe with reasonable particularity the items or categories of items sought, must specify a reasonable time, place, and manner of inspection, and must specify the form in which electronic information should be produced.[43] As with interrogatories, responses generally are due within 30 days.[44] Unlike interrogatories, it is possible to compel the production of documents from nonparties through the use of a Rule 45 subpoena.[45]

1. DRAFTING DOCUMENT REQUESTS

When drafting document requests you must designate each item or category of documents with sufficient specificity so that the responding party understands what you are requesting.[46] For example, in a breach of contract case, the defendant may focus its discovery on the extent of plaintiff's claimed damages by serving the following document request:

> Produce all DOCUMENTS containing Plaintiff's financial records from 2008 to the present that were created in the normal course of its business. For purposes of this request, "financial records" includes all balance sheets, income statements, audited and unaudited tax returns, cash flow statements and analyses, departmental budgets, marketing and advertising budgets, and any other discrete budgets.

Trial preparation materials generally are protected from discovery,[47] but statements of parties and non-parties are discoverable and must be produced even without a showing of substantial need.[48] For example, the opposing party gave a written statement to its insurance company regarding a loss. That document is discoverable.

Rule 34 does not contain a presumptive limit on the number of document requests a party may serve. Nonetheless, it is important to keep in mind the proportionality rule contained in Rule 26(b)(1). Some courts impose a limit, so, based upon the complexity of the case you should be prepared to ask for a specific limit.

---

[43] FED. R. CIV. P. 34(b)(1). For more on the production of electronically stored information, see Chapter 10.

[44] FED. R. CIV. P. 34(b)(2)(A).

[45] *Id.* 34(c).

[46] The "reasonable particularity" requirement is not susceptible to an exact definition; what is reasonably particular is subject to the facts and circumstances in any given case. Mallinckrodt Chem. Works v. Goldman, Sachs & Co., 58 F.R.D. 348, 353 (S.D.N.Y. 1973); *see also* Smith v. Dow Chem. Co., 173 F.R.D. 54, 58 (W.D.N.Y. 1997). Requesting electronically stored information presents special challenges. Refer to Chapter 10, which is devoted entirely to ESI discovery.

[47] See FED. R. CIV. P. 26(b)(3).

[48] *Id.* 26(b)(3)(C).

2. RESPONDING TO DOCUMENT REQUESTS

The first thing to do when you receive a request for documents is to identify and gather responsive documents[49] and then determine whether any of them are subject to a privilege or some other protection. Next, you should segregate privileged or otherwise protected documents. You will need to identify these documents in a privilege log that you should serve with your response.[50] Responses to document requests must include specific objections, if any, on a request-by-request basis, and if you withhold documents as a result of an objection, your response must clearly indicate that fact.[51]

When you produce documents, you must do so "as they are kept in the usual course of business or must organize and label them to correspond to the categories in the request,"[52] unless otherwise stipulated by the parties or ordered by the court. Oftentimes, this means making responsive documents available to the requesting party for review rather than just copying everything and producing it. The requesting party then selects the documents it wants copied, and the producing party arranges for copies to be made.

If the case involves a substantial number of documents, the parties should agree during the Rule 26(f) meet and confer process that documents shall be Bates stamped, with a prefix that clearly indicates which party produced which documents. Then, responses to document requests should reference documents responsive to each request by Bates number designation.[53]

For example:

RESPONSE TO DOCUMENT REQUEST NO. 1:

[Objections.] Subject to, and without waiving the aforementioned objections, documents responsive to this request are Bates labeled: WID000123–WID000200. These documents are enclosed and are incorporated by reference to this response.

---

[49] If you have done a thorough pre-discovery investigation, you likely have already gathered many of the documents that the opposing party will request in formal discovery. However, it is rare that counsel can anticipate every avenue that adverse counsel may explore. Therefore, once you receive document requests, you must engage in a reasonable effort to gather the documents requested.

[50] *See* Appendix for an exemplar privilege log.

[51] FED. R. CIV. P. 34(b)(2)(C).

[52] *Id.* 34(b)(2)(E)(i).

[53] For more on Bates stamping, see Chapter 14.

With regard to production of ESI, the response may be:

RESPONSE TO DOCUMENT REQUEST NO. 1:

[Objections.] Subject to, and without waiving the aforementioned objections, documents responsive to this request are produced, consistent with the court's pretrial order dated June 1, 2019, in a flat ascii format on a CD-ROM labeled "Disc 1." Disc 1 is enclosed and incorporated by reference to this response.[54]

While the above is the appropriate way to respond to a document request, the following, wholly inadequate response, is all too common:

RESPONSE TO DOCUMENT REQUEST NO. 1:

[Objections.] Subject to, and without waiving the aforementioned objections, documents responsive to this request shall be produced at a time and place mutually agreeable to the parties.

A response such as this does not satisfy the letter or the spirit of the Rule. If you receive such a response, you should immediately send a meet and confer letter specifying a time and place that the documents are to be produced, and indicating that counsel fully expects that the documents will be produced as they are kept in the usual course of business, or that they shall be organized and labeled to correspond to the categories in the request.

In addition to Bates stamping (or using some other unique identifier), if some or all of the documents are subject to a protective order, they may need to be stamped, labeled or otherwise denoted "confidential, subject to court order" before they are produced. In other words, there are logistical considerations that may bear upon how responsive documents shall be produced. Counsel should work cooperatively through the logistics of document productions so as to avoid unnecessary disputes over these ministerial functions.

D. REQUESTS FOR ADMISSIONS

If interrogatories are akin to open-ended questions, requests for admission ("RFAs") are akin to leading questions, that is, the answer is contained in the request. A request for admission may ask a party to admit any fact, application of law to fact, or opinion,[55] or the genuineness of any document.[56] This is a potentially powerful, sometimes overlooked, tool in your discovery arsenal. Be careful when you receive RFAs—requests are

---

[54] There are numerous ways to produce ESI, including uploads and granting access to the documents stored in the cloud. Another way is to simply copy the requested documents to a thumb drive. More will be said about this in Chapter 10.

[55] FED. R. CIV. P. 36(a)(1)(A).

[56] *Id.* 36(a)(1)(B).

deemed admitted if not denied or objected to within 30 days.[57] There is no presumptive limit on the number of RFAs that may be served, although the rules do explicitly note that the court may impose a limit on the number of RFAs.[58]

1. DRAFTING RFAs

RFAs should be narrowly tailored. Each RFA should pertain to a single fact or matter, should be clear and unambiguous, and should use plain English. Think of RFAs as going for individual base hits, rather than home runs. For example:

> "Admit the light was red for southbound traffic on Main Street when your car entered the intersection at Elm Street on May 5, 2019."

> "Admit that the speed limit on southbound Main Street at the intersection of Elm Street was 35 m.p.h. on May 5, 2019."

> "Admit that the brakes in the vehicle you were driving were in proper working condition when it entered the intersection at Elm Street on May 5, 2019."

Overly broad and conclusory RFAs, such as "Admit that the defendant is liable for the harm caused to the plaintiff" will get you nowhere and will simply result in a denial. However, if each RFA is pegged to a specific element of an individual claim or defense, then admissions (or denials with explanations) can be quite useful.

If the RFA pertains to the genuineness of a document, Rule 36(a)(2) requires that the document must accompany the RFA unless it already has been produced. As a practical matter, counsel often will stipulate to the genuineness of documents without resort to RFAs, but in the event the genuineness of a given document is in question, an RFA is the appropriate means by which to conduct discovery into the matter.

2. RESPONDING TO RFAs

If a party fails to respond to an RFA within 30 days, the matter is deemed admitted.[59] In other words, if counsel blows the 30-day time limit, she has (1) admitted on behalf of the client every RFA, and (2) committed malpractice.[60]

---

[57] *Id.* 36(a)(3).

[58] *Id.* 26(b)(2)(A).

[59] *Id.* 36(a)(3).

[60] Failure to timely respond to requests for admission results in an automatic admission of the matters requested, even if the requesting party makes no motion to establish these matters; the rule is self-executing. Smith v. Pac. Bell Tel. Co., Inc., 662 F. Supp. 2d 1199, 1229 (E.D. Cal. 2009). Courts may entertain motions for relief from the automatic admission rule, generally upon a showing of good cause and lack of prejudice to the non-moving party. Good cause ≠ "I forgot."

There are five possible responses to an RFA:

(1) Admit. If a party admits a given RFA, then the matter is conclusively established, unless the court, on motion, permits the admission to be withdrawn.[61]

(2) Deny. If a party denies an RFA and the matter denied is later proven true, the requesting party may move for its reasonable expenses, including attorney's fees in making that proof.[62]

(3) Partially admit, but deny the balance. A partial admission must specify the part admitted and deny the remainder.[63]

(4) Neither admit nor deny. If the responding party cannot admit or deny an RFA, the response must state in detail why it cannot do so.[64] A party may assert a lack of knowledge or information as a basis for a refusal to admit or deny only if the party has made a reasonable inquiry.[65] Presumably, if the party subsequently acquires information that enables a more specific response, it is under a continuing duty to supplement the response with either an admission or denial.[66]

(5) Object and refuse to either admit or deny. If an objection is interposed, and no response is made beyond the objection, the grounds for objecting must be stated. It may not include a general objection that "the request presents a genuine issue for trial."[67] Typically, an objection may lead to a meet and confer, and if the dispute is not resolved, then to a motion to compel. Unless the court finds an objection justified, it must order that an answer be served and may award expenses for bringing the motion.[68]

---

[61] FED. R. CIV. P. 36(b). A court generally will require a showing of good cause and/or a lack of unfair prejudice before it will permit withdrawal of an admission. *See, e.g.,* Am. Auto. Ass'n Inc. v. AAA Legal Clinic of Jefferson Crooke, P.C., 930 F.2d 1117, 1119 (5th Cir. 1991) ("[T]he court may permit withdrawal or amendment when the presentation of the merits of the action will be subserved thereby and the party who obtained the admission fails to satisfy the court that withdrawal or amendment will prejudice that party in maintaining the action or defense on the merits."); Jones v. Tauber & Balser, P.C., 503 B.R. 162, 175 (N.D. Ga. 2013) ("Both criteria weigh in favor of granting the motion to withdraw. First, allowing the withdrawal aligns the record to reality, and thus provides a more accurate basis upon which the Court can reach the merits of Plaintiff's case. Second, the withdrawal of the admissions does not prejudice Plaintiff in any material way.").

[62] FED. R. CIV. P. 37(c)(2).

[63] *Id.* 36(a)(4).

[64] *Id.*

[65] *Id.*

[66] *Id.* 26(e), 37(c).

[67] *Id.* 36(a)(5).

[68] *Id.* 36(a)(6).

CHAPTER 8

DEPOSITIONS

■ ■ ■

Second only to trial, depositions can be the most challenging aspect of civil litigation. And while trials are few and far between for many practitioners, depositions are a staple of litigation. Like interrogatories, depositions are limited in number, and also are limited in duration. Unlike interrogatories, the witness must directly answer each question without assistance or intervention from counsel.

This dynamic give-and-take gives depositions a special power. In fact, depositions can make or break a case. Therefore, it is important to master the skills necessary to take effective depositions. It is equally necessary to understand the inherent group dynamics and human factors that play an important role in this form of discovery. Before launching into the "when, where, why and how," of taking and defending depositions, we think an allegory (and a true story) may be apt.

On a spring break during law school, the author of this chapter was visiting with his parents. His father had just bought a backyard play set for his granddaughters. He pulled out of the large box what looked like a thousand parts. At the bottom of the box was a thick book of instructions. When the old man opened the book to page 1, he burst out laughing. The very first instruction was:

> "You are about to endeavor on a complicated task. Therefore, it is important to remain calm."

Actually, it was excellent advice, and thoroughly applicable to deposition practice. There are a lot of moving parts, some of which are intuitive, others not at all. A calm and deliberative approach is as important to deposition practice as it is to a complicated construction project.[1]

A. OVERVIEW OF THE TYPES OF DEPOSITIONS

Rules 27 through 32 (with the exception of Rule 29) govern the taking and defending of depositions. Rather than parse each rule, we begin with a

---

[1] For an excellent, concise and practical guide to defending and taking depositions, see BRADLEY G. CLARY ET AL., SUCCESSFUL FIRST DEPOSITIONS (West, 4th ed. 2017).

general overview and then we outline the types of, and purposes for, various depositions.[2]

Depositions are a powerful and time-efficient form of discovery. They afford counsel the opportunity to elicit testimony, under oath, from both parties and non-parties. Rule 30 presumptively limits the number of depositions each party may take to ten.[3] Unless otherwise stipulated, each deposition is limited to a single day not to exceed seven hours.[4] Counsel may take depositions at any time after commencement of discovery, unless otherwise limited pursuant to stipulation or court order.

Counsel must provide reasonable notice to take the deposition of a party,[5] and may compel a non-party to appear for a deposition through use of a subpoena.[6] The rules allow for various forms of depositions, each serving a particular purpose. Following is a brief summary of the forms of depositions allowed under the rules.

1. DEPOSITIONS TO PRESERVE TESTIMONY

Rule 27 governs the perpetuation of testimony by deposition. A Rule 27 deposition is not a tool of discovery,[7] but instead is a means to preserve testimony of a witness who may be unavailable for trial.[8] Depositions to preserve testimony are most common when a potential party expects an action to be filed and also expects a witness to be unavailable once the suit is brought. A person seeking to take a deposition to preserve testimony must petition the court for leave to do so.[9] If you take a deposition to preserve testimony, it is critical to keep the rules of evidence firmly in mind as the testimony elicited is, essentially, trial testimony.[10]

---

[2]   We will not spend time on depositions by written questions, governed by FED. R. CIV. P. 31, as this form of discovery is rarely employed and is of dubious utility unless it is the only practical way to proceed, generally when deposing distant witnesses for whom the cost of a live deposition outweighs the potential benefit.

[3]   FED. R. CIV. P. 30(a).

[4]   *Id.* 30(d)(1).

[5]   *Id.* 30(b)(1).

[6]   *Id.* 45(a).

[7]   *See* Penn Mutual Life Ins. Co. v. United States, 68 F.D.R. 1371, 1376 (D.C. Cir. 1995).

[8]   For example, the potential witness or party may be elderly, *In re* Town of Amenia, 200 F.R.D. 200 (S.D.N.Y. 2001), ill, Kurz-Kash, Inc. v. United States, 115 F.R.D. 470 (S.D. Ohio 1986), or likely to leave the jurisdiction, *see In re* Boland, 79 F.R.D. 665 (D.D.C. 1978). If the witness is in fact unavailable at trial, admissible portions of the deposition may be used in lieu of live testimony pursuant to FED. R. EVID. 804(b)(1).

[9]   FED. R. CIV. P. 27(a).

[10]   FED. R. CIV. P. 27 refers to FED. R. CIV. P. 32(a), which states at subd. (1): "[A] deposition may be used against a party on these conditions: . . . (B) it is used to the extent it would be admissible under the Federal Rules of Evidence if the deponent were present and testifying."

2. LAY WITNESSES (PARTY AND NON-PARTY)

Governed by Rule 30, lay witness depositions are by far the most common form of deposition. They primarily are for discovery, but may be useful at trial for impeachment, to aid a witness's recollection, or as a substitute for testimony if a witness becomes unavailable and the questions would be permissible at trial. You may take depositions of parties and non-parties, but there are several important distinctions between the two:

Party	Non-Party
Privilege attaches to witness preparation; opposing counsel may not inquire into the content of attorney-client communications.	No privilege attaches to witness interviews or preparation; opposing counsel is free to inquire into conversations between the witness and opposing counsel and/or her investigators.
Party admissions—everything the party testifies to will be treated as a party admission under Federal Rule of Evidence 801(d)(2).	Not admissions, but may be admissible at trial if the witness becomes unavailable or for other limited purposes if otherwise admissible under the Rules of Evidence.
Deposition testimony is compelled via notice of deposition.	Deposition testimony is compelled via subpoena (Rule 45).
The party-deponent typically is represented at the deposition by counsel.	Non-parties often are not represented by counsel.

Illus. 8-1.

3. EXPERT DEPOSITIONS

Expert depositions typically take place after completion of "fact" discovery.[11] Expert depositions usually come late in the discovery process for two reasons: (1) oftentimes the experts need to review and rely upon "fact" discovery as part of their analysis; and (2) expert discovery is expensive. If you can favorably settle your case prior to incurring the costs associated with expert discovery, or at least prior to expert depositions, you may save your client a substantial amount of money. If expert depositions go forward, the order in which these depositions take place often is subject

---

[11] During the Rule 26(f) meet and confer process, counsel should work through expert discovery, including the order of depositions. The exemplar Rule 26(f) report form that can be found in the Appendix distinguishes fact discovery from expert discovery.

to negotiation, as there usually is a tactical advantage to having your expert deposed last.

4. DEPOSITIONS OF ORGANIZATIONS (INCLUDING RECORDS CUSTODIANS)

Rule 30(b)(6) governs depositions of an organization or its records custodian. This is a powerful but often neglected discovery tool that is especially useful when you do not know who within an organization has knowledge of issues into which you wish to inquire and when you want to be sure you are deposing someone who can speak for, and bind, the organization with his or her testimony. The deposing party must serve notice on the organization, including a list of subjects to be inquired into. It is incumbent on the organization to designate a person or persons with knowledge of those subjects to speak on behalf of the organization.

B. GROUP DYNAMICS AND HUMAN FACTORS

A deposition usually takes place in a conference room at counsel's offices. Present are the court reporter (whose job it is to swear in the witness and faithfully record the proceedings), the witness (who may or may not be a party), the witness's lawyer,[12] opposing counsel, and sometimes the clients. Ideally, deposing counsel asks non-objectionable questions of the witness, who provides straightforward, truthful responses, while defending counsel rarely speaks, and when she does, states her objections in a succinct, non-argumentative manner. Based upon experience, this type of deposition is rare.

Individual litigation styles (for example, aggressive, passive-aggressive, accommodating, inept), counsels' level of preparation, personality types of both counsel and the witness, and deposition tactics often create a dynamic and sometimes volatile environment. In order to take an effective deposition, deposing counsel must control the room.

When we say deposing counsel must control the room, we do not mean that counsel should be domineering. What we mean is that counsel must stay focused on achieving the goals of the deposition. A witness who evades questions or attempts to intimidate deposing counsel is trying to control the room. Defending counsel who engages in long-winded objections, aggressive behavior, or constantly interrupts is trying to control the room. Behavior like this can be extremely frustrating and the temptation to respond in kind can be strong. Resist. Your job as deposing counsel is to use the time you have to fully explore the witness's knowledge, to obtain helpful admissions (if you are deposing the opposing party), and to make a clear record. Engaging in a battle of wills with the witness or his counsel

---

[12] The witness will almost always be defended by counsel if the witness is a party. Non-party witnesses may or may not be represented.

cedes control to them. They are succeeding in preventing you from achieving your goals. On the other side of the equation, as defending counsel, most of what you can do to control the room happens *before* the deposition takes place, during the witness preparation process.

In other words, the best way to control the room is to not become distracted by, or get sucked into, other participants' tactics. This may seem self-evident but in practice it can be extremely hard to do. Later in this chapter we will discuss how to deal with bad behavior during depositions. For now, the advice we impart is this: it is important to remain calm.

C. TAKING DEPOSITIONS

1. OBJECTIVES

Taking depositions serves multiple purposes. The chief discovery-related purposes are to:

- Discover the evidence supporting the adverse party's claims;
- Discover the evidence supporting your client's claims;
- Narrow or define disputed issues;
- Create evidence (e.g., by obtaining party admissions).

Further, taking a party or non-party witness deposition also allows counsel to:

- Assess the witness, including the witness's credibility;
- Lock in the witness's anticipated trial testimony;
- Determine the scope of the witness's knowledge and limits of that knowledge;
- Obtain information that has not been wordsmithed or filtered by opposing counsel.

The only way to effectively and efficiently meet these objectives is through careful preparation.

2. PREPARATION

Most of what a lawyer does (or should do) in relation to depositions takes place *before* the deposition. Whether taking or defending, advance preparation can, and often does, take longer than the deposition itself. You get one shot to take the witness's deposition.[13] It is important to make it count. Even the most experienced lawyer should not "wing it."

To properly prepare to take a deposition you must know the case—all of it. You must review all discovery responses. You must establish clear

---

[13] FED. R. CIV. P. 30(a)(2)(A)(ii) (leave of court required to re-depose a witness).

objectives for the deposition. And you must organize by preparing an outline and gathering exhibits you intend to use during the deposition. To establish specific objectives for the deposition, you should:

- Review your theory of the case and evidence map in order to identify weaknesses and gaps that may be filled by the witness's testimony;[14]

- Identify specific admissions (if the witness is a party) and other information you hope to extract;

- Determine how to either bolster or undermine the witness's credibility, depending on whether the witness is favorable or adverse to your client's case.

As an organizational aid, and to ensure you meet all of your objectives, you should prepare a comprehensive outline.[15] An outline is not simply a list of questions. Your outline should reflect your strategy and objectives, and should logically order topics and exhibits you intend to use. Depending on the complexity of the case and whether you may need to use the deposition in lieu of testimony at trial, you may choose to organize your deposition outline chronologically, around a series of individual events, around important documents, or in any other way that facilitates a coherent, thorough examination.

Further, you should formulate you lines of questioning in a way that will advance your specific goals. For instance, if you wish to exhaust the witness's knowledge of a certain subject, you should outline a series of open-ended questions. As an example, assume you are deposing an eyewitness to an auto crash. The outline for exhausting the witness's knowledge may look like this:

Witness's personal knowledge of the accident:

[Exh.: Police report]

[Exh.: Witness's 6/20/12 statement to police]

Q. When? [June 20, 2012]

Q. Where? [Intersection of Main and Elm]

Q. Where were you standing? [SE corner]

Q. How far away? [20–30 ft.]

Q. Any limitations on your ability to observe the accident (such as people or objects in your line of sight, not wearing corrective lenses, etc.)? [No.]

Q. What did you see?

---

[14] *See* Chapter 1, Section E.

[15] For an example of a deposition outline, see Appendix.

Q. What did you hear?

Q. What did you do after the collision?

Q. Who did you talk with? [D, P, police]

Q. What was said to/by each?

Note that these are all open-ended questions. At the deposition, you will need to follow up each of these open-ended questions with more specific questions, but the initial questions of "who, what, when, where, why and how" should be in your outline.

On the other hand, if you hope to extract helpful admissions from the opposing party, it is most useful to draft precise, leading questions. For example, plaintiff's counsel in an auto crash case may ask of the defendant:

Events just before the accident:

[Exh. ___: Police report]

[Exh. ___: D's Responses to Interrogatories, Nos. 3, 4, 7, 12]

[Exh. ___: Hard copy of text messages]

Q. You were the driver of the blue Pontiac that was involved in the June 20, 2019 accident, correct? [Police report]

Q. You were heading west on Main St. toward Elm St., correct? [Police report]

Q. You know the intersection well since you grew up in the neighborhood, correct? [Interrogatory No. 3]

Q. You know the intersection has a 4-way stop, indicated by stop signs, correct?

Q. You were texting on your cell phone as you approached the intersection, correct? [Hard copy of text messages; [Get witness to authenticate]

Q. Because you were texting, you were looking at your cell phone, correct?

Q. While you were texting, you were not looking in the direction you were driving, correct?

Q. You did not come to a stop at the stop sign, did you?

Q. At no time did you apply your brakes as you approached the intersection, did you? [Police report: no skid marks noted.]

Whether you are asking open-ended or leading questions, it is useful to note in your deposition outline all anticipated responses, including the specific sources of information that suggest the party's responses. That way, you can pull, mark, and use as an exhibit a document that can help refresh the witness's recollection, confront the witness with evidence that contradicts the witness's deposition testimony, or otherwise obtain the concession you seek.

In addition to preparing an outline, you should gather, organize, and copy all documents you may want to use as exhibits. Make three copies of each: one for the court reporter to mark, one for opposing counsel (though not required, it is considered a courtesy), and one for your own use during the deposition. Place each exhibit, along with its copies, in its own folder. This aids organization and will save time at the deposition when pulling exhibits to be marked.

3. TAKING THE DEPOSITION

It is your job, as deposing counsel, to set specific goals for the deposition and then execute your plan in order to achieve those goals. Simply sitting across from the witness and mechanically asking your pre-written questions will likely not be effective.

a. Set the Tone

You will get more from your deposition if you control the room and control the witness. In most circumstances, this means directing all details and attempting to put the witness at ease.

When the witness comes into the room, introduce yourself. If the deposition is in your offices, offer the witness a beverage. Explain where the bathrooms are. Ask the witness if she is ready to begin. In other words, be civil. In fact, try to be likable.

Once the witness is sworn in, go through preliminary instructions on how the deposition will proceed.[16] This is an important step not only because you are establishing the ground rules, but because you are making clear to the witness that you are in charge. Do this in a friendly, but professional tone. For example:

Q. You are under oath, just as if you were testifying at trial. Do you understand that?

Q. Should I ask you a question that you don't understand please let me know and I will try to rephrase it. Okay?

Q. It is important that you answer questions verbally; nods of the head or other gestures will not be clear on the record, so please answer with a "yes," "no," or other oral response.

Q. If you wish to take a break, please let me know, but I will finish the current line of questioning before we do so. Do you understand?

---

[16] *See* Appendix for an exemplar outline of preliminary instructions.

After establishing the ground rules, our time-tested advice is that you begin slowly. Start with non-controversial, preliminary questions. The purpose of these questions is twofold: (1) to gather potentially useful background information on the witness; and (2) to get the witness used to the back-and-forth of question and answer. All the while, by being civil and friendly, you are building rapport with the witness and hopefully getting the witness to relax. In most cases, a relaxed witness who thinks you are friendly, or at least not confrontational, may be more likely to let their guard down and more readily offer information.[17]

As an important part of the effort to establish rapport with the witness and to maintain control of the deposition, you should maintain direct eye contact. Observe carefully the witness's demeanor—look for non-verbal cues that the witness is withholding information, is fearful, or is angry. Do not let your outline get in the way of careful observation of the witness. If you are glued to your outline, you may miss vital information. Therefore, the outline should be used as an outline, *not as a script*. Every time you break connection with the witness by studying the outline or reading from it, you are interfering with the connection you should be trying to make with the witness.[18]

b. Get the Witness Talking

Get the witness talking. This is the flipside of what defending counsel will attempt to prevent as part of the witness's preparation. Generally, ask open-ended questions. For example:

Q. Tell me more about your training as a welder.

Q. What, in your opinion, is the difference between a competent welder and one who isn't?

Q. What do you like most about your job?

Q. What do you like least about your job?

Use non-verbal cues, such as nodding your head in agreement. If you sense the witness is going to say more, don't interrupt; let him continue. If he hesitates, it is perfectly acceptable to say:

Q. You were about to say something more, what was it?

---

[17] Some attorneys are of the opinion that it is best to ask key questions right from the start on the theory that it will not allow the witness the time to prepare to answer those questions. We have found that this approach may backfire, especially if the witness has been properly prepared. It has a tendency to put the witness on guard and can make the rest of the deposition unduly tense.

[18] Which begs the question: "Then why bother having an outline?" Because it is there if you need it. During the flow of "q and a" there will be natural times to break eye contact, to give the witness a little breathing room. Review the outline then to make sure you have not missed anything. If you have, then you have the opportunity to double back and cover what you missed.

Remember, a casual, even friendly tone, so long as it appears genuine, tends to be more probative than one that is intimidating or confrontational.[19]

c. Boxing in, Boxing out and Exhausting the Witness's Knowledge

An important goal of any deposition should be to get the witness to commit to his version of the facts. Therefore, you should make sure that the witness is "boxed in" on whatever topic you explore. By "boxing in" we mean you have gotten the witness to unequivocally, unambiguously, and fully testify to *everything* he knows about the topic. For example:

Q. How do you know the plaintiff?

Q. When did you first meet?

Q. Do you consider the plaintiff a friend of yours?

Q. When did you become friends?

Q. How often do you socialize?

Q. Do you have any kind of financial relationship with the plaintiff?

Q. Do you owe her money or does she owe you money?

Q. What discussions have you had with the plaintiff regarding the accident that is the subject of this lawsuit?

Q. When?

Q. Where?

Q. Others present?

Q. What did you discuss?

Q. Anything else?

Q. Have you told me everything you recall regarding discussions with the plaintiff pertaining to the accident?

This can go on for some time but you get the idea.

Conversely, if the witness professes to lack knowledge about a given subject, then you must fully "box out" the witness. It may be that the witness has no knowledge whatsoever of the subject matter, or that the witness lacks sufficient foundation. Following is an example of boxing out the witness who professes to know nothing of the subject matter:

---

[19] There are lawyers who would disagree with this advice. Some lawyers are very effective by engaging in a hard-edged cross-examination. However, experience has taught us that they are in the minority, and many who engage in this style of cross-examination end up shutting the witness down and missing useful information.

Q. Is it your testimony that you don't know the defendant?

Q. You never met the defendant?

Q. You wouldn't recognize the defendant if you were shown a photo?

Q. You have never spoken to the defendant?

Q. Nor do you know anything about the defendant's reputation for truthfulness?

Q. Or anything else about the defendant's reputation?

Q. Would it be fair to say that you know absolutely nothing about the defendant?

Q. And at no time in the past did you know anything about the defendant?

This may seem like overkill but you would be surprised how witnesses may suddenly "remember" facts at trial. By boxing out the witness you will be in a position to impeach the witness at trial with her prior inconsistent statements. In the alternative, the witness may have some unfavorable information about a subject but may lack adequate foundation to testify to that subject. In that situation, the goal is to establish that lack of foundation, and therefore "box out" the witness on the basis of lack of foundation. For example:

Q. It is your testimony that my client caused the accident?

Q. But you didn't see the accident?

Q. And you didn't hear the accident?

Q. Nor has my client discussed the accident with you?

Q. Would it be fair to say that the only basis you have for testifying that my client caused the accident is what the plaintiff told you?

Q. And there is no other basis for your opinion?

Essential to either boxing in or boxing out the witness is making sure that the subject has been fully exhausted. In other words, you must make sure that the witness has testified to everything he knows or has unequivocally disqualified himself. Exhausting the subject ensures that there will be no surprises at trial, or if the witness embellishes, the record is clear that the witness is testifying inconsistently with his deposition testimony.[20] Following is an example of exhausting a subject with the witness:

Q. Have you told me everything you know about the defendant?

---

[20] And in such instances, FED. R. EVID. 613 allows counsel to impeach the witness with his prior inconsistent statement.

Q. There is nothing else you can tell me about the defendant?

Q. And your answers to the questions I have put to you today are based upon your best recollection?

Q. And sitting here today, your recollection is clear?

Again, counsel can then effectively impeach the witness at trial if he "suddenly" remembers additional "facts," or otherwise embellishes his story. Likewise, if the adverse counsel proffers the witness's affidavit in connection with a summary judgment motion, and that affidavit is inconsistent with his deposition testimony, then there exists a sound basis to request that the court disregard the affidavit.[21]

d. Admissions

This section applies solely to the depositions of parties and their agents because only parties or those enumerated under Federal Rule of Evidence 801(d)(2) can make party admissions. Sometimes the adverse party spontaneously offers testimony that is helpful to your case, adverse to his own, or both. However, usually the adverse party needs help in making those useful admissions. That help comes in the form of a well-crafted leading question. Take, for example, deposition testimony of the plaintiff in a trade secrets case. Counsel is attempting to establish that plaintiff failed to properly safeguard its data:

Q. Were you the only person with a password to the computer that contained what you claim are trade secrets?

A. No.

Q. How many people knew the password?

A. Not sure; maybe ten or more.

Q. Were all these people employees of WidgetCo at the time the alleged trade secrets were taken?

A. No. A few were outside consultants. One or two may have been subcontractors.

Q. Were each of these individuals advised that the information on the computer contained trade secrets?

A. Oh sure.

Q. How?

A. Um, well, I think they were all told by me or someone in the office.

---

[21] *See, e.g.,* Philips v. Bronx Lebanon Hosp., 701 N.Y.S.2d 403, 405 (N.Y. App. Div. 2000) (affidavit submitted in opposition to summary judgment that is inconsistent with prior deposition testimony rejected by court.)

Q.   But you are not sure.

A.   Not for everyone, no.

Q.   You would agree, then, that it is possible that someone with access to the alleged trade secrets may not have been told by WidgetCo that the information on the computer constituted trade secrets?

A.   I guess so.

In a case where one of the elements of proving that a trade secret exists is that the party claiming protection took reasonable steps to safeguard its information, the above cross-examination, and particularly the final, leading question in that exchange, would effectively undermine the claim. But before the cross-examiner got to the "kill shot," she first led the witness to the inevitable conclusion by asking a series of predicate questions.

Going after key admissions, such as in the example above, takes careful planning. The predicate questions, as well as the ultimate, leading question, should be mapped out. Depending upon how the witness responds, counsel must be prepared to adjust. For example, assume the previous Q. and A., but with different, unexpected responses from the witness:

Q.   Were each of these individuals advised that the information on the computer contained trade secrets?

A.   Oh sure.

Q.   How?

A.   It was company policy. [Unexpected response]

Q.   A formal policy?

A.   Yes.

Q.   Can you identify any document or any form of communication that contains that policy?

A.   No.

Q.   Because no such document exists?

A.   I don't know if it does or doesn't.

Q.   If you don't know if such a writing exists, then how would you expect others to know it exists?

A.   I guess I wouldn't.

Q.   Let's assume it does. How would this writing be conveyed to those who were given access to what you claim are trade secrets?

A. Since I don't know if we have it in writing then I can't answer your hypothetical question.

Q. But is it your position that this policy is important in order to safeguard company secrets?

A. Yes.

Q. Do you specifically recall informing each and every person with the password to the computer that the information contained in it was considered by WidgetCo to be trade secrets?

A. Not specifically, but I'm sure I did.

Q. But you have no record of any of these communications?

A. No.

Q. You would agree, then, that it is possible that WidgetCo did not communicate to everyone with access to the alleged trade secrets that the information on the computer constituted trade secrets?

A. I guess so.

It took counsel more time and effort to get to the key admission, but by knowing that no such document existed (or, at least had not been disclosed in discovery), she was able to adjust her cross-examination in order ultimately to extract the admission she was after.

Of course, there is no single method for obtaining desired admissions. The best advice we can offer is that you think about what, exactly, you want to get the witness to say, think about how best to lead the witness to the admission, and be prepared to cut off escape routes by knowing the facts of the case as well, or better, than the witness.

e. Asking About Emotionally Charged or Controversial Matters

It is not uncommon for a case to involve difficult, emotionally charged or embarrassing issues. Think of a sexual harassment case in which a manager is accused of engaging in nonconsensual sexual activity with an employee of the company. The manager vehemently denies the accusation. In both the manager's deposition and the employee's deposition the sexual encounter will be explored in some detail. Publicly. On the record. How will the witnesses react?

In such cases, it is not unusual for the witness to become emotional, or even enraged or distraught. If you expect to get into emotionally charged or controversial matters with the witness we recommend the following:

- **Hold off until later in the deposition** before getting into the sensitive subjects. Getting into it too early, before you establish rapport and before easier Q and A, could sour the entire proceeding and make it much more difficult to get even the most basic information from the witness later on.

- **Do not ambush the witness** with a highly sensitive question; give the witness a sense as to what is coming. Some lawyers go right for the throat, without warning. We have found this approach generally to be counter-productive. If the witness knows the difficult questions are coming, he is more likely to provide coherent, responsive testimony.

- **Avoid judgmental questions**, such as "How could someone in your position do something so despicable?" Instead, ask the question in a manner that does not betray a personal judgment on your part. For example, "My client claims you exposed yourself on [date] in the copy room. What is your response?"

If the witness denies or otherwise provides unambiguous responses, then you have a record and the witness is boxed in. If, however, the witness is evasive or otherwise does not provide clear testimony, then you may need to become more assertive and push the witness to unambiguously answer the questions. In any event, even if the subject matter makes you, as cross-examiner, uncomfortable, it is your job to get at the facts, to elicit clear testimony, and hopefully to extract useful admissions.

f.   Handling Exhibits

Identify in your outline all exhibits you plan to use, and come to the deposition with at least three copies: one for the court reporter to mark and give to the witness, one as a courtesy copy for opposing counsel (and if there are multiple parties, a copy for each attorney in attendance), and one for yourself, which you may want to annotate or highlight in advance, so you can quickly find the relevant sections of the document.

Once the court reporter marks an exhibit, you should thereafter refer to the document by its exhibit number. This is particularly important in document-intensive cases, or cases in which there may be multiple iterations of the same document. Always give the witness an opportunity to review the document before you proceed with questions. If the witness can authenticate the document (assuming no stipulation exists regarding authenticity) you should get that authentication properly on the record:

Q.   Are you familiar with Exhibit X?

Q.   How is it that you are familiar Exhibit X?

Q.   Is this a true and correct copy of Exhibit X?

g. Handling Objections

Objections are a routine part of depositions, but all too often lawyers misuse them. The rules explicitly require lawyers to state objections "in a nonargumentative and nonsuggestive manner," and to refrain from instructing the witness not to answer unless "necessary to preserve a privilege, to enforce a limitation ordered by the court, or to present a motion under Rule 30(d)(3)."[22] In other words, defending counsel should succinctly state her objection on the record, without giving a speech, suggesting a response, or otherwise coaching the witness.

Sometimes, an objection is well-taken and actually may be a helpful signal that you need to rephrase. For example:

Q. What did he say to you about that?

By Ms. Smith: Objection. The question is vague and ambiguous.

Actually, Ms. Smith may be right. Accept the help and re-state the question so it is clear who "he" is and what "that" is referring to. Making the deposition record clear will be important if you need to later use the transcript during summary judgment or at trial.

Oftentimes, however, objections are improper. For example:

Q. Sitting here today, can you specifically recall what the defendant Jack Jones said immediately after his vehicle crashed into the plaintiff's vehicle?

By Ms. Smith: Objection. Calls for hearsay, calls for a narrative, calls for speculation. I don't think the witness should be required to quote what was said, especially since it happened over two years ago and the witness's memory may not be photographic. Counsel, I suggest you ask a reasonable question.

This objection is wholly improper. Hearsay is an *evidentiary* objection governed by the Rules of Evidence and appropriate at trial; hearsay is not a proper discovery objection. Further, the narrative accompanying the objection coaches the witness by suggesting that the witness's memory may have faded. What should counsel do when opposing counsel makes improper objections, so-called "speaking objections," coaches the witness, or otherwise interferes with your deposition?

- Remain calm. Do not lose your temper. If you lose your temper, you lose control of the room and likely also lose control of your ability to think clearly. If you cannot think straight, you cannot effectively represent your client.

---

[22] *See* FED. R. CIV. P. 30(c)(2). FED. R. CIV. P. 30(d)(3)(A) allows for suspension or termination of the deposition if defending counsel determines that the deposition "is being conducted in bad faith or in a manner that unreasonably annoys, embarrasses or oppresses the deponent or party."

- Remind counsel that Rule 30(c)(2) specifically prohibits speaking objections, and that under Rule 26(b), information need not be admissible in evidence to be discoverable.

- If counsel persists in obstructing the deposition, then remind counsel that Rule 30(d)(2) allows you to seek sanctions against a "person who impedes, delays, or frustrates the fair examination of the deponent."

- If counsel's conduct is egregious, consider making a record that counsel has prevented you from conducting discovery, then suspend the deposition until a motion for sanctions can be brought.[23]

- Alternatively, particularly when opposing counsel is obstructing a particularly important line of inquiry, take a break and call the judge or magistrate judge with opposing counsel present and seek a ruling on the questions and objections at issue. If the judge is willing to hear you, have the court reporter read to the court the portion of the record in which opposing counsel has acted inappropriately.

h. Dealing with Witnesses Behaving Badly

Witnesses may lie. They may obfuscate. They may evade. They may become petulant. What should counsel do with a difficult witness? It depends.

If you are getting the testimony you came for, then be patient and plow ahead. If the witness is lying, let him. Assuming you have done your homework, you will know that the witness is lying and you should be able to prove it later. Lying witnesses raise tactical challenges. You may have documents or other evidence at the ready to expose the lie. Or you may choose not to, but instead keep the impeaching evidence in your back pocket for use at trial. Depending on the case, your theory of the case, and your discovery plan, a lying witness may be quite welcome. For example, if the witness provides testimony supposedly helpful to the adverse party, or harmful to your client's case, to the extent you can establish the witness is a liar (using his own sworn deposition testimony), the more likely you will be able to neutralize the witness.

What if the witness seems to have difficulty recalling? Witnesses who are selective amnesiacs are frustrating. If the witness feigns memory loss,

---

[23] You should do this only as a last resort. If you are able to achieve your goals for the deposition notwithstanding adverse counsel's bad behavior, it is generally better to plow forward. However, if you are completely thwarted in your efforts due to counsel's bad behavior, you should suspend the deposition and seek your remedies. Generally, judges hate this kind of behavior but equally hate having to deal with it. By suspending the deposition, you run the risk that the court may have little sympathy for your plight and your inability to manage it yourself and not give you the relief you are seeking.

there are several things you can do. First, attempt to completely box out the witness. Make sure the record is clear about everything the witness has forgotten. That way, you can effectively prevent the witness from testifying later, or can discredit him with the on-the-record amnesia he suffered at his deposition. Second, consider getting the witness to testify in great detail about trivial matters. That will help discredit the witness's convenient lack of memory relating to centrally important facts. Third, you should ask the witness if he is taking any medications or drugs, or suffers from any psychological or medical condition that impairs his memory. This may offend the witness, but if she is playing games, it may not matter.

What if the witness obfuscates or is evasive? Fortunately, there is a rule for that. Rule 37(a)(4) specifically states that an evasive or incomplete answer should be treated as a failure to answer.[24] Read the rule into the record and advise counsel to instruct the witness to respond. Caution counsel and the witness that the failure fully to respond to the question will lead to a motion to compel and for sanctions *against both counsel and the witness.*

i. Never Forget the Record/Making the Record

A deposition is useful only to the extent the record is clear. A garbled record is not useful for dispositive motions, impeachment of witnesses at trial, or much of anything else. Therefore, counsel always must be mindful of the record.

Following are a few basic rules:

- **Speak slowly and deliberately.** The court reporter is there to make a complete record, but if you are a fast talker, or run your words together, you will make the court reporter's job difficult. Slow down.

- **Do not talk over the witness.** Wait for the witness to finish his response before beginning your next question. This seems pretty simple, but in practice it is not. People tend to talk over each other, but the court reporter cannot record two people speaking at the same time.

- **Once an exhibit is marked, refer to it by its exhibit number.** It is no longer "that memo" or "the letter." It is "exhibit 3" or "exhibit 4."

- **Narrate or clarify witness gestures and other significant communication that otherwise may not be made part of the record.** For example, if the witness shakes his head in response to a question, follow up with "You

---

[24] FED. R. CIV. P. 37(a)(4) ("For purposes of this subdivision (a), an evasive or incomplete disclosure, answer, or response must be treated as a failure to disclose, answer, or respond.").

are shaking your head. Is that a no?" Or the witness may testify, "I was about from here to the wall away from the plaintiff." Follow up: "Would that be about 15 feet?"

If the witness (or his lawyer) raises his voice, note as much on the record, e.g., "Counsel has risen from his seat and is yelling." Or consider: "Counsel is leaning toward the witness and whispering into his ear."

- **Do not agree to go off the record.** Sometimes opposing counsel will ask to go off the record in order to prevent the court reporter from transcribing the full extent of an argument with you, or from transcribing veiled attempts to coach the witness. Be vigilant about the record, which should capture everything that happens; not just the questions and answers.

j. Concluding the Deposition

Before concluding your examination, take a short break to review your outline and your notes. It is easy to skip over a portion of your outline and then forget to go back to it later. Always take a few moments before you conclude to make sure you have covered everything.

When you have concluded your examination, other counsel (including the witness's counsel) may choose to follow up with their own questions, which they are allowed to do. Once they have concluded, you may follow up again with additional questions.

Once questioning is completed, advise the witness that he has the right to "read and sign" his deposition transcript.[25] If the witness is represented, it is incumbent on that lawyer to advise the witness whether to exercise his right, or to waive it. If the witness is unrepresented, you may only advise the witness of the right, but you may not direct the witness as to what he should do. Either way, get the witness to state on the record whether the witness wants to exercise or waive the right to read and sign. Reading and signing allows the witness to review the transcript for errors and note them on an errata sheet. Be aware that any changes in the testimony does not negate the prior testimony and, in fact, may be the basis to impeach the witness if the "corrected" testimony is inconsistent with the original testimony.

D. DEFENDING DEPOSITION WITNESSES

The primary goal when defending a deposition witness is this: *minimize damage.* This is not the time to volunteer information you or your client hope may persuade opposing counsel of the rightness of your client's

---

[25] *See* FED. R. CIV. P. 30(e).

cause. The client may have a nearly uncontrollable urge to argue her case during the deposition. It is your job to prevent this.

1. PREPARING THE WITNESS

If you are a control freak (and many litigators are), defending a deposition can feel like a horrible loss of control. To the extent counsel can control the deposition, it needs to happen *before* the witness appears to testify: it happens via thorough witness preparation.

Witness preparation begins even before you meet with the witness—witness preparation begins by first preparing yourself. You should review the file, including pleadings and discovery responses served by both sides. Take extra care with documents that may bear upon this particular witness's testimony. Prepare an outline of potential subjects. In other words, you should master the subject matter and think through everything you would ask the witness if you were the one taking the deposition.

When you meet with the witness, whether the witness is the client or a non-party, do not treat this meeting in a perfunctory manner. Preparing your witness can take hours or even days in some instances. Be efficient by organizing yourself in advance, but be thorough.

How the prep session proceeds is largely dependent upon whether privilege attaches to your communications with the witness. If the witness is a non-party, then there is no cloak of privilege and you must be particularly circumspect. Opposing counsel will be free to inquire into the substance of all of your communications with the non-party witness and you will have no valid objection to the inquiry. So the basic rule regarding prep of non-party witnesses is this: *do not say anything to the witness that you do not want the other side to hear.*

If the witness is a client, then privilege attaches and the preparation can be more rigorous and the discussion more frank. The question of whether the witness is, or will be deemed a client, is beyond the scope of this book, but counsel should be aware, at minimum, that if your client is an organization, not every employee or affiliate of that organization will be considered a client for privilege purposes.[26]

For most witnesses, a deposition is not part of their routine. The witness may be anxious or even frightened. He may be worried about taking time away from work or family. He may be worried that his testimony might get him in trouble with his boss, his co-workers, even his spouse. Therefore, first and foremost, it is important to establish rapport and build a relationship of trust with the witness. This is an essential part of witness preparation: if the witness does not trust you, he is less apt to

---

[26] *See* Diversified Indus. v. Meredith, 572 F.2d 596 (8th Cir. 1977) (overview of the "control group," "Harper & Row," and "modified Harper & Row" tests to determine if corporate employee is covered by the attorney-client privilege).

be forthcoming and he is less apt to be receptive to your guidance. This is one of those "human factors" that you always should be alert to.

Always ask the witness what questions or concerns he has about the process. Listen closely for clues to what motivates the witness: fear, anger, a desire to settle scores? This will help inform how that witness may perform during the deposition. Show an interest in the *person*. From counsel's perspective, this is a witness, a source of evidence. True, but he also is a person and should be treated with respect.

Some lawyers will sit the witness in a room and have him watch a videotape on how to be a witness. This is not witness preparation. Witness prep should be a *conversation*: you should both advise the witness and learn from the witness. There may be things the witness knows that you may not, especially if the witness is a non-party. Therefore, part of deposition prep is conducting a thorough interview of the witness so that, hopefully, there will be no surprises during the deposition.

As you learn from the witness, the witness also should be learning from you. Certainly explain the process:

- What the room will look like (a conference room in an office building);

- That the witness will be sworn in by a court reporter who will be taking down everything that is said (but no judge will be there to rule on objections);

- That opposing counsel may be aggressive, or friendly, or seem uninformed, but no matter how that lawyer comes across, a deposition is not a friendly conversation—it is testimony (and because it is testimony, the witness must be truthful);

- That the witness should not answer a question unless it is crystal clear—if the question is at all confusing or ambiguous, the witness should ask that it be rephrased (the witness should not guess at the questioner's meaning);

- That if the witness does not know an answer, or cannot recall it at that moment, he should specifically say so, and make that distinction (there is an important distinction between not knowing something and not presently recalling it);

- That there may be objections and some back-and-forth between the lawyers, but that unless you instruct the witness not to answer a question, he should do so (even if he doesn't want to);

- That the witness may ask for and take breaks when needed (a deposition is not, nor should it be, a test of endurance);

- That at the end of the deposition, he will have the right to "read and sign" the transcript.[27]

If the witness is the client, you may discuss the theory of the case, how the witness's testimony fits within the larger picture, the implications of the witness's testimony, and so forth. With non-party witnesses, divulging this information could, and probably will, result in it becoming a subject of the witness's testimony.

Regardless of whether the witness is a client, we begin and end all prep sessions with these admonitions:

1. You will be under oath; therefore, you must not lie.

2. Do not volunteer information;

3. DO NOT volunteer information;

4. DO NOT VOLUNTEER INFORMATION![28]

Once you explain the basics of the deposition process, it is important to get the witness talking. Ask opened-ended questions about the witness's knowledge of the case. Prompt the witness with phrases like "go on" and "can you recall anything else?" and "say more about that." Part of the witness prep is to exhaust the witness's knowledge because during the deposition itself opposing counsel will be attempting to do the same.

When you are satisfied that the witness has told you everything he knows, rehearse. It may be helpful to have another attorney in the office conduct a mock cross-examination so that the rapport and trust that you have worked so hard to build is not undermined by a seemingly harsh or unfair cross-examination. The cross-examination need not be extensive, but it is important to get the witness used to the back-and-forth of question and answer. It also will give you the opportunity to remind the witness to keep responses short and to not volunteer information (in our experience, witnesses are unable to fully internalize the "do not volunteer" instruction until going through a practice round). Do not avoid the most difficult or problematic areas of the witness's testimony. In fact, it is best to focus on those areas to make sure the witness is fully prepared.

By the end of the prep session, you should be confident that you know what the testimony will be, and the witness should be confident that he is well-prepared.

---

[27] If the witness is your client, you will further advise the witness to not waive this right.

[28] The following anecdote helps to drive this important point home, and is useful to share as an example of what not volunteering information means:

You are walking down the street and a car pulls up next to you—the driver asks, "Do you know how to get to the Interstate from here?" In the real world, you would presumably give the driver detailed instructions. In a deposition, the response should simply be, "Yes." In the real world, this response would be considered odd and rude. In a deposition, it is wholly appropriate.

2. DEFENDING THE WITNESS DURING THE DEPOSITION

When you defend a witness during a deposition, your job is to listen closely to questions, object only when necessary to make a record, protect the witness, preserve a privilege, and make sure the witness gets adequate breaks and is treated appropriately. Beyond that, once the deposition begins, you may feel an uncomfortable loss of control over the process.

When you object, state the objection concisely and without argument. Be alert. Questions and answers will keep coming and you need to stay focused on each and every one. This can become a challenge over the course of a long deposition. If your mind begins to wander, or you find that you are objecting *after* the witness has responded, it may be time to take a break, get a cup of coffee, or just stretch your legs for a minute. In some ways, it takes more focus to defend a deposition than to take one.

If the form of the question is objectionable (e.g., it is vague or compound), and could be cured through rephrasing, you waive the objection if you fail to timely assert it at the deposition. Then, if opposing counsel attempts to use the objectionable question and answer at trial or in dispositive motions, you no longer may object. Even if the "form of the question" objection is waived, questions may still be subject to objection later if they run afoul of the Rules of Evidence.

If a question seeks privileged information, information that is otherwise confidential, or information that is attorney work product, you should object *and* instruct the witness not to answer. Once you do, that particular inquiry ends unless and until a court orders the witness to answer. The other situation in which you may instruct a witness not to answer is if questioning is being conducted in bad faith. Your client has the right to be treated respectfully. If opposing counsel harasses or otherwise treats your client unfairly, you should object. In extreme cases, you may need to instruct the witness not to answer a particular question or line of questioning whose purpose is to harass, and you may suspend the deposition and seek an order to have the deposition terminated or limited.[29]

On behalf of the witness, take frequent breaks. Being deposed can be grueling and exhausting. The witness will become both physically and mentally tired. It is important that the witness be allowed to stretch his legs, use the restroom, and perhaps most importantly, confer with counsel in private. Though counsel is prohibited from "coaching" the witness during the deposition itself,[30] during breaks there is no prohibition against talking with the client. You may reassure him, remind him not to volunteer information, and you may talk through questions that were confusing or

---

[29] *See* FED. R. CIV. P. 30(c)(2), (d)(3).

[30] "No coaching" means you may not answer for the witness, you may not tell the witness what to say, and you may not "signal" the witness.

answers that seemed incomplete. *However,* counsel may not coach the witness during breaks. Some courts have gone so far as to order the witness to disclose the substance of the conversation with his counsel during a break when the deposition resumes.[31]

Once opposing counsel has completed her examination, as defending counsel you may elect to ask some questions of your own. This is a right you should exercise only in limited circumstances. If adverse counsel has garbled the record or has failed to inquire into a substantive area for which the witness has knowledge, it is not your job to help her by asking clarifying questions. If, however, the witness has misstated something, you should have the witness explain, correct, or clarify his previous misstatement. It is better to do this at the deposition itself rather than later, when the witness is afforded the chance to "correct" testimony on an errata sheet during the reading and signing of the deposition.

Finally, the witness has the right to read and sign the transcript of the deposition, offering "corrections" on an errata sheet. The witness should state on the record prior to the deposition's conclusion whether the witness chooses to exercise or waive the right to read and sign. In almost every instance, the witness should exercise the right. The purpose should be to correct transcription errors, not to change substantive testimony. Substantive changes to testimony can be treated as inconsistent statements, which in turn will leave the witness exposed to impeachment. If you instead make these corrections on the record during the deposition, the witness has an opportunity to explain and hopefully minimize any impeachment potential.

E. EXPERT DEPOSITIONS

Chapter 9 focuses on the role of expert witnesses in case development. Here, we briefly delve into the subject of expert depositions.[32] What holds true for lay witness depositions largely holds true for expert depositions. There are, however, additional rules and considerations unique to experts.

As a practical matter, most of the expert witness's deposition preparation takes place in relation to the preparation of the expert report. That is not to say, however, that you may forego a witness prep session. Depending upon the expert's experience as a witness, the expert's preparation may require as much attention as a lay witness's deposition

---

[31] *See* HANDBOOK FED. CIV. DISC. & DISCLOSURE 5.38 (4th ed. 2019).

[32] FED. R. CIV. P. 26(b)(4) governs discovery of testifying expert witnesses. It states:

(A) *Deposition of an Expert Who May Testify.* A party may depose any person who has been identified as an expert whose opinions may be presented at trial. If Rule 26(a)(2)(B) requires a report from the expert, the deposition may be conducted only after the report is provided.

prep. In fact, sometimes prepping experts can take longer, depending upon the complexity of the subject matter the expert is expected to address.

You must ensure the expert has reviewed every detail of his report, has all relevant facts at his fingertips, and has considered how he will respond to difficult cross-examination. Further, if the expert has testified in the past, the possibility exists that opposing counsel will use that prior testimony during cross-examination. You should consider whether it might be worthwhile to obtain whatever deposition and trial transcripts are available and review them for possible inconsistencies with the expert's expected testimony.

When taking an expert's deposition, you should consider what your goals are, particularly in the context of the Federal Rules of Evidence 702 through 704. At risk of oversimplification, there are five areas of inquiry that examining counsel should focus on:[33]

1. Whether the expert is, in fact, an expert on the subject of his offered testimony;

2. Whether his testimony will assist the trier of fact;

3. Whether the data or underlying information the expert is relying on is reliable;

4. Whether the expert's methodologies are valid and reliable;

5. Whether the opinions offered invade the province of the jury.[34]

It is not unusual to work closely with your own expert while preparing to depose the opposing expert. You should have already gained a measure of mastery of the subject matter by conducting your own research. However, prepping your expert can expand and deepen your knowledge of the subject matter. This heightened preparation is the best way to ensure that you will have the ability to effectively probe the opposing expert's testimony.

Your goal is to create a record intended to discredit or undermine the adverse expert's testimony and to persuade the court to limit or exclude that testimony.[35] It is unlikely that cross-examining the expert will result in his recanting whatever opinions he is offering. The goal, instead, is to

---

[33] *See* FED. R. EVID. 702.

[34] Although FED. R. EVID. 704 permits experts to testify to the "ultimate issue" in the case, whether the opinion would go so far as to simply tell the jury how to decide the case has been the subject of many appeals. *See, e.g.*, Richman v. Sheahan, 415 F. Supp. 2d 929, 949 n.20 (N.D. Ill. 2006) ("The lingering fear that merely because an expert gives an opinion that even touches on an ultimate legal issue the jury may be overawed by the expert is at odds with the liberalizing thrust of Rules 702–704 and the deeply felt conviction that juries are assumed capable of deciding the most complicated of cases.").

[35] Courts may consider whether the expert may testify via several vetting processes: (1) by way of a *Daubert* hearing, (2) based upon a motion in limine, or (3) by conducting a *voir dire* of the expert witness during trial.

unpack the bases of the expert's opinions (i.e., thoroughly probe the foundation of the expert's opinions) and to build a record sufficient for the court to either keep the expert off the stand or to prepare you for a cross-examination at trial that will discredit the expert's opinions.[36]

F.   SPECIAL ISSUES RELATING TO RULE 30(b)(6) DEPOSITIONS

In the civil litigation context, an organization may be called upon to testify pursuant to Rule 30(b)(6). This form of discovery can be extremely useful, but the rule has created a plethora of practical problems arising from the reality that organizations are not people, and therefore they do not independently possess "knowledge" or "memories." Whatever an organization "knows" must be found through its employees, former employees, agents, and records. Someone has to gather that information and then a living, breathing person must be prepared to testify to it.

1.   RULE 30(b)(6) DEPOSITION NOTICES

Rule 30(b)(6) depositions may be taken of "a public or private corporation, a partnership, an association, a governmental agency, or other entity,"[37] regardless of whether the organization is a party. Because a Rule 30(b)(6) deposition notice is directed generally to an entity and not to a specific person, the notice "must describe with reasonable particularity the matters for examination."[38] The purpose of this notice is to give the organization an opportunity to prepare and to designate an appropriate person to speak on its behalf. Because of this unique notice requirement, you must identify the goals of your Rule 30(b)(6) deposition by the time you prepare the notice or subpoena.

2.   PREPARING THE WITNESS

A Rule 30(b)(6) deposition notice sets in motion a complex process for preparing the organizational witness to testify.[39] Defending counsel must gather information responsive to the notice, identify a witness or witnesses within the organization best suited to testify to the subject matter, then assist the witness with organizing and internalizing the information in order to provide meaningful and accurate testimony. In a complex case, the amount of information to be gathered and organized can be overwhelming.

---

[36]   Also keep in mind that some expert depositions are used directly at trial, in lieu of live testimony. When this is likely to happen, you should consider a videotaped deposition, and you should take special care with both the wording and order of your questions. Treat such a deposition as if it were an examination at trial.

[37]   FED. R. CIV. P. 30(b)(6).

[38]   *Id.*

[39]   For a general discussion of Rule 30(b)(6) depositions, and particularly the challenges of witness preparation, *see* Craig M. Roen & Catherine O'Connor, *Don't Forget to Remember Everything: The Trouble With Rule 30(b)(6)*, 45 U. TOL. L. REV. 29 (Fall 2013).

Nonetheless, courts have been less than sympathetic with regard to the burden Rule 30(b)(6) places on the witness.[40]

Fortunately, it appears Rule 30(b)(6) will have been amended by the time this edition goes to print. The amendment will require counsel to meet and confer before taking a Rule 30(b)(6) deposition. The Committee on Rules of Practice and Procedure of the Judicial Conference of the United States has recommended this change in order to head off disputes that may arise during a Rule 30(b)(6) deposition that, in turn, may result in unnecessary motion practice. The authors consider this to be a substantial improvement to the Rule.[41]

Though somewhat controversial and not routinely used, you may consider working with Rule 30(b)(6) witnesses to create testimonial summaries to use as an aid during the deposition.[42] This approach, which provides the witness a coherent summary of information responsive to each topic identified in the notice, has potential benefits but also is fraught with hazards and challenges. Other methods of preparing Rule 30(b)(6) witnesses also present potential difficulties (such as trying to get the witness to memorize all relevant information). Therefore, when faced with a Rule 30(b)(6) deposition you should carefully review the law in the particular jurisdiction regarding the manner and extent to which the witness should be prepared.

3. PREPARING FOR AND TAKING RULE 30(b)(6) DEPOSITIONS

As you prepare to take a Rule 30(b)(6) deposition, keep in mind that you are not deposing the person, you are deposing the *organization*. Therefore, you should focus your deposition inquiries on two areas: (1) what the organization did to educate the witness on the subject matter; and (2)

---

[40] *See, e.g.,* Starlight Int'l Inc. v. Herlihy, 186 F.R.D. 626 (D. Kan. 1999).

[41] *See* Committee on Rules and Practice of the Judicial Conference of the United States, Transmittal of Proposed Amendment to the Federal Rules of Civil Procedure (Oct. 23, 2019). The Committee Notes state:

> Candid exchanges about the purposes of the deposition and the organization's information structure may clarify and focus the matters for examination, and enable the organization to designate and to prepare an appropriate witness or witnesses, thereby avoiding later disagreements. It may be productive also to discuss "process" issues, such as the timing and location of the deposition, the number of witnesses and the matters on which each witness will testify, and any other issue that might facilitate the efficiency and productivity of the deposition.

> The amended rule directs that the parties confer either before or promptly after the notice or subpoena is served. If they begin to confer before service, the discussion may be more productive if the serving party provides a draft of the proposed list of matters for examination, which may then be refined as the parties confer. The process of conferring may be iterative. Consistent with Rule 1, the obligation is to confer in good faith about the matters for examination, but the amendment does not require the parties to reach agreement. In some circumstances, it may be desirable to seek guidance from the court.

[42] For a lengthy discussion regarding preparation and use of testimonial summaries in depositions, see Roen & O'Connor, *supra* note 39.

what the organization knows or does not know about the given subject. In other words, for each topic, your inquiry should be: what did the witness do to establish adequate foundation to testify, and what is the substantive knowledge of the organization based upon what is hopefully adequate foundation.

The reason for this two-part inquiry is to determine whether the designated witness has adequately prepared himself (or has been prepared) to testify, and if not, to make a record in order to compel the organization to do a more complete job of preparing the witness for further testimony at a later date. In the alternative, as a matter of litigation tactics, if the witness is unprepared to testify to properly designated subjects, and the responses from the witness are "I don't know," or "I haven't been prepared to testify to that subject," then examining counsel may use that testimony to box out the organization from offering evidence in the summary judgment context or at trial on the subject matter.

The full range of complexities relating to Rule 30(b)(6) deposition strategies and tactics are beyond the scope of this book. Suffice it to say that, whether defending or taking an organization's deposition, you must be extremely thorough in your preparation, and you must remember that the person sitting in the witness's chair is not the witness: the witness is the organization. If the organization is a party, that testimony will be treated as party admissions and therefore the stakes at a Rule 30(b)(6) deposition can be high.

G. USING DEPOSITIONS IN COURT PROCEEDINGS

We will revisit this topic in Chapter 15, but it is apt that we close the loop here in terms of how effective deposition practice can have an impact on later proceedings.

1. AS PARTY ADMISSIONS

Any statement by a party will be treated as an admission and may be used as substantive evidence. This means if the statement is relevant it may be used as evidence against that party. It is all the better when the statement is made under oath in a deposition.

You are entitled to have the deposition testimony entered into the record (which is quite common in the context of a summary judgment motion). In addition, at trial, if the opposing party does not remember something or equivocates, you may cross-examine the witness by getting her to agree with her prior deposition testimony.

2. WHEN THE WITNESS IS UNAVAILABLE

There are times when a witness is unavailable for trial. For instance, she may have died, is no longer subject to the court's subpoena power, or is too ill to attend trial. Under these circumstances Rule 32 governs.[43]

In order to use a deposition in lieu of live testimony, the proponent must show (1) that the witness is unavailable, and (2) the proffered testimony must be admissible pursuant to the Rules of Evidence.[44] Assuming those two requirements are met, the deposition testimony may come in if the witness is deemed unavailable.[45]

With regard to the admissibility of the proffered testimony, too often counsel—and sometimes judges—fail to insist that the testimony comport with the Rules of Evidence just as if the witness were present.[46] Yet, Rule 32(b) specifically requires it. This is why it is important to not only think about the testimony you hope to elicit from the witness but to do so in a manner that will satisfy the Rules of Evidence.

To the extent one party offers a portion of deposition testimony, the opposing party is entitled to "counter-designate" testimony from the deposition.[47] This should be done through a meet and confer process. The mechanics of doing so can become rather involved, but for our purposes suffice it to say that each side should mark the deposition transcript to reflect the proposed testimony and then the opposing side should be given the opportunity to note objections. Once this process is completed, the annotated transcript should be given to the judge for review and rulings.

Once the court has ruled on the objections, it is common to have a reader "testify" on the stand and literally read from the transcript the answers to the questions posed by the attorney. In the alternative, if there is a visual recording of the witness, the recording can be edited consistent with the designated testimony and played back to the jury. Indeed, if you anticipate the witness will not be available for the proceeding, you should consider visually recording the deposition. It will be much less stilted and artificial, and it will allow the fact finder to assess the demeanor of the witness.

3. TO IMPEACH AND TO REFRESH RECOLLECTION

Recall we presented the concepts of "boxing in," "boxing out," and "exhausting" the subject during the deposition. Here is where it comes into play. Deposition testimony may be used to impeach a witness if the

---

[43] FED. R. CIV. P. 32(a) sets forth the circumstances in which a witness is determined unavailable.

[44] *Id.*

[45] *Id.* 32(a)(4).

[46] *Id.* 32(b).

[47] *Id.* 32(a)(6).

testimony elicited on the stand is inconsistent with the prior testimony from the deposition.[48] This can be a very effective form of impeachment, i.e.: "Were you lying under oath then or are you lying now?"

Similarly, if the witness cannot recall certain events (or conveniently forgets), you may use the deposition to "refresh" the witness's memory. If the witness testifies she simply cannot remember some matter, you may ask the witness if her prior deposition testimony would help her recall. If she says "yes," you are entitled to show it to her. This technique may be used both on direct and cross-examination.[49]

To the extent a deposition is useful at trial, or as part of the record for a motion, is highly dependent upon the clarity and completeness of the testimony you elicit from the witness. A garbled record is not of much use, nor is one in which the questions are imprecise or the answers are unclear. Trial is not the time to find out that the witness's deposition is of little use.

---

[48] FED. R. EVID. 613.

[49] *Id.* 612.

CHAPTER 9

EXPERTS

■ ■ ■

Does your case need a termite control expert? Or an acupuncture expert? Perhaps your case would benefit from the testimony of an expert on mucus? For just about any issue in any type of civil case, there are experts (or those professing to be experts) who are available to serve as witnesses.[1] This chapter addresses expert witness development, discovery, and testimony, and discusses the rules of civil procedure and evidence that bear upon expert witnesses.

Early on in the case development process, ideally before the case is joined, you will identify those claims or defenses for which expert testimony will be necessary or helpful. On the liability side of a case, for example, it may be helpful to employ an expert to provide testimony on the appropriate standard of care, breach of that standard, or causation. On the damages side of a case, an expert may help calculate lost income or profits, or the extent of personal injury or harm to reputation. Sometimes the type of expert you need will be self-evident; other times you will need to do some homework before you will know who you really need.

To determine whether you need an expert and what kind of expert you need, always begin with the theory of the case and the evidence map. For each element of each claim or defense, ask yourself two questions:

> Is the proof necessary to support the claim or defense of such a kind that only someone with special knowledge, skill, experience, training, or education will be competent to offer an opinion?[2]

and

> Will use of an expert help the fact-finder better understand the issues?[3]

If the answer to these questions is "yes," you need an expert. And if you need an expert, you need to become an expert on selecting experts. That is

---

[1] You can find experts through legal associations, word-of-mouth, ads in legal journals, or in directories such as the SEAK Expert Witness Directory. *See* SEAK EXPERT WITNESS DIRECTORY, www.seakexperts.com (last visited Sept. 28, 2020). You also can search databases like Westlaw for similar types of cases; sometimes an opinion will identify experts by name and provide useful information about their level of expertise or the credibility of their testimony. Best of all, get recommendations from lawyers who have worked with the type of expert you need.

[2] *See* FED. R. EVID. 702.

[3] *Id.*

to say, in addition to determining the subject matter for which you need an expert, you also need to be discerning about the qualities your expert needs in order to be effective.

A. TESTIFYING VS. NON-TESTIFYING EXPERTS

This chapter focuses on testifying experts. However, you should be aware there are two categories of experts: testifying and non-testifying. Testifying experts provide evidence to assist the fact-finder, that is, they are designated as trial witnesses. Non-testifying experts, on the other hand, provide assistance to the attorney who hires the expert, but their role is limited to consulting, and their identity generally need not be disclosed.

Rule 26 sets forth a number of requirements relating to testifying experts that do not apply to non-testifying experts. Specifically, before offering opinions at trial, testifying experts generally are required to produce detailed reports that must be disclosed to the opposing party. Similarly, testifying experts are subject to being deposed (though in some state courts the disclosure requirement is limited to responding to an "expert interrogatory"). At trial, a witness designated as an expert will not be allowed to testify unless the expert's opinions, and the bases for them,, satisfy the Rules of Evidence.

A non-testifying expert, or a consulting expert, works behind the scenes. This type of expert provides subject-matter or technical assistance to the attorney. For example, a consulting expert may provide advice regarding information to seek during discovery. A consulting expert may provide candid evaluations and assessments that can help guide a settlement strategy, or can help decide whether to file a lawsuit in the first place. A consulting expert may help with evaluating the opposing expert's analysis and opinions, and may provide valuable assistance in preparing to depose or cross-examine an opposing expert at trial. Such an expert may also assist with other aspects of discovery, such as electronically stored information, and with trial preparation.

Because a consulting expert provides direct assistance to counsel and not testimony, the expert's work generally is protected from disclosure. In fact, Rule 26 explicitly protects from discovery "facts known or opinions held" by a consulting expert, unless the opposing party demonstrates the presence of exceptional circumstances.[4] This protection is consistent with, and based upon, the work product doctrine.[5]

Sometimes, an attorney may initially retain an expert as a consulting expert, but later decide to use the expert as a testifying expert. Retaining someone initially as a consulting expert is especially valuable as a means

---

[4]   FED. R. CIV. P. 26(b)(4)(D).

[5]   *See* 8A WRIGHT & MILLER, FEDERAL PRACTICE AND PROCEDURE § 2032 (3d ed.).

of fleshing out the theory of the case and determining the strengths and weaknesses of your client's claims or defenses. If the candid advice you receive from your consulting expert supports your theory of the case, you may decide to use the expert as a testifying expert. Be careful, though. Once you disclose the expert as a testifying expert, the expert's work—even the initial work done as a consultant—may become subject to discovery.[6]

B. SELECTING AN EXPERT

Careful selection of an expert witness is one of the most important decisions a lawyer makes in the litigation context. Her testimony may be necessary to make out a *prima facie* case. Experts educate the jury on matters generally not familiar to the fact finder. And the expert's testimony may play an outsized role in advancing your theory of the case. Therefore, you need to know how to select the best possible expert for your case. In some instances this may involve meeting with and evaluating several experts before finding the right one.[7]

1. IS THE EXPERT AN EXPERT ON THE SUBJECT MATTER YOU NEED?

The first step in hiring an expert is identifying what kind of expert you need.[8] Do you need an economist or an accountant? An accident reconstruction expert or a brake failure expert? Sometimes you may not know exactly what kind of expert you need until you begin to talk to potential experts or until you get further into your case. Consider the following real-life example:

> Your client lost a hand when the barrel of a muzzle-loaded musket replica exploded. The client had tripled the recommended amount of gunpowder. So you look for someone who will opine that the manufacturer was at fault for selling a firearm that blows up when overfilled with gunpowder (a foreseeable problem).

The real lawyer in this case had to interview approximately ten potential experts before identifying the type of expert needed: a firearms designer with an expertise in forensic metallurgy.

---

[6] *See, e.g.*, Greenwood 950, LLC v. Chesapeake Louisiana, LP, No. 10–CV–0419, 2011 WL 1234735, at *1–2 (W.D. La. Apr. 1, 2011).

[7] There is a question of whether an expert that you meet with, but for whatever reason reject, may then be retained by opposing counsel. Case law runs both ways. In order to be safe, it is wise to have the expert sign a non-disclosure agreement that essentially prevents her from being retained by adverse counsel.

[8] There are times when not only is the type of expert you need self-evident, but that the expert "comes with the case." For example, in an auto crash case, it may be that your expert witness who can best testify to the plaintiff's injuries is the patient's own doctor. When this is the case, no expert report is required.

Once you identify the particular subject for which you need expert testimony, be sure to verify that your potential expert truly is an expert on the precise subject upon which you need testimony. There are individuals who hold themselves out as experts who are willing to take on cases for which they may not be qualified. It is your job to ensure that the potential expert actually is an expert on the particular subject matter you need—do not rely solely on the expert's representation regarding the scope of his expertise. Remember, in order to lay the foundation for offering an expert's opinion, you must be able to qualify the expert as expert *in the exact subject on which the expert will testify*.[9] It is a bad day in court when the judge excludes your expert because you mistakenly took the purported expert at his word.

Another example may be instructive. It is common in automobile accident cases that plaintiffs with soft tissue injuries will retain a chiropractor to testify to the appropriate chiropractic care and treatment for those injuries. Defense counsel who hires, say, a neurologist to opine about chiropractic care runs the risk of having the testimony from the neurologist excluded. It might be proper for the neurologist to opine about the cause, nature and extent of the plaintiff's injuries,, but the neurologist is not qualified to opine about the proper course of chiropractic care for that patient since the neurologist has not been trained as a chiropractor.

2. WILL THE EXPERT SUPPORT YOUR THEORY OF THE CASE?

Before formally retaining someone as a testifying expert, be sure the potential expert supports your theory of the case. In other words, you will need to talk through the case with the putative expert, and perhaps provide some case materials for the expert to review, in order to determine if the expert will give you what you need. There is nothing unethical or untoward about this. Various experts, examining the same facts and data, may draw differing conclusions. You need to find one that supports your case. Here is an example from an actual case:

> Plaintiff contracts to have the defendant build a prefabricated storage building to hold mountains of human food waste the plaintiff intends to convert into animal feed. The building collapses. Plaintiff sues, claiming the building was poorly designed. Defense claims that the plaintiff caused the building to fall down by improperly compacting the waste with a front-end loader, thus causing the walls to tip outward. Each side retained construction engineers. Each had roughly the equivalent credentials. Both reviewed the same underlying facts. Not

---

[9] FED. R. EVID. 702; Kumho Tire Co. v. Carmichael, 526 U.S. 137 (1999); Daubert v. Merrell Dow Pharm., Inc., 509 U.S. 579 (1993).

surprisingly, the plaintiff's expert opined that the building was poorly designed. Defendant's expert opined that the design was proper, and that the failure was due to the plaintiff's own conduct.

Depending on the nature of the case and the work that must be done before an expert can form an opinion, it may not be immediately clear whether your expert will support your theory of the case. In these situations, it is best to retain the expert first as a consulting expert. This protects your communications with the expert in case the expert's opinions end up not supporting the case.[10]

3.　DOES THE EXPERT PRESENT WELL?

It is not enough that the expert is an expert on the subject matter and that his opinions will support your case. The expert must present well as a witness. Expert testimony can be powerfully persuasive, but not if the expert does not present well. If the case goes to trial, it will become very important that the expert can relate to the jury, make his subject understandable, and not be off-putting. You do not want an expert who comes across as pompous, or flippant, or who simply cannot translate the complexities of the subject matter into understandable lay terms. You also do not want an expert who comes across as an advocate. Your expert should seem unbiased, approachable, trustworthy, confident but not arrogant, and impressively credentialed.

These criteria cannot all be gleaned from a resume. You must interview your possible experts, and try to view them through the eyes of a jury. Then you have to trust your gut: Does the expert seem authoritative without coming off like a know-it-all? Does the expert possess the skills of a good teacher? Can the expert make what may be dry subject matter interesting? These are not secondary considerations. Aloof, boring, condescending experts are not persuasive. Experts to whom jurors can relate tend to be more compelling.

4.　WHAT IS THE EXPERT'S HISTORY?

Do some research on your potential expert. Has the expert been identified in any published cases? Has the expert ever failed to be qualified by a judge as an expert? If the answer to the second question is "yes," you may need to look for another expert. Past disqualifications of the expert may come back to haunt you if opposing counsel also finds those problem cases. You do not want to be in the position of trying to convince your judge

---

[10]　FED. R. CIV. P. 26(b)(4)(D).

to allow expert testimony that has previously been excluded by another judge.[11]

Similarly, if the expert's profession has a governing body, association or licensing organization that self-polices, you will need to know if the expert has ever been censured, suspended, or otherwise disciplined. It is your job to know whether there is anything in the potential expert's background that may undermine his credibility or detract from the expert's persuasiveness.

Further, has the expert published? You will need to know if the expert has written on the topic for which he has been retained. If so, you will need to review his writings to determine if he has taken positions counter to those about which he is being asked to testify.

C. BE AWARE OF THE RULES OF EVIDENCE RELATING TO EXPERTS

Essential to selecting, preparing, and using an expert is knowledge of the evidentiary rules relating to experts, that is, Rules 702–704. These rules are the prism through which the judge will look when determining whether to allow your expert to testify.[12] Unless you pay attention to these rules at the time of hiring and preparing your expert, you risk paying for a witness whose work may never make it in front of the fact-finder.

1. THE EXPERT MUST BE AN EXPERT IN THE FIELD

Federal Rule of Evidence 702 allows a proffered expert witness to offer opinions only if the witness "is qualified as an expert by knowledge, skill, experience, training, or education." Therefore, before a court will allow a designated expert to offer an opinion, the court first must determine whether the expert is truly qualified to speak as an expert.[13] But more than that, the court will determine whether the expert is qualified to speak as an expert *on the particular subject*.[14] Therefore, as described above, be careful to ensure that your potential expert is an expert in the specific field for which you seek an opinion.

---

[11] In addition to asking the putative expert if his opinions have ever been excluded from a trial or hearing, make sure you conduct your own research on Westlaw or LexisNexis. Both services have extensive databases relating to experts.

[12] Whether your expert can testify before the fact-finder may be determined at a pretrial evidentiary hearing, so-called a *Daubert* hearing, or during the trial itself. Either way, you will need to establish that the expert's opinions, and the bases for them, satisfy the foundational requirements of Rule 702.

[13] *See* FED. R. EVID. 104(a).

[14] *See, e.g.*, Stevens v. Nat'l Liab. & Fire Ins. Co., No. 13–12920, 2015 WL 5567758, at *3–4 (E.D. Mich. Sept. 21, 2015).

2. THE EXPERT'S TESTIMONY MUST BE RELIABLE

Not only must the court find your expert to be appropriately credentialed, the court also must find that the testimony will be reliable.[15] There are two broad aspects to the reliability question: the expert's methodology must be reliable, and the expert's conclusions must draw on sufficient facts and data.

First, let's consider methodology. In the context of a science-based analysis, relevant questions might include whether the methodology, technique or theory has been subject to peer review, whether there is a known error rate when the technique or theory is applied, and whether the theory or the technique is generally accepted in the scientific community.[16] These factors are not exclusive or necessarily dispositive,[17] but they indicate the type of inquiry a court should make when assessing whether the proffered testimony is likely reliable. And although the seminal case of *Daubert v. Merrell Dow Pharmaceuticals, Inc.,*[18] concerned scientific expert testimony, the Supreme Court subsequently confirmed that the trial court also must assess the reliability of non-scientific expert testimony.[19]

With regard to non-scientific expert testimony, consider, for example, a case involving water damage to a home, allegedly caused by a plumber's substandard work. The case requires the testimony of an expert plumber to prove that the defendant plumber's work was not performed in a "workmanlike" manner. There probably is not going to be a scientific technique or methodology employed by your expert. He likely will make a visual inspection of the work, manually check fittings, soldered joints, etc. His opinions will be based upon his experience and the thoroughness of the inspection. This, in and of itself, may be a sufficiently reliable manner of determining the quality of work performed.

Reliability also requires sufficient facts or data. The adage "garbage in, garbage out" applies here. For example, if an expert's opinion relates to random or systemic sampling, there must be a sufficiently large sample set in order for the data to be deemed reliable. Asking two individuals whether Celebrity X's reputation has been damaged by false statements in the

---

[15] *See* FED. R. EVID. 702:

   A witness who is qualified as an expert . . . may testify in the form of an opinion or otherwise if:

   . . .

   (b) the testimony is based on sufficient facts or data;

   (c) the testimony is the product of reliable principles and methods; and

   (d) the expert has reliably applied the principles and methods to the facts of the case.

[16] *See* Daubert, 509 U.S. at 589–590.

[17] *See id.* at 594; *see also* Kumho Tire Co. v. Carmichael, 526 U.S. 137, 149 (1999).

[18] Daubert, 509 U.S. 579.

[19] Kumho Tire Co., 526 U.S. 137.

media is neither sufficient nor reliable.[20] Similarly, asking 10,000 people chosen at random whether "Celebrity X, who is a true humanitarian and calls his mother every Sunday, suffered damage to his reputation when the evil publisher, without checking a single fact, published lies about Celebrity X?" would not be a valid basis for drawing any meaningful conclusions. The sample size may be sufficient, but the question is phrased in such a way as to make the responses inherently unreliable.

Facts and data may come from the expert's first-hand observation, such as a doctor drawing conclusions from a medical exam, but first-hand observation is not necessarily required in order to pass the reliability threshold. Counsel may provide the data or information to the expert, or even may present the expert with a hypothetical. But if you intend to ask the expert to assume facts that the expert is not independently verifying, make sure the facts are accurate. Opposing counsel is certain to inquire, and the court may exclude the expert's opinion as unreliable if the opinion is based on unverifiable facts or data.

Facts or data upon which the expert relies need not be admissible. Unlike lay witnesses, experts may offer an opinion based upon information provided by someone else. An expert orthopedic surgeon may not have personally taken the x-ray of the plaintiff, but the surgeon can read it and offer opinions based upon it, so long as it is shown to be an x-ray of the plaintiff. Similarly, a forensic accountant need not have personally observed every transaction of a corporation accused of tax fraud, as experts in the field routinely rely on their review of documents such as balance sheets, profit and loss statements, and their supporting documents. So long as the information is the kind of information upon which an expert in the relevant field would reasonably rely, your expert can rely upon it even if the information would not otherwise be admissible at trial.[21]

The bottom line is that as you select an expert and as you work with him to formulate opinions, you must be vigilant about reliability of methodology and sufficiency of facts and data. You are not yourself the expert, and therefore it is tempting to simply defer, but you must ask probing questions along the way or your whole effort may be for naught. Ask, for example, why this method and not another? Why this learned treatise and not the contrary one? Why these facts and not others? Why this assumption and not that assumption? Be sure you understand every step of the expert's methods and are confident about the facts and data upon which the expert relies.

---

[20] *See, e.g.*, Countrywide Fin. Corp. Mortgage-Backed Sec. Litig., 984 F. Supp. 2d 1021, 1033 (C.D. Cal. 2013).

[21] FED. R. EVID. 703.

3. THE EXPERT'S TESTIMONY MUST ASSIST THE JURY

Before a court will allow expert testimony, the court must be persuaded that expert testimony will assist the fact-finder to "understand the evidence or to determine a fact in issue."[22] If the expert intends to simply share a subjective opinion rather than an opinion based on specialized knowledge, that will not qualify as testimony whose purpose is to aid the jury's understanding. It is helpful to think of this caution not as a limitation, but as an invitation to work with the expert to develop testimony that will *teach* the jury about the subject matter. Once the expert educates the jury, then the expert may offer an opinion that fits within the context of what the jury has learned.

In cases of a magnitude that warrant the investment, it may be appropriate to hire two experts relating to a given issue: one that simply educates the jury on the subject, i.e., a "teaching expert," and another who provides specific opinions. For example, in an asbestos bodily injury case, the plaintiff may offer an expert to provide testimony relating to what asbestos is, how it is ingested, and how it affects the lungs or other organs of the body over time. Counsel may then offer the testimony of the treating physician regarding the specific diagnosis and prognosis of the plaintiff. By separating the functions of the experts, each tends to add credibility to the other's testimony and therefore present a stronger case overall.

4. PERMISSIBLE SCOPE OF AN EXPERT OPINION

Under appropriate circumstances, an expert may express an opinion even on an ultimate issue.[23] What does that mean? May an expert express the opinion, "The defendant is liable," or "Plaintiff cannot prove a contract was formed"? No. That would usurp the role of the fact finder. Opinions that merely tell the trier of fact what result to reach or that state a legal conclusion in a way that says nothing about the facts are objectionable.[24] So, how far can an expert go in offering an opinion on the "ultimate issue"?

Although Rule 704 uses the term "ultimate issue," the expert may not "invade the province of the jury." As a practical matter, to the extent counsel can have the expert focus his opinions on factual matters, the less likely the expert will be found to have overstepped. Therefore:

"The brakes failed due to a design defect," *not* "The defendant is liable."

---

[22] *Id.* 702(a).

[23] *Id.* 704 ("An opinion is not objectionable just because it embraces an ultimate issue.").

[24] 29 CHARLES ALAN WRIGHT & ARTHUR R. MILLER, FEDERAL PRACTICE AND PROCEDURE § 6284 (1st ed.).

"The widget design is publicly available," *not* "The widget design is not a trade secret."

"Plaintiff's lost profits total $1 million" *not* "The jury should award $1 million in damages."

It is your job to make sure your expert stays on track and states his opinions in a way that does not appear to usurp the role of the jury. Keep in mind though, per *Daubert*, the court makes an initial finding regarding admissibility. If you don't satisfy *Daubert* and its progeny, the jury will never hear your expert's testimony.

D. EXPERT DISCOVERY

Rule 26 includes provisions that explicitly govern the discovery process relating to experts, including disclosure requirements, protections and timing.

1. EXPERT DISCLOSURES

Mandatory disclosures relating to experts include the requirement to identify any expert you intend to use at trial,[25] and to accompany that identification with information regarding the substance of the expert's expected testimony.[26] The nature and extent of the disclosures regarding the expert's expected testimony depend on whether the expert is one you retained specifically for the purpose of providing expert testimony.

If you specifically retained the expert for the purpose of testifying in your case, then you must accompany disclosure of the expert's identity with a report written and signed by the expert.[27] Rule 26 describes in detail the extensive required contents of this mandatory report.[28]

If your expert is not someone you retained for the purpose of the litigation at hand, for example, a treating physician, then the rule exempts the expert from the requirement of preparing a written report.[29] As counsel, however, you still need to disclose both the subject matter on which the expert will testify along with a summary of the facts and opinions about which the expert will testify.[30]

The effect of these expert disclosures, whether written by the expert or by counsel, is to set in stone the opinions of the expert as well as the bases for those opinions. Because the expert's report governs the scope of

---

[25] FED. R. CIV. P. 26(a)(2)(A).

[26] *See id.* 26(a)(2)(B)–(C).

[27] *Id.*

[28] *Id.* 26(a)(2)(B)(i)–(vi).

[29] *Id.* 26(a)(2)(C).

[30] *Id.* 26(a)(2)(C)(i)–(ii).

the expert's testimony, you must make sure the report contains everything you intend to have the expert testify to at trial.

Note, however, that Rule 26(b)(4)(B) and (C) protect from disclosure draft reports that run between the expert and counsel, as well as communications regarding the substance of the report. These rules afford counsel and testifying experts the ability to work more cooperatively in preparing the expert's report without risking disclosure of counsel's work product. Nonetheless, take precautions not to become a "co-author" of the report. To that end, it generally is best to provide oral rather than written feedback to the expert.

Generally, the court will direct the timing of expert disclosures in the court's scheduling order. Therefore, it is important to work through disclosure issues as part of the Rule 26(f) meet & confer process.[31] If, however, the scheduling order fails to address expert disclosures, watch your calendar and disclose on your own within at least 90 days before trial,[32] and before the expert's deposition.[33]

2. EXPERT DEPOSITIONS

We touched on expert depositions in Chapter 8. Here, we delve more deeply.

The need to be vigilant about the rules of evidence also applies to expert depositions. The opinions the expert intends to offer must satisfy those rules or else, presumably, be excluded. Therefore, whether you are taking an expert's deposition or preparing an expert for deposition, always consider the following:

- Is the expert really an expert on the subject matter?

- Is there adequate factual foundation for the opinions offered?

- Are the expert's methods, and their application, sound?

- Are the expert's opinions within the bounds of Federal Rule of Evidence 704?

If you are proffering the expert, the answer to each question had better be yes. If you are deposing the opposing party's expert, look for areas where the expert does not meet the requirements of Rules 702 through 704. If you find deficiencies, then you have the opportunity to make a record upon which to seek to exclude, or limit, the opinions of the opposing expert.

---

[31] For more on the Rule 26 meet & confer process, see Chapter 5.

[32] *See* FED. R. CIV. P. 26(a)(2)(D).

[33] *See id.* 26(b)(4)(A).

a.   Defending the Expert Deposition

Just because the witness is an expert, and just because the witness may have been deposed numerous times in the past, a careful and thorough prep session is essential. In part, such a prep session helps you to better understand the expert's work and conclusions. But it also, importantly, gives you the opportunity to help with tone and presentation. A careful deposition preparation and practice session also will reveal any potential gaps or other problems in the expert's report. Hopefully there are no problems at this point, but if there are, have the expert revise the report and be prepared to testify to the reasons for doing so.

With regard to the deposition itself, make sure the expert does not bring any information exempt from discovery, such as draft reports[34] and communications between counsel and the expert.[35] Neither should the expert bring any extraneous information, such as articles or other documents that the expert may have referred to but not relied upon. The expert should bring to the deposition all underlying documents containing information upon which the expert relied in formulating his opinions.

As with lay witness depositions, once the deposition begins, there is little you can do to "defend" the expert. You are not allowed to coach or otherwise advise the expert during the deposition. You must state any objections succinctly and in a non-suggestive manner. Even so, if you have adequately prepared beforehand, then the expert should be well positioned to provide accurate, useful testimony.

b.   Taking the Expert Deposition

Before taking an expert's deposition, review the expert's complete file. You can do this by way of agreement with opposing counsel or through a subpoena. Review the file to identify documents to be copied for use as exhibits, and to generally prepare to examine the witness. For example, you may identify gaps in the underlying facts presented to and considered by the expert. If so, you can prepare a cross-examination that shows the expert lacks sufficient factual foundation to offer valid opinions. Or there may be notes the expert took that give you insight into his thinking.

Once you have familiarized yourself with the expert's file, you will be in a better position to complete a thorough outline and to focus on potential areas of weakness. You will also be able to conduct a much more efficient deposition.

A well-taken expert deposition can affect the course of a case. Typically, such a deposition will have three possible components: probing the purported expert's credentials; exploring the expert's previous

---

[34]   *Id.* 26(b)(4)(B).

[35]   *Id.* 26(b)(4)(C).

testimony; and meticulously testing the expert's opinions and the bases therefore.

i. Probe the Expert's Credentials

Make sure the expert is not simply credentialed, but is an expert in the particular subject at issue. Review the expert's *curriculum vitae* and consult with your own expert to determine whether there might be cracks in the expert's armor that you can explore and exploit. But if the witness's expertise is plainly obvious, do not waste valuable deposition time going through a lengthy resume.

ii. Explore Previous Testimony

If the expert has testified previously—and most have—you should see if the expert is mentioned in either a positive or negative light in any online judicial opinions. But also consider reviewing transcripts of prior testimony.[36] Transcript review can be time consuming, expensive, and tedious, but it may help to uncover information you can use to impeach or otherwise undermine the expert's testimony.[37] During the deposition, you may elect to explore prior problematic rulings or testimony, or you may, for tactical reasons, prefer to wait until pretrial hearings or trial in order to confront the witness with the adverse information.

iii. Meticulously Test the Expert's Opinions

The meat of the expert deposition involves review of the expert's report and the opinions contained therein. By the time the deposition concludes, you should understand every word in the report, you should know everything the expert relied upon, you should understand the basis for every opinion contained in the report, and you should have effectively boxed in and boxed out the expert so there is no possibility of the expert subsequently adding, "clarifying," or changing his opinions, the contours of those opinions, or the bases for the opinions.

Start by establishing the entire body of facts or data the expert reviewed, considered, or relied on in forming the expert's opinion. If you later can establish that the expert's underlying facts or data are incomplete or otherwise insufficient, you will have a basis to move to exclude the testimony. Therefore, for each opinion offered by the expert, you should ask:

---

[36] A number of legal associations maintain files of the testimony of experts who appear in cases relating to the association's practice areas. Some transcripts are now available through online services provided by Westlaw and LexisNexis.

[37] FED. R. CIV. P. 26(a)(2)(B)(v) requires the expert to identify at the time of expert disclosures all cases in which the expert testified, whether by deposition or trial, in the previous four years.

"Identify all information upon which you relied in rendering your opinion."

Do not allow the expert's report or other disclosed information to speak for itself on this issue. You need to ask the expert to specifically identify all facts, data, treatises, articles, and theories upon which the expert relied in reaching his conclusions, including anything outside the file. It is common that experts will rely upon learned treatises, technical manuals, quick reads on the Internet, or any number of other outside sources, but fail to include them in the expert's report or other information the expert and counsel turn over. It may just be that the article, or book, or other source contains information useful for impeachment at trial.

Make sure you not only understand everything in the expert's report, but make sure you understand the expert's methodology or tests used or theories relied upon. Find out whether those methods, tests, or theories are commonly used, are subject to being tested, and are generally accepted by experts in the field. Basically, you need to gauge the reliability of the expert's testimony in order to set the stage, when appropriate, for a motion to exclude the testimony for lack of necessary foundation.

E. *DAUBERT* HEARINGS AND OTHER MEANS BY WHICH TO CHALLENGE EXPERT TESTIMONY

Many times, an expert will easily qualify as an expert for purposes of offering testimony, even though the expert's opinion is contested. In other cases, the witness's qualifications as an expert and the acceptability of the witness's methodology or theories may be less clear. When these foundational issues are sufficiently complex, the court may hold a so-called *Daubert* hearing.[38] This is a hearing, usually held before trial, which helps the court determine whether the expert's proffered testimony satisfies Rules 702 through 704. Essentially, the proponent of the expert testimony must demonstrate by a preponderance of the evidence that the expert is qualified and that the testimony is both reliable and helpful to the fact-finder.[39]

---

[38] In *Daubert*, the Supreme Court held that the district court, prior to admitting expert testimony, must make a "preliminary assessment of whether the reasoning or methodology underlying the testimony is scientifically valid and of whether that reasoning or methodology properly can be applied to the facts in issue." 509 U.S. at 593. In Kumho Tire Co. v. Carmichael, 526 U.S. 137 (1999), the Court held that all types of proffered expert testimony should be subject to this kind of preliminary assessment, not just the testimony of scientific experts. Now, when a court holds a hearing to assist it in making this preliminary admissibility assessment, the hearing is called a *Daubert* hearing.

[39] For a nice description of the applicable legal standard, see Castro v. Sanofi Pasteur Inc., No. CV 11–7178, 2015 WL 5770381, at *4 (D.N.J. Sept. 30, 2015). Whether to hold a *Daubert* hearing is within the trial court's discretion. United States v. Ashburn, 88 F. Supp. 3d 239, 243 (E.D.N.Y. 2015).

Other times, the court will defer ruling until trial on whether the expert's opinions may be considered by the fact finder. Deferring such rulings presents a number of problems for trial counsel, but for purposes of this discussion, once the expert takes the stand and begins his testimony, opposing counsel may rise to object and ask to *voir dire* the witness outside the hearing of the jury. Essentially, this is the opportunity to show the court, by way of cross-examination of the witness, that the expert lacks some requisite to offer his opinions.

One other way to challenge expert testimony is through a motion in limine. Experience dictates that it may be difficult to exclude expert testimony simply by relying on a written record, but it can be done in appropriate circumstances. For example, if the expert's opinion clearly would usurp the role of the jury, e.g., the opinion to be offered is "the defendant is liable," then a motion in limine challenging the expert's opinion may be the most efficient means to blocking the testimony.

No matter how you challenge the testimony of an opposing expert, it is critical to start with a clear and thorough deposition record. You can use a good deposition record at a *Daubert* hearing, to *voir dire* or otherwise cross-examine the witness, or as the basis for a motion in limine. Even when the expert is allowed to testify, if you are careful during the deposition to lock in the expert's testimony, you can eliminate after-the-fact fudging or supplementing.

F. COST CONSIDERATIONS

Experts are expensive. Because of that, some lawyers try to delay for as long as possible retaining them. In fact, some wait until the end of fact discovery and an attempt at settlement before they rush to find an expert who can be available on short notice. This approach may be tempting, but it is not good practice.

Expert witnesses can provide more than just opinions designed to help the trier of fact; experts can help counsel develop a coherent theory of the case, guide discovery, promote a favorable settlement, and ultimately help counsel save time (and thus, money). Our advice is this: retain your experts early, and if cost is a factor, use them sparingly until it becomes necessary to prepare the expert report, prepare for and attend the deposition, and, absent settlement, testify at trial.

CHAPTER 10

ELECTRONICALLY STORED INFORMATION AND E-DISCOVERY

■ ■ ■

INTRODUCTION

Electronically stored information ("ESI") presents an enormous challenge to the 21st century litigator. Virtually all business is now conducted through digital communications, analysis, and recordkeeping. Individuals and organizations regularly communicate through e-mail, text messaging, and a variety of other social and business-related media. When something goes wrong, either in business or personal dealings, and ends up in litigation, important parts of the evidentiary record may come from ESI.

Discovery relating to ESI is commonly referred to as e-discovery and generally falls within the ambit of Rule 34. There are additional rules specific to e-discovery that will be discussed below.

Thus, in addition to mastering the rules related to civil litigation, the subject matter of the case, case development strategies, discovery strategies, and the art of persuasion, counsel must also have a working knowledge of ESI.[1] Some litigators seem to resist or avoid ESI-related issues. However, in today's digitized world, failing to understand the world of ESI does a disservice to the client. There is no avoiding it, so take a deep breath and read on.

Please note that this chapter only touches on a limited number of potentially complex issues regarding ESI and e-discovery. This rapidly evolving area of civil litigation will continue to present challenges to lawyers and judges, probably indefinitely. Our intention is to give you an overview, though we do provide in footnotes a number of good sources for further reading.

---

[1] There is an ethical imperative to competently represent the client, including the obligation to maintain the requisite knowledge and skill; a lawyer should keep abreast of changes in the law and its practice, including the benefits and risks associated with relevant technology. MODEL RULES OF PROF'L CONDUCT R. 1 cmt. 8 (2020). The California State Bar is more explicit: "Attorney competence related to litigation generally requires, at a minimum, a basic understanding of, and facility with, issues relating to e-discovery, i.e., the discovery of electronically stored information ("ESI")." Cal. State Bar Standing Comm. on Prof'l Responsibility & Conduct, Proposed Formal Op. 11–0004 (2014).

A. ESI: WHAT IT IS

ESI is any information that is communicated and/or stored electronically.[2] Following are some current examples, although as technology changes, so must this list:

- E-mail;

- Text messages and other forms of instant messaging;

- Facebook, Twitter, and other social media postings;

- Digital images (such as photographs);

- Animated and moving images (such as digitized movies and video surveillance);

- Publicly available software programs (including computer applications for consumers and commercial use);

- Proprietary software programs (such as data tracking systems and applications for manufacturing products);

- Voicemail;

- Data on tracking and GPS devices;

- Aircraft and vehicle "black box" data;

- Financial transaction data;

- Word processing documents, including data embedded within those documents;

- Spreadsheets;

- Computer slideshows;

- Websites;

- Metadata (data on data that resides in many of the forms of ESI listed above).

These examples of ESI would be inaccessible without the operating systems (the software that makes computers and other electronic devices run) and applications (such as Word and iTunes) that "interpret" ESI data. Without an operating system and application to interpret the data, you would be unable to read or use the electronic information. In the context of discovery, therefore, ESI must be produced in a manner that can be interpreted by the recipient via software that can recognize and read it.[3]

---

[2] BARBARA J. ROTHSTEIN ET AL., FED. JUDICIAL CTR., MANAGING DISCOVERY OF ELECTRONIC INFORMATION: A POCKET GUIDE FOR JUDGES 2 (2d ed. 2012).

[3] A major issue relating to discovery of ESI is the form in which the information is produced. Many litigators insist ESI be produced in its "native form," that is, in the form it was originally created. For example, if a document is created in Microsoft Word, but produced as a pdf (essentially, a picture of the Word document), it is not being produced in its native form.

ESI may involve the production of massive amounts of data. Consider this: Johnson & Johnson was involved in a major case in which many categories of its ESI were potentially relevant and thus needed to be reviewed. Here is what the litigants were facing:

- Collection of documents from over 350 records custodians;

- Over 56 *million* documents;

- After key word searches and elimination of duplicates, the universe of ESI was winnowed down to 13 million documents;

- After further limiting the fields of data, at trial, the parties presented approximately 200 documents.[4]

As you consider the many forms of ESI, you also should keep in mind the distinction between "personal ESI" and "enterprise ESI." Enterprise ESI consists of data maintained and used by an organization as well as the applications maintained and used by organizations that allow multiple individuals within an organization to access and use that data. Inventory data and inventory management software are good examples of enterprise ESI.[5] Personal ESI, on the other hand, consists of data such as digital photographs or audio files on an individual's cell phone. This sounds like a neat and easy distinction, but it is not unusual for individuals to use personal devices to communicate enterprise information, or to use enterprise devices to communicate personal information. It is important to keep this in mind as you draft and respond to ESI discovery requests.[6]

B. ESI: WHERE IT IS

One of the many ESI-related challenges is to determine where relevant ESI resides—both your client's ESI and the adverse party's ESI. Depending upon the nature of the data, its relation to commercial or personal matters, the sophistication of the data users, and a variety of other factors, there are a plethora of possible locations. These could include:

- Laptop computers;

- Personal electronic devices (e.g., mobile phones and tablets);

- Local-area network (LAN) servers;

- Internet-based servers (i.e., "cloud" storage systems);

---

[4] Comments from deputy counsel and head of litigation for J&J (Feb. 2014) submitted to the FRCP Committee.

[5] SHIRA A. SCHEINDLIN ET AL., ELECTRONIC DISCOVERY AND DIGITAL EVIDENCE 50 (2012).

[6] A term used to refer to mixed-use devices is "BYOD," or, bring your own device. For example, many people use their mobile phones for both business and personal use. If litigation involves business communications that reside on a personal mobile phone it can present a plethora of problems, not the least of which would be the discovery of very personal communications that can prove embarrassing.

- Flash drives, CDs, DVDs, and other external memory devices;

- Vehicle on-board diagnostics (OBD) systems;

- Aircraft in-flight recording systems (i.e., "black boxes");

- "Smart" TVs;

- Industrial robot or equipment control units;

- Home automation systems;

- Network routers;

- Cable converter boxes;

- Network backup tapes;

- "The cloud."

Indeed, practically anything employing computer technology has the potential for housing ESI.[7] Moreover, electronic devices may house ESI in a variety of locations, including archives and discontinued or disabled databases. Often, even "deleted" data remains in some format on ESI storage media. For the litigator, locating relevant ESI can be like looking for a needle in a whole lot of haystacks.

C. THE RULES RELATING TO DISCOVERY OF ESI

In 2006, the Rules of Civil Procedure were substantially revised in order to address a number of discovery-related issues pertaining to ESI. The Rules were again amended in 2015, providing further guidance on ESI-related discovery issues. Rules 16, 26, 34, 37 and 45 each contain specific references to ESI. Because the rule changes are relatively new, courts continue to grapple with how best to manage e-discovery.[8]

---

[7] Many employers allow their employees to use personal devices, such as home computers and mobile phones, to conduct business. This seemingly innocuous practice can create major discovery headaches. For example, company communications that become the subject of discovery may become extraordinarily difficult to gather and review if they do not reside on a central server. For this (and other) reasons, some employers create policies prohibiting the use of personal electronics for business purposes.

[8] The Federal Judicial Center produced a pocket guide to assist judges with ESI-related issues. *See* ROTHSTEIN, *supra* note 2, at 1. We recommend you familiarize yourself with this handbook.

The following chart summarizes the procedural rules relating to ESI:

Rule	Purpose and Function
Rule 16(b)(3)(B)(iii)	Authorizes the court to order the parties to preserve ESI in anticipation of discovery.
Rule 26(a)(1)(A)(ii)	Requires parties to make ESI part of their initial disclosures.
Rule 26(b)(2)(B)	Limits discovery of ESI that is not reasonably accessible due to undue burden or cost.[9]
Rule 26(f)(3)(C)	Requires the parties to meet and confer about discovery issues relating to ESI, including the forms in which it should be produced, and to discuss preservation of ESI in anticipation of discovery.
Rule 34(a)(1)(A)	Authorizes the parties to request ESI that is in the responding party's possession, custody, or control.
Rule 34(b)(1)(C)	States that the requesting party may specify the form in which ESI is to be produced.
Rule 34(b)(2)(D)	States that the responding party may object to the form in which its ESI is requested, and if no form is specified in the request, the responding party must specify the form it intends to use.
Rule 34(b)(2)(E)(ii) and (iii)	Specifies that, unless otherwise stipulated, ESI shall be produced in the form it is ordinarily maintained or in a usable form, but the ESI need not be produced in multiple forms.

Illus. 10-1.

The Rules impose a "two-tiered" approach to determining whether ESI is subject to discovery. First, the burden is on the responding party to assert that ESI is not reasonably accessible because of undue burden or cost.[10] Once such a showing is made, it falls to the requesting party to show that discovery is nonetheless warranted by good cause. If the good cause

---

[9]   Rule 26(b)(2)(B) states:

Specific Limitations on Electronically Stored Information. A party need not provide discovery of electronically stored information from sources that the party identifies as not reasonably accessible because of undue burden or cost. On motion to compel discovery or for a protective order, the party from whom discovery is sought must show that the information is not reasonably accessible because of undue burden or cost. If that showing is made, the court may nonetheless order discovery from such sources if the requesting party shows good cause, considering the limitations of Rule 26(b)(2)(C). The court may specify conditions for the discovery.

[10] FED. R. CIV. P. 26(b)(2)(B).

showing is made, discovery may proceed. The court may impose conditions and limitations on the discovery if necessary.[11]

The Rules give little guidance as to what comprises "reasonably accessible" or "undue burden or cost." The analysis is highly fact based, however, often requiring detailed information regarding technical characteristics, search capabilities, business disruption, economic costs, labor required, and the potential value of the information that might be retrieved.[12] Because of this, some amount of discovery may be necessary to test the responding party's assertion.[13]

The Rules give significantly more guidance, however, for determining whether good cause exists to compel discovery regardless of accessibility. The advisory committee notes provide seven factors to consider:

1)   the specificity of the discovery request;

2)   the quantity of information available from other and more easily accessed sources;

3)   the failure to produce relevant information that seems likely to have existed but is no longer available on more easily accessed sources;

4)   the likelihood of finding relevant, responsive information that cannot be obtained from other, more easily accessed sources;

5)   predictions as to the importance and usefulness of the further information;

6)   the importance of the issues at stake in the litigation; and

7)   the parties' resources.[14]

Consideration of these factors, however, is subject to the general proportionality requirements of Rule 26(b)(1): where burden or expense nonetheless outweighs the likely benefit—even if "good cause" exists—the court may limit the extent of discovery.

It should be noted that the cost of storing ESI has plummeted since 2006 when the Rules were first amended to take into account e-discovery as has the cost of conducting searches. Much of this is due to the ability to inexpensively store massive amounts of data in the cloud. In terms of

---

[11]   *Id.*

[12]   Jared S. Hosid & Courtney Ingraffia Barton, *Rule 26(b)(2)(B): Not Reasonably Accessible Because of Undue Burden or Cost, in* MANAGING E-DISCOVERY AND ESI: FROM PRE-LITIGATION THROUGH TRIAL 563, 572–3 (Michael D. Berman, Courtney Ingraffia Barton & Paul W. Grimm eds., 2011).

[13]   FED. R. CIV. P. 26(b)(2)(B) advisory committee's note (2006).

[14]   *Id.* The similarity to the *Zubulake* factors is clear, but note the slightly different purpose: *Zubulake* uses these factors to determine whether, during discovery, cost-shifting is appropriate; the Rules suggest these factors as considerations relevant to whether discovery is appropriate *at all.*

searching the data, the use of artificial intelligence in the search for responsive documents has made the discovery process much more efficient. These topics are beyond the scope of this book, but there are any number of organizations and individuals that track the development of ESI and e-discovery.[15]

D. LEARNING ABOUT YOUR CLIENT'S ESI

As soon as your client retains you, you need to gain an understanding of your client's ESI systems, policies and procedures (if it has any). This is true for two important reasons: (1) you are less likely to locate evidence helpful to the case without knowing where and how to look for it; and (2) you have a duty to conduct a reasonable search for information sought by the adverse party.[16] Unless you develop an intimate understanding of how, where, and for how long your client stores its ESI, you inevitably will miss important data.

1. GET A "TOUR" OF THE CLIENT'S ESI

Regardless of whether your client is an individual or a major corporation, you should get a "tour" of the client's ESI. If the client is an individual, the tour may simply be a review of the client's personal computer and other personal electronic devices, such as a cell phone or tablet. If the client stores data in the cloud or uses various social media sites, you also need to review that data.

Consider the following scenario. A husband sues for divorce, claiming that his wife has been unfaithful. The wife claims that her husband, who owns his own business, has been hiding marital assets from her. With just these bare-bones allegations, consider the implications for ESI discovery:

- E-mail, text messages, and Snapchat "selfies" may contain evidence of the wife's infidelity;

- Shared photo files in the cloud may tell where the wife was when she claimed she was visiting a sick relative;

- Online banking transactions and records will show where the couple's money was, and where it went;

- Digital records obtained from the husband's business, such as sales and accounting records, will reflect company revenue,

---

[15] Two leaders in the field of ESI and e-discovery are EDRM (the developer of the Electronic Discovery Reference Model) that operates under the auspices of Duke University School of Law and a consultant by the name of Craig Ball at craigball.com.

[16] JAY E. GRENIG & JEFFREY S. KINSLER, HANDBOOK OF FEDERAL CIVIL DISCOVERY AND DISCLOSURE § 12:16 (2014); *see also* Brown v. Tellermate Holdings, Ltd., No. 2:11–cv–1122, 2014 WL 2987051, at *1 (S.D. Ohio 2014) (counsel failed to ensure client's "cloud-based" ESI, which was under client's control, was accessed and produced, resulting in the levy of issue sanctions against the non-producing party).

expenditures, payments of salaries, bonuses, expense reimbursements, etc.

The point is that the outcome of even a personal dispute involving individuals may hinge on the existence and discovery of ESI.

When the dispute is complex and involves sizeable organizations, the task of identifying what relevant digitized information exists, and where, can be daunting. The amount of ESI may be measured not in gigabytes, but in terabytes. Although you should meet with your client's chief information officer or liaison (if there is one) to get a tour of the organization's ESI, do not allow yourself to simply be led through the tour; always listen with a critical and inquiring ear.[17]

For example, assume the client accuses a competitor of stealing the design of an advanced and proprietary widget that the client developed and carefully guarded. Counsel meets with the chief design engineer of the company, as well as the company's computer systems manager. They show counsel that all company designs are kept on a main server, which is password protected. Only management-level employees are given the password, which is changed daily. It would appear that the client has taken reasonable steps to safeguard its trade secrets. However, counsel asks the following questions:

1. Does the company use encrypted communications when sharing sensitive information with outside vendors? [Answer: Um, no.]

2. Once someone gains access to the server, can they download designs and specs to their personal PC? [Answer: Yes.]

3. Are all the company's employees' personal PCs password protected? [Answer: They should be. We are pretty sure. We'll look into it.]

4. Is data ever stored on external memory devices, such as flash drives? [Answer: Yes.]

5. Are all the flash drives accounted for? [Answer: Gee, we're not sure. We'll find out.]

From the perspective of the client, it has taken reasonable steps to protect its proprietary information. But once counsel digs deeper, problems with the client's assumption become apparent. The point is that getting a tour of the client's ESI is not a passive exercise; it is part of counsel's overall

---

[17] In many smaller businesses, the person most knowledgeable about the company's ESI may be a secretary, or it may be the tech company that helps the business with both its hardware and software. In a case litigated by one of the authors, the person who knew the most about how and where the company's data was stored was a former employee who had been in charge of the accounting department.

investigation of the case, and it is incumbent on you as counsel to be sure you obtain all the information you need.

2.   DATA MAPS

Some organizations create and maintain so-called data maps. At their most basic level, data maps are schematics or summaries of the information an organization maintains along with the location of that information. Data maps also may include information such as access and editing rights to certain data, retention and backup practices, metadata descriptions and so on. In other words, data maps can range from simple to incredibly complex. If the client has a data map, and it is current, it can save you a lot of time and help to avoid much confusion and cost when responding to discovery. If the client does not maintain a data map, it may be appropriate to advise the client to create one and keep it current, particularly if the client has ongoing litigation matters.[18]

There is no standard form or template for data maps. In fact, many law firms and consulting companies that regularly deal with ESI issues work with clients to develop custom data maps suited to the needs of both the client and the needs presented by the given litigation. At a minimum, a data map should answer the following questions:

- What forms of ESI exist, and where is each form stored?

- How far back in time does the ESI go?

- What ESI has been purged, overwritten, deleted or otherwise disposed of, and when?

- What is the native file format of the ESI?

- Who has access/editing rights to each form of ESI?

- Who is the person to be contacted regarding questions or obtaining access to each form of ESI?

- Is access limited by password or other?

- Is the ESI backed up, and if so, where?

- What is the relevant retention policy? When is data purged?

A data map of any size and sophistication would be too detailed to show here, and actual data maps tend to be highly proprietary and not available for publication. However, to give the reader a sense of what *one element* of

---

[18]   For a helpful discussion of data maps and client data management practices, see Mark P. Diamond, *Steps for Managing Electronically Stored Information (ESI) Under FRCP*, FINDLAW, http://technology.findlaw.com/electronic-discovery/steps-for-managing-electronically-stored-information-esi-under.html (last visited June 29, 2015).

a data map may look like, consider the following illustration of a fictitious human resources department data map:

Data Source Name:	HRMain	
Department	Human Resources	
Data Location(s)	Main server; HR Director's PC; cloud back-ups	
Main Contact	HR Director: Joan Smith	jsmith@ZYX.net
IT Contact	IT Director: John Jones	jjones@ZYX.net
Access rights	HR, IT Directors; Assistant HR Director; HR Secretary; President	
Data Descriptions	1. Employee files (1999–present) 2. Employee compensation records (1999–present) 3. Work comp files (2012–present)	1. Retention: 7 years post-employment 2. Retention: 7 years post-employment 3. Retention policy: 3 years
Backups	Google Cloud (2015–present)—daily	Hard copies in Nor-Cal storage (1999–2015)
Production Formats	.doc, .xls, .pdf	Hard copies to be imaged in .pdf format
Password Protected? Encrypted?	Yes No	
Accessibility	Easy for documents in 2012–present timeframe	Moderate to hard for copies in 1999–2011 timeframe

Illus. 10-2.

An actual ESI data map likely would be much more extensive, including information descriptions for research and development, sales, marketing, accounting, legal, human resources, insurance and risk management, customer data, and more.

With or without the benefit of a data map, counsel must be able to: (1) find relevant data, (2) assess the difficulty of accessing and producing the data (which may involve a painstaking review of the data for confidential and/or privileged information), and (3) see to it that properly discoverable ESI is retained and timely produced.

3. PRESERVATION OBLIGATIONS

The client may have specific ESI retention and destruction policies. In the normal course, data may be deleted or overwritten. However, if you, as counsel, anticipate the possibility of litigation, you have a duty to ensure that the client preserves evidence (including ESI) that may relate to the dispute—regardless of the normal retention policy.[19] The best way to meet your professional obligation and make sure the client does not destroy or alter ESI is to: (1) advise the client in writing that it may not destroy any potentially relevant information, regardless of its normal retention practices; (2) identify the ESI that may be subject to discovery; and (3) instruct the client to safeguard the ESI.

E. CONDUCTING DISCOVERY INTO THE ADVERSE PARTY'S ESI

In order to increase the chances that ESI discovery will go relatively smoothly, it is important to address a number of issues during the Rule 26(f) meet and confer stage of the case. It is at this early stage that you should attempt to get an agreement on the manner in which ESI will be produced, along with any applications that will make the ESI readable.[20] Further, you should attempt to agree upon such things as cost-sharing, the media to be used to convey the ESI, as well as protocols for the inadvertent disclosure of privileged or otherwise protected information. The Rules also obligate you to discuss preservation of ESI.[21]

Some larger firms now have in-house ESI experts and employ attorneys who specialize in ESI discovery. However, most firms lack the economies of scale necessary to make separate ESI experts or departments economically feasible. Therefore, for cases of sufficient size and complexity, it is prudent to retain the services of a consulting expert to assist with the

---

[19] *See* MODEL RULES OF PROF'L CONDUCT R. 3.4(a) ("A lawyer shall not . . . destroy or conceal a document or other material having potential evidentiary value.").

[20] FED. R. CIV. P. 26(f)(3)(C) specifically requires counsel to meet and confer regarding ESI as part of their efforts to draft a joint discovery plan. *See* Chapter 5 for a discussion of the Rule 26(f) meet and confer as it relates to ESI.

[21] FED. R. CIV. P. 26(f)(3)(C).

ESI discovery process.[22] Indeed, there is an expectation that the discovery process of ESI shall be both cooperative and transparent.[23]

1. LITIGATION HOLD LETTERS

At the earliest possible time, and certainly no later than when initial pleadings are served, it is imperative to send a litigation hold letter to the opposing counsel (or putative adverse party even before the inception of litigation). The purpose of a litigation hold letter is to apprise the adverse party that it must preserve any evidence that may relate to the subject matter of the litigation.[24] Although the adverse party has an affirmative duty to preserve ESI that may be the subject of discovery, it would be unwise to simply assume it will choose to do so. A letter directing the categories of ESI to be retained, therefore, is best.

2. WRITTEN DISCOVERY, SUBPOENAS, AND DEPOSITIONS

ESI discovery can be complicated. To best ensure that you get what you need, you must carefully craft your document demands and/or subpoenas. This starts with your definition of the term "document." Rule 34 explicitly identifies ESI as an appropriate subject of a document demand, though it does not provide any definitional language.[25] Likewise, Rule 45 acknowledges that subpoenas may require non-parties to produce their ESI, again without definition.[26] Simply including ESI within your definition of documents is not a sufficient guarantee you will get the ESI to which you are entitled. The term should be separately defined.[27]

Further, you must be ever vigilant to ensure that the opposing party has conducted a reasonable inquiry into what ESI is in its possession, custody, or control. For example, if the production contains no email, or attachments to the email are not produced, it is a pretty good indicator that the adverse party and its counsel have failed to conduct a reasonable search. Similarly, if you are aware of various iterations of the same document (such as drafts of contracts), but the iterations are not produced, you should suspect that the adverse party has failed to conduct an adequate search, or that discoverable ESI has been destroyed.

In cases where ESI will be a significant focus of discovery, you should consider taking a Rule 30(b)(6) deposition[28] at the earliest possible

---

[22] If the consultant is a non-testifying expert, then the work performed for counsel should not be subject to discovery per FED. R. CIV. P. 26(b)(4)(D).

[23] *See* The Federal Judges' Guide to Discovery 2.0 (2015) (The Electronic Discovery Institute).

[24] *See* Zubulake v. USB Warburg (Zubulake IV), 220 F.R.D. 212 (S.D.N.Y. 2003).

[25] *See* FED. R. CIV. P. 34(a)–(b).

[26] *Id.* 45(c)(2)(A).

[27] For a definition of ESI, *see* Appendix.

[28] See Chapter 8 for more on 30(b)(6) depositions of an organization.

opportunity in order to learn what, where, and how the adverse party maintains and stores its ESI, what technical terminology it uses in relation to its ESI, what its retention and destruction policies are, and whether it follows its own policies. By taking an early Rule 30(b)(6) deposition, you will be in a better position to make clear, unambiguous, targeted requests for ESI.

Without a 30(b)(6) deposition, you may miss important documents. If you lack specific information regarding how, when, and where the adverse party maintains its ESI, how confident are you—or should you be—that your opposing counsel knows what responsive ESI might be available and how to retrieve it? Thus, a Rule 30(b)(6) deposition not only helps you to properly frame your ESI discovery requests, it can help inform opposing counsel and thereby better ensure that you get the information to which you are entitled.

A potential problem is that Rule 30(a)(2)(A)(ii) generally allows counsel to depose a given witness only once. If you take the organization's deposition for the sole purpose of educating yourself on its ESI, you have arguably used up your one allotted deposition of the organization and may not get the chance to depose the organization later regarding substantive matters. Therefore, it is important to either: (1) get opposing counsel to stipulate that the ESI-related organizational deposition will not count toward the "one and done" rule, or (2) get the court to so rule.

F. PARTICULAR ESI DISCOVERY ISSUES

The sheer quantity of ESI that may be maintained by parties lends itself to expansive discovery requests, and the expense of both accessing and sifting through such data can be substantial. In an effort to lay down a fair and coherent doctrine addressing these problems while sticking to the basic tenants of the Federal Rules,[29] the *Zubulake v. UBS Warburg LLC* line of cases[30] have proven to be the seminal opinions on ESI discovery.

The *Zubulake* cases arose out of a garden-variety employment discrimination case in which the plaintiff sought to discover emails to support her claim.[31] Because these emails supposedly existed only on back-up tapes and in archival format, the defendant estimated the cost of restoration and retrieval of the emails at $175,000 and refused to produce

---

[29] FED. R. CIV. P. 1 (The Rules "should be construed, administered, and employed by the court and the parties to secure the just, speedy, and *inexpensive* determination of every action and proceeding.") (emphasis added).

[30] Zubulake v. USB Warburg LLC (*Zubulake IV*), 220 F.R.D. 212 (S.D.N.Y. 2003); Zubulake v. USB Warburg LLC (*Zubulake III*), 216 F.R.D. 280 (S.D.N.Y. 2003); Zubulake v. USB Warburg LLC (*Zubulake I*), 217 F.R.D. 309 (S.D.N.Y. 2003).

[31] *Zubulake I*, 217 F.R.D. at 312.

them.[32] *Zubulake I* centered around two questions: (1) to what extent is ESI discoverable; and (2) which party must bear the potentially high cost of production?[33]

The court had little trouble determining that the emails contained on the back-up tapes were indeed discoverable.[34] The second question, however, proved to be much more complex. In determining which party had to bear the high costs of discovery, *Zubulake I* set out a three-part process. First, the court must determine whether the data is "accessible" or "inaccessible." Second, if the data is inaccessible, the responding party must sample the ESI to further refine cost estimates and the benefits of production. Finally, the court must use the sampled data to inform a seven-factor balancing test to determine whether cost-shifting for full production is appropriate.[35]

1. DETERMINE ACCESSIBILITY OF THE DATA

The accessibility of data turns largely on the format in which the ESI is maintained.[36] The court recognized five categories of data storage, each varying in its accessibility:

- *Active, online data:* data used in the active stages of electronic recordkeeping, which therefore is easily accessible;

- *Near-line data:* data stored on removable media that is quickly accessed via robotic means;

- *Offline storage/archives:* data stored on removable media that must be manually organized and retrieved;

- *Backup tapes:* data preserved on tape that generally is recorded in a linear, sequential manner, that frequently is compressed to save storage space, and that requires the reading of *all* data previously recorded on the tape in order to identify and retrieve the requested data;

- *Erased, fragmented, or damaged data:* data files that have been broken up in the saving process or otherwise damaged or erased.

Under this division, the court considered online, near-line, and offline data to be accessible due to its readily usable format.[37] Retrieving such data can be done with relative ease. Such data, therefore, must be produced under

---

[32] *Id.*

[33] *Id.* at 311.

[34] *Id.* at 317.

[35] *See* Bradley T. Tennis, Comment, *Cost-Shifting in Electronic Discovery*, 119 YALE L.J. 1113, 1114 (2010).

[36] *Zubulake I*, 217 F.R.D. at 318.

[37] *Id.* at 321.

the presumption that the responding party will bear the costs of production.[38] In other words, if the data is accessible, the analysis ends.

On the other hand, data that has been damaged or stored on back-up tapes generally requires extensive restoration in order to produce it in a reasonably usable format.[39] The court found that such inaccessibility made it appropriate to consider the possibility of shifting the cost of discovery—fully or partially—to the requesting party.[40]

2. ENGAGE IN DATA SAMPLING IF THE DATA IS "INACCESSIBLE"

For data that is not easily accessible, the question becomes whether it still needs to be produced and, if so, who should bear the cost of the production. In order to obtain a factual basis to help answer these questions, *Zubulake* required the defendant to produce all the requested emails from a small sample of the back-up tapes.[41] The court then used this information to inform a balancing test for determining the ultimate appropriateness of cost-shifting.

3. THE BALANCING TEST TO DETERMINE THE APPROPRIATENESS OF COST-SHIFTING

The third and final portion of the *Zubulake* cost-shifting analysis is the seven-factor balancing test. The *Zubulake* balancing test seeks not only to list, but to prioritize the relevant balancing factors. By prioritizing the factors and giving each one a corresponding weight, the test attempts to determine whether an "undue burden or expense" would be placed on the responding party.[42] From greatest weight to least weight, the factors are listed in the following order:

1. The extent to which the request is specifically tailored to discover relevant information;

2. The availability of such information from other sources;

3. The total cost of production, compared to the amount in controversy;

4. The total cost of production, compared to the resources available to each party;

---

[38] *Id.* at 320; *see also* Oppenheimer Fund, Inc. v. Sanders, 437 U.S. 340, 358 (1978) ("Under [the discovery] rules, the presumption is that the responding party must bear the expense of complying with discovery requests . . . .").

[39] *Zubulake I*, 217 F.R.D. at 320.

[40] *Id.*

[41] *Id.* at 324.

[42] *Id.* at 322.

5. The relative ability of each party to control costs and its incentive to do so;

6. The importance of the issues at stake in the litigation; and

7. The relative benefits to the parties of obtaining the information.[43]

Employing this balancing test, the court determined that some cost shifting would be appropriate.[44] When considering the appropriateness of cost-shifting under the seven-factor test, litigators must remember that it is "not merely a matter of counting and adding [the relevant factors; the factors are] only a guide."[45] Ultimately, it is at the court's discretion to determine whether to shift any or all of the costs of production.

Though the *Zubulake* cases appear to still be good law, with the advent of artificial intelligence as used in e-discovery, the calculus of cost vs. benefit has been dramatically altered. As we discussed in the Johnson & Johnson case, what was once completely cost-prohibitive is now within reach to larger numbers of litigants.[46]

G. CONCLUSION

As complicated as some of the preceding sections appear, this chapter is no more than a brief overview of some of the issues relating to discovery of ESI. Litigators and the courts continue to grapple with both the conceptual and practical problems relating to rapidly advancing technology. The point is this: all litigation counsel need to be sensitive to the probability that ESI will be a subject of discovery in many cases, and therefore you must possess, at minimum, a broad understanding of what it is, where it may reside, and how best to manage its production.

---

[43] *Id.* at 324.

[44] *Zubulake III*, 216 F.R.D. at 289.

[45] *Id.*

[46] *See* Ajith Samuel, *Artificial Intelligence Will Change E-Discovery in the Next Three Years*, LAW TECHNOLOGY TODAY (April 4, 2019) (www.lawtechnologytoday.org/2019/04/artificial-intelligence-will-change-e-discovery-in-the-next-three-years/) (Last visited on June 16, 2020).

CHAPTER 11

INSPECTIONS AND TESTS, PHYSICAL AND MENTAL EXAMS

■ ■ ■

INTRODUCTION

There are cases in which discovery extends beyond an exchange of words and documents. Rules 34 and 45 permit discovery of physical things, and Rule 35 permits examinations of the litigants themselves. Moreover, Rules 34, 35 and 45 not only allow the parties to document physical conditions, but also to build their cases by *creating* evidence. This type of discovery can yield dramatic and highly probative evidence: a photograph of the scene of a fatality, a videotaped re-enactment of a propane tank explosion, an investigation of a litigant's claimed post-traumatic stress disorder. Consider the following hypothetical:

> A woman is driving her car on a private road in a light afternoon rain. A deer leaps onto the road and the woman hits the brakes. The rear brakes lock up, causing the car to spin and then flip. Faint skid marks are left on the roadway.

> Though the woman's neck is broken, she survives. The accident has left her a quadriplegic and even after multiple surgeries, she is wheelchair-bound. She begins to experience horrible nightmares and suffers near-continuous anxiety attacks.

> Shortly after the accident, the woman's lawyer takes possession of the vehicle and has it stored in a warehouse. Her counsel's expert determines that the brake design is faulty, and that, based upon his inspection of the vehicle and research into similar accidents, the auto manufacturer is at fault. Counsel sues the manufacturer and litigation ensues.

Based upon this hypothetical, there are multiple inspections, tests and examinations that both the plaintiff's counsel and defense counsel may want to arrange, including:

- Inspection and testing of the vehicle, and particularly its braking system, presumably by an engineer who later will opine about the brake failure (or lack thereof) [Rule 34];

- Inspection of the private roadway, perhaps by an accident reconstruction expert to determine if something about it may have contributed to the accident [Rule 45];

- An examination of the plaintiff by a medical doctor to document the extent of her physical injuries, to explore whether there exist contributing causes of her paralysis (such as substandard medical care), and to determine her prognosis [Rule 35];

- An examination of the plaintiff by a psychologist or psychiatrist relating to the plaintiff's claimed emotional disturbances [Rule 35].

Each inspection or test of the car, its component parts, the roadway and re-creation of the conditions at the time of the accident may be videotaped and photographed and may include measurements or other analytical processes. Any physical and psychological examinations must be documented and made available to the plaintiff.[1] In each instance, the parties' respective experts likely would (and should) be directly involved with the inspections and examinations.

Inspections, tests, measurements, and examinations may do more than simply yield useful evidence—they may inform the whole theory of the case. Because of this, you may need to proceed with these tests and examinations early in the case, possibly even before the case is joined. Even when it is necessary to wait until the formal discovery period begins, it may be prudent to begin discovery with an inspection rather than with written discovery, as the inspection may inform the discovery that follows.

The data or information collected as a result of these forms of discovery often provide the basis, i.e., the *foundation* necessary to satisfy the requirements for expert testimony pursuant to Rule of Evidence 702. The "data" that is collected, as well as the methods applied to obtain expert opinions, are often derived from Rule 34 or 45 inspections or Rule 35 examinations. Therefore, as you conduct this type of discovery, you must remain acutely aware of the Rule 702 requirements that any expert testimony which is based upon this type of discovery will need to meet.

A. RULES 34 AND 45: INSPECTION AND TESTING OF THINGS, ENTRY UPON LAND

Rule 34 provides the authority to "inspect, copy, test, or sample" tangible things in another party's possession or control.[2] The rule is broad.

---

[1] The subject of any physical or psychological examination is entitled to a report regarding the exam and the examiner's conclusions. *See* FED. R. CIV. P. 35(b).

[2] FED. R. CIV. P. 34(a). Rule 45 provides similar permission with respect to non-parties. *Id.* 45(a)(1)(A)(iii).

It allows for discovery of "tangible things," "designated land," and "premises." The rule allows parties to "inspect," "test," "sample," "measure," "survey," and "photograph" the subject of the discovery. But remember, discovery under Rule 34 still is subject to the Rule 26(b) restriction that the discovery sought must be relevant and proportional to the needs of the case.

Inspections and testing may be simple and straightforward, involving only a visual examination and the taking of a few photographs. It also may be quite elaborate. In the real case example above, an identical vehicle, with identical brakes, was run on a test track with repeated "braking events" in order to wear down the brakes to the condition they were in at the time of the accident. Thereafter, a professional driver was retained in order to attempt to replicate the spinout (with outriggers attached to the vehicle to prevent rollover). The entirety of the testing was videotaped with elaborate measurements taken throughout. Imagine the cost.

If inspection or testing would cause the "tangible thing" to be permanently altered—or even destroyed—then it is imperative that anyone who potentially has a claim or who may be liable is given notice of the inspection and testing so they may attend.[3] Failure to do so may result in a claim of spoliation (a subject we will cover in Chapter 13), with all the attendant risks of sanctions.[4]

Discovery of tangible items and inspection of premises requires use of a subpoena under Rule 45 when the discovery request is directed to a non-party.[5] Failure to comply with a properly-issued subpoena may result in a contempt citation.[6] If the inspection would result in an undue burden on the subject of the subpoena, then the subject may seek to quash the subpoena.[7] In the event an accommodation may be worked out, compensation may be appropriate for the burden imposed or for any disruption caused by the inspection.[8]

As a matter of practice, we have found that it generally is best to contact the subject of the subpoena before he is served. Working with the subject to accommodate his schedule or otherwise make arrangements before a process server is sent out to serve a subpoena usually receives a

---

[3] *See generally* Mirchandani v. Home Depot, U.S.A., Inc., 235 F.R.D. 611 (D. Md. 2006) (noting that the existence of adequate safeguards against prejudice to other parties—including notice of destructive testing—is a relevant consideration in determining propriety of destructive testing by any party).

[4] *See* Vodusek v. Bayliner Marine Corp., 71 F.3d 148 (4th Cir. 1995) (holding that it was within the district court's discretion to allow the jury to draw an adverse inference from spoliation caused by an expert witness's destructive investigation and examination of evidence).

[5] FED. R. CIV. P. 34(c).

[6] *Id.* 45(g).

[7] *Id.* 45(d)(3).

[8] *Id.* 45(d)(3)(C)(ii).

better response than surprising the individual, which can cause consternation, anger and result in a lack of cooperation.

B. RULE 35: PHYSICAL AND MENTAL EXAMINATIONS

Rule 35 permits, upon a showing of good cause, examination of the mental or physical condition of a party whose mental or physical condition is at issue.[9] For example, if a plaintiff claims bodily injury resulted from the defendant's negligence, that plaintiff's physical condition is at issue. Rule 35 allows the defendant to have the plaintiff physically examined by an expert of the defendant's choosing so that the defendant may evaluate and challenge the claim.

Unlike most other forms of discovery, Rule 35 requires the party seeking the examination to show good cause.[10] This is because physical and mental examinations are inherently invasive.[11] The court must be assured that the requested examination is relevant, and that the nature and scope of the examination are appropriate to the circumstances.[12]

Although Rule 35 provides that the party seeking an examination will move the court for an order compelling the adverse party to attend, oftentimes physical and mental examinations are simply agreed to between the parties.[13] However, counsel may not agree on the nature and scope of such an examination, or sometimes even to the need for one. Because examinations are within the discretion of the court, it is important to specifically tailor a request for an examination to the requirements contained in Rule 35 as applied to the particular facts and allegations in the case at hand. Therefore, we will go through each element of Rule 35.

---

[9]   Rule 35 examinations are often referred to as "independent medical examinations." Such examinations are usually requested by defense counsel when a plaintiff claims physical or emotional harm. In fact, there is nothing independent about these examinations since the examinations are conducted at the behest of a litigant.

[10]   FED. R. CIV. P. 35(a)(2)(A).

[11]   Guilford Nat. Bank of Greensboro v. S. Ry. Co., 297 F.2d 921, 924 (4th Cir. 1962) ("[u]nder Rule 35, the invasion of the individual's privacy by a physical or mental examination is so serious that a strict standard of good cause, supervised by the district courts, is manifestly appropriate."), *cited with approval* in Schlagenhauf v. Holder, 379 U.S. 104, 117–18 (1964).

[12]   *See* Schlagenhauf, 379 U.S. at 118 (Good cause is "not met by mere conclusory allegations of the pleadings—nor by mere relevance to the case—but require[s] an affirmative showing by the movant that . . . good cause exists for ordering each particular examination. Obviously, what may be good cause for one type of examination may not be so for another.").

[13]   FED. R. CIV. P. 35(b)(3) advisory committee's note (1970).

1. MENTAL OR PHYSICAL CONDITION IN CONTROVERSY

Rule 35(a)(1) states that the court may order a mental or physical examination of a party if the party's mental or physical examination is "in controversy." What does this mean?

A plaintiff who alleges in his complaint a mental or physical injury places that mental or physical injury in controversy.[14] A generic claim of emotional distress or mental anguish may not, however, be enough to place a plaintiff's mental state "in controversy" for purposes of requiring a Rule 35 exam. Instead, courts typically require that mental injury be "an important component" of plaintiff's damage claim before finding that plaintiff's mental state is in controversy in the way intended by the rule.[15] Likewise, a defendant who asserts a mental or physical condition as a defense places the condition in controversy.[16]

A party's mental or physical condition also may be considered "in controversy" even absent any specific allegation raised by that party. For example, in a case in which a codefendant claimed that the defendant's physical condition caused an accident, the court ordered an examination of the defendant even though the defendant did not raise his condition as a defense.[17] Similarly, the court ordered the defendant to undergo a paternity test in a case in which the plaintiff alleged that the defendant engaged in sexual activity with her while she was in a residential treatment facility, causing pregnancy and emotional distress.[18]

2. GOOD CAUSE SHOWN

When a party objects to an examination request, the requesting party must do more than simply show that a mental or physical condition is "in controversy." Rather, the requesting party also must show good cause for the examination.[19] To meet that good cause standard, the normal showing for discovery—mere relevance—is not enough.[20] Moreover, what constitutes good cause tends to be quite case-specific. The following examples provide a sense of how courts view examination requests:

> Good cause did not exist to support a repetitive vocational rehabilitation examination on the issue of mitigation where the

---

14 Schlagenhauf, 379 U.S. at 119.

15 *See generally* Turner v. Imperial Stores, 161 F.R.D. 89 (S.D. Cal. 1995) (discussing at length precedent on both sides of the issue, and deciding that a claim of emotional distress alone does not warrant a Rule 35 exam).

16 Schlagenhauf, 379 U.S. at 119.

17 *See* Schlagenhauf, *supra* note 11, 379 U.S. 104.

18 Doe v. Senechal, 725 N.E.2d 225 (Mass. 2000).

19 FED. R. CIV. P. 35(a)(2)(A).

20 Guilford Nat. Bank of Greensboro v. S. Ry. Co., 297 F.2d 921, 923–25 (4th Cir. 1962).

plaintiff already had an expert evaluate his employability, where the expert's results and report had already been shared with the defendant, and where the defendant already had deposed the examining expert as well as prospective employers the plaintiff had contacted, and had additionally received written discovery relevant to the mitigation issue.[21]

In a police brutality case in which the defendant officer's mental health at the time of the alleged use of excessive force was admittedly in controversy, there was an insufficient showing of good cause to justify a Rule 35 examination because there was no credible and specific evidence to indicate that a current examination would be sufficiently relevant to determining the officer's mental status at the time of the incident, which was four years earlier.[22]

3. NATURE AND SCOPE OF THE EXAMINATION

A motion to compel an examination must specify the time, place, manner, conditions, and scope of the examination, as well as the person or persons who will perform it.[23] In issuing an order, the court usually will require that the examination take place at a time and location convenient for the party to be examined.[24]

Other questions, however, are more critical and more difficult than location and timing. How comprehensive, or in-depth may an exam be? How many consulting experts may be involved? For physical examinations, to what extent may physicians use invasive procedures, such as taking tissue for biopsy? For mental examinations, to what extent may the psychiatrist or psychologist conduct testing of the subject's overall personality, inquire into highly personal history, or otherwise explore the intimate details of the subject's most private thoughts?

How much background information shall the examiner be entitled to obtain? In a simple auto crash case, should the insurance company's doctor be given access to all of the plaintiff's medical records? If not, where should the line be drawn? In a sexual harassment case in which the plaintiff claims emotional harm, to what extent should the examiner be given access to previous mental health counseling records and other records that might evidence some kind of preexisting condition that could have contributed to the plaintiff's emotional trauma?

---

[21] Acosta v. Tenneco Oil Co., 913 F.2d 205 (5th Cir. 1990).

[22] McLaughlin v. Atl. City, No. CIV 05–2263 RMB, 2007 WL 1108527 (D.N.J. Apr. 10, 2007).

[23] FED. R. CIV. P. 35(a)(2)(B).

[24] *E.g.*, Scipione v. Advanced Stores Co., Inc., No. 8:12–CV–687–T–24AEP, 2013 WL 646405, at *2 (M.D. Fla. Feb. 21, 2013).

Courts consider Rule 35 requests on a case-by-case basis. When the nature or scope of the examination is at issue, it is prudent to obtain affidavits from the putative examiners that can support the motion to compel the given examination. Such affidavits should help answer the fundamental question most judges would ask before allowing such invasive and discretionary discovery: "Counsel, why should I grant your motion?"

4. QUALIFICATIONS OF THE EXAMINER AND THE EXAMINER'S REPORT

Rule 35 requires that examinations be performed by "a suitably licensed or certified examiner."[25] Further, the examiner is required to produce a written report containing "the examiner's findings, including diagnoses, conclusions, and the results of any tests."[26]

Put another way, the examiner likely will be a testifying expert witness who will need to be qualified as an expert and produce an expert report. Therefore, always read the requirements of Rule 35 in conjunction with the expert disclosure requirements of Rule 26(a)(2). Rule 26 requires a broader disclosure than set forth in Rule 35 but, as a practical matter, only a single report typically is generated. If you want the examiner to be able to testify as an expert and if you want the expert's opinions to be admissible at trial, be mindful of the Rule 26 requirements and Evidence Rules 702–704.

5. WAIVER OF PRIVILEGE

A litigant who places her physical or mental condition in issue not only opens herself up to discovery into her physical or mental condition, she also must waive any privilege that otherwise might attach to the communications between the litigant and the examiner. In fact, the waiver may be much broader than that. The adverse examiner may need to do more than conduct an exam. The examiner may also want to obtain and review the litigant's existing medical and/or psychological records, and courts may well require their disclosure.[27] Depending upon the breadth of the waiver, some of the litigant's most private information may become the subject of discovery. For some litigants, this may cause them to reconsider going forward with their claims. In a sexual harassment lawsuit, for example, the possibility of providing psychological records pertaining to a previous divorce or sexual assault may cause the litigant to abandon part or all of her claim.

---

[25] FED. R. CIV. P. 35(a)(1).

[26] *Id.* 35(b)(2).

[27] *See* Dochniak v. Dominium Mgmt. Servs., Inc., 240 F.R.D. 451 (D. Minn. 2006) (noting that where the Rule 35 "in controversy" requirement is fulfilled, there may be waiver of protection of general medical records).

Therefore, in any case where the physical or mental condition of your client may be placed in issue, it is incumbent on you to have a frank discussion with your client about the likelihood that some measure of her past medical or psychological history may be subject to discovery. Sometimes the desire for privacy trumps any benefit that could result from litigation.

6. PREPARING THE CLIENT WHO IS THE SUBJECT OF AN EXAMINATION

Lawyers typically do not—and may not—attend Rule 35 exams.[28] Therefore, if your client becomes the subject of a Rule 35 examination, either mental or physical, it is not enough to simply tell him where and when to show up. You must prepare your client for the examination.

Before any Rule 35 exam, explain the following to your client:

- The examiner is *not* treating the client and is *not* meeting with the client to provide advice or to help him get better;

- There is no cloak of confidentiality to protect communication between the examiner and the client; anything the client tells the examiner will likely show up in the examiner's report and become part of the record in the case;

- The client should *not* share with the examiner any communications between you and the client;

- The client should answer the examiner's questions fully and truthfully, but should *not* argue with the examiner or otherwise try to persuade the examiner of the merits of his case.

If the client feels that the examiner has been unfair or otherwise unprofessional during the examination, the client should contact you immediately after the examination in order to make a detailed and contemporaneous record of the specific problems that arose during the examination.

7. OBTAINING A PROTECTIVE ORDER

Any time a Rule 35 examination is scheduled, or existing medical or mental health records are requested during discovery, you should get a protective order under Rule 26 prior to releasing those records. The protective order should explicitly limit dissemination of any of the information contained in the records, limit the number of copies made, require anyone with access to the records to read and sign the protective

---

[28] Hertenstein v. Kimberly Home Health Care, Inc., 189 F.R.D. 620, 629 (D. Kan. 1999) (noting that federal cases generally prohibit attorney attendance at Rule 35 examinations).

order restrictions, and require their return or confirmed destruction within a particular time period following the conclusion of the litigation.

The last thing the client wants is her most personal information disseminated to people who have no business seeing it. Nor do you, as her lawyer, want to explain to her how the problem could have been avoided had you just requested an agreement from opposing counsel or an order from the court to protect it.

CHAPTER 12

PRIVILEGES AND OTHER REASONS FOR WITHHOLDING INFORMATION

■ ■ ■

Chapter 4 addressed the scope of discovery, touching on limitations relating to privilege and other reasons to withhold otherwise discoverable evidence. This chapter provides a more in-depth overview of the most common bases for withholding information and how to address these issues throughout the litigation process.[1]

It is the lawyer's responsibility to protect privileged or otherwise confidential information during discovery and throughout the course of the litigation.[2] In essence, counsel must act as an information filter. In order to fulfill this obligation, it is important to become familiar with the law of the particular jurisdiction in which the case is pending as it relates to privilege and other bases for claiming confidentiality.

A. FOUR COMMON REASONS FOR WITHHOLDING INFORMATION

While the scope of the discovery rules is broad, Rule 26 does recognize limits with respect to privileged information[3] and attorney work product.[4] Proprietary information and information subject to a recognized privacy right also receives some protection, as discussed below.

---

[1] Privilege, work product, and other doctrines that protect information from discovery are highly complex and nuanced. This chapter provides no more than a general overview designed to identify potential issues and offer some guidance on how to anticipate and manage them.

[2] This responsibility also extends to the confidential information of third parties that the client is obligated to keep private.

[3] *See* FED R. CIV P. 26(b)(1) ("parties may obtain discovery regarding any *nonprivileged matter*") (emphasis added).

[4] *See* FED. R. CIV. P. 26(b)(3)(A) ("Ordinarily, a party may not discover documents and tangible things that are *prepared in anticipation of litigation or for trial* by or for another party."). Although Rule 26(b)(3)(A) refers specifically to protecting "documents and tangible things," Black's Law Dictionary defines work product to include "[t]angible material *or its intangible equivalent, in unwritten or oral form*, that was either prepared by or for a lawyer or prepared for litigation, either planned or in progress." BLACK'S LAW DICTIONARY 1843 (10th ed. 2014) (emphasis added). Courts similarly recognize work product protection as extending beyond "tangible things." *See, e.g.*, United States v. Deloitte LLP, 610 F.3d 129, 136 (D.C. Cir. 2010) ("Rule 26(b)(3) only partially codifies the work-product doctrine announced in *Hickman*. Rule 26(b)(3) addresses only 'documents and tangible things,' but *Hickman*'s definition of work product extends to 'intangible' things.) (citations omitted).

1. PRIVILEGES

In addition to the federal body of law relating to privilege, each state has its own privilege-related statutory and common law. Therefore, the range and extent of privileges may vary, depending on which jurisdiction's law governs. In cases brought in federal court, federal common law and statutory law apply in non-diversity cases, but in diversity actions, state law governs.[5]

For example, under Minnesota law, there is a range of privileges afforded by statute: attorney-client; doctor-patient; psychotherapist-patient; clergy-parishioner; chemical dependency counselor-client; and parent-child, just to name a few.[6] Other jurisdictions do not confer such broad privilege rights. Therefore, you must consider and resolve choice of law issues before you can be certain as to which jurisdiction's privilege laws will apply.

This chapter addresses only the most commonly invoked privileges.

a. Attorney-Client Privilege

The attorney-client privilege protects communications between the attorney and client when the communication relates to giving or receiving legal advice. The client holds the privilege, which cannot be waived without the client's consent.[7] The privilege applies only when attorney and client ensure that the communication is, and remains, confidential. If a third party is present during conversations between attorney and client, no privilege attaches to those conversations. Similarly, if the client shares an attorney communication with, for instance, a friend, the client has waived any privilege that otherwise would have attached to the communication.[8]

The application and scope of the attorney-client privilege becomes more complicated when the client is an organization. Does the privilege apply to the CEO and all the way down to the guy in the mail room? No. The precise contours of the privilege and the test to be applied varies, but generally speaking, high-level employees and those in a need-to-know chain will be covered.[9] If your client is an organization, you need to determine very early on whom within that organization will be covered by the attorney-client privilege. You also need to counsel those individuals about the privilege and how to protect it.

---

[5]   *See* FED. R. EVID. 501.

[6]   *See, e.g.,* MINN. STAT. § 595.02 (2013).

[7]   *See* 24 CHARLES ALAN WRIGHT & ARTHUR R. MILLER, FEDERAL PRACTICE AND PROCEDURE § 5487 (1st ed.).

[8]   *See, e.g.,* Chase v. City of Portsmouth, 236 F.R.D. 263, 265 (E.D. Va. 2006).

[9]   The two primary approaches are the Upjohn test, *see* Upjohn Co. v. United States, 449 U.S. 383, 392 (1981), and the control group test, *see, e.g.,* Caremark, Inc. v. Affiliated Computer Servs., Inc., 192 F.R.D. 263 (N.D. Ill. 2000).

i. Waiver of the Attorney-Client Privilege

Waiver of the attorney-client privilege most typically occurs when otherwise privileged communications are disclosed to third parties. If the disclosure is intentional, the privilege is waived. If the disclosure is inadvertent, the privilege may survive. For example, if a party produces documents in response to a document request, but mistakenly includes in the production a letter from counsel to her client, the disclosure would likely be deemed inadvertent. There would be no waiver, and in fact, the opposing party would be obliged to return the errant document and could not rely upon or otherwise exploit its contents in the litigation.[10]

Attorney-client communications also become discoverable if a party puts the advice of its counsel "in issue." For example, if a party asserts that it relied upon its counsel's advice as a defense, the advice itself becomes an issue in the case and therefore will become subject to discovery. A party may not claim, for instance, that it is not liable because it acted on advice of counsel, while at the same time assert the attorney-client privilege with regard to that advice.[11] The attorney-client privilege cannot be used both as a sword and a shield.

ii. Crime-Fraud Exception

Clients may not obtain advice of counsel in order to plan or commit a crime or a fraud. Therefore, as a matter of public policy, an exception to the attorney-client privilege applies in these circumstances, commonly known as the "crime-fraud exception."[12]

In order for the exception to apply, the party challenging the privilege must show: (1) that the client was planning or engaged in criminal or fraudulent conduct when the client sought advice from counsel; and (2) the communication was related to the criminal or fraudulent conduct (either to facilitate it or conceal it).[13] The exception applies even if counsel is unaware that the client is using the advice to further a crime or fraud. However, a party challenging privilege on this basis must make a sufficient showing to the court that the communication furthered a crime or fraud, or helped to conceal the criminal or fraudulent activity.[14]

b. Doctor-Patient Privilege and Medical Records Protections

Virtually every jurisdiction protects doctor-patient communications. In addition, federal law (and many state statutes) explicitly prohibit

---

[10] FED. R. EVID. 502(b); FED. R. CIV. P. 26(b)(5)(B).

[11] *See* McGrath v. Nassau Cnty. Health Care Corp., 204 F.R.D. 240, 245–46, 247 (E.D.N.Y. 2001).

[12] *See* United States v. Zolin, 491 U.S. 554, 564–65 (1989).

[13] *In re* Napster, Inc. Copyright Litig., 479 F.3d 1078, 1090 (9th Cir. 2007).

[14] *Id.*

holders of medical information from releasing that information absent consent of the patient.[15] This leads to two issues: (1) what is the extent of the privilege; and (2) what are the mechanics for obtaining medical records.

i. *Extent of the Privilege*

Generally, a doctor-patient privilege applies if: (1) there was a medical provider-patient relationship; (2) the communication at issue took place during the relationship; and (3) the communication was related to the treatment of the patient.[16] The patient holds the privilege, which generally cannot be waived without the patient's consent.[17] A litigant who puts his physical or psychological condition in issue, however, waives the right to shield relevant medical records from discovery.[18] The question then becomes to what extent the privilege has been waived. For instance, a plaintiff claiming permanent disability caused by a car accident certainly opens the door to discovery into the treatment received for the claimed injuries. But what about records pertaining to previous injuries or pre-existing conditions that may have affected the extent of the claimed disability or other damages?

Like almost every other issue that comes up in discovery, the extent to which the court will allow inquiry will largely depend upon whether the party seeking the information can articulate a rational explanation as to why the discovery request is relevant and proportional to the needs of the case. This is an important step. If the parties cannot agree on the appropriate scope of medical record discovery, you should have your own medical expert assist you in articulating the basis for your need or the basis for opposing the release of records.

Remember, too, that if your client is the injured party, you need to explain medical waivers before you make any claim that may require one. The client's interest in privacy may affect the claims the client is willing to litigate.[19] In cases where it is likely the client will be required to waive medical privilege, it is important that counsel advise the client of that eventuality before claims are made relating to the client's physical or mental status. The client should be made aware, for example, that by

---

[15] See Health Insurance Portability and Accountability Act of 1996 ("HIPAA"), Pub. L. No. 104–191, 110 Stat. 1936 (codified in scattered sections of 18, 26, 29, and 42 U.S.C.).

[16] See, e.g., State v. Deases, 518 N.W.2d 784, 787 (Iowa 1994).

[17] See 25 WRIGHT & MILLER, FEDERAL PRACTICE AND PROCEDURE § 5537 (1st ed.).

[18] See, e.g., Lind v. Canada Dry Corp., 283 F. Supp. 861 (D. Minn. 1968) (claim of personal injury waives doctor-patient privilege).

[19] Remember, too that whenever a litigant's physical or mental condition is at issue, not only may the court order release of the party's medical records, the court also may order the litigant to undergo an exam performed by an expert hired by the opposing party. See FED. R. CIV. P. 35(a)(1). Because these types of examinations are usually conducted by a health care practitioner selected by the adverse party and not for purposes of care and treatment, the "patient" should reasonably assume that any communications with the Rule 35 examiner will be conveyed to the adverse party, typically in the form of a report. *See also* Chapter 11.

making a claim for physical or emotional harm, the client's past medical care may become something of an open book and that the adverse party will be privy to what may be private information.

ii. Mechanics for Obtaining Medical Records

Assuming there is a waiver of a medical or psychological treatment privilege, in the civil litigation context there are three mechanisms for discovery of health care information: (1) patient authorizations; (2) court orders; and (3) certain types of subpoenas or discovery requests.[20]

Patient authorizations are the most efficient mechanism for getting health care records. If the parties agree on which health care providers' records are subject to discovery, the party seeking discovery may request the adverse party to sign authorizations for the release of records. Often, what is authorized is a matter of negotiation between the parties.

If the parties cannot agree on the scope of disclosure, then a motion to compel or for a protective order may be necessary. The court may issue an order delineating what is discoverable or otherwise directing the party whose health care records are in issue to sign an authorization consistent with the court's order.[21]

Third, a properly issued subpoena *duces tecum* that either contains the patient's authorization for release of records or a copy of the court order requiring their release will satisfy HIPAA so long as representations are made to the subject of the subpoena that notice has been given to the patient or that a protective order that meets HIPAA requirements is in place.

c. Spousal Privilege

Most states provide some kind of privilege relating to communications between spouses. Some provide immunity from testifying against a spouse, and a few states maintain laws that absolutely disqualify one spouse from testifying against another. Other states make the non-testifying spouse the privilege holder, giving that spouse the right to enforce the privilege. Others leave to the testifying spouse discretion whether to invoke or waive the privilege.

Regardless of the particular rule, there must be an initial showing that the communication took place between spouses and that it was meant to be confidential.[22]

---

[20] JAY E. GRENIG & JEFFREY S. KINSLER, HANDBOOK OF FEDERAL CIVIL DISCOVERY & DISCLOSURE § 18.3 (3rd ed.).

[21] *Id.*

[22] See WRIGHT & MILLER, *supra* note 17, at § 5577.

2. ATTORNEY WORK PRODUCT

Protections afforded under the attorney work product doctrine rule do not arise from a privilege but rather as a qualified immunity protecting from discovery materials created in anticipation of litigation or trial.[23] The work product doctrine is intended to protect counsel's strategies, research, and other thought processes from opposing counsel. Although Rule 26(b)(3) refers to "documents and tangible things," in practice, the work product doctrine extends to counsel's thoughts, whether documented or not.[24]

In order for the protection to attach, the material must be created in anticipation of, or during, litigation. For example, counsel's notes of a witness interview, or legal research regarding possible claims and defenses would be typical work product. The protection extends to investigators and others working at the direction of counsel.

Further, Rule 26(b)(4)(d) disallows, with narrow exceptions, discovery of the work product of consulting experts retained by counsel in anticipation of litigation or trial. These are experts retained to advise or guide counsel, but who will not be called as trial witnesses, and they typically fall within the ambit of work product protections. For instance, if litigation counsel retains an ESI expert to help conduct discovery into a party's electronically stored information, ordinarily the work product of that consulting expert is not discoverable.

There are two kinds of work product: ordinary work product and opinion work product.[25] Ordinary work product includes raw factual information while opinion work product includes counsel's mental impressions.[26] Ordinary work product is usually not discoverable absent a showing of substantial need. To meet this burden, the party seeking the work product must show that it has substantial need for the material to prepare its case and cannot, without undue hardship, obtain the substantial equivalent by other means."[27] Opinion work product, on the other hand, receives near absolute protection.[28]

That is not to say that *evidence* gathered by litigation counsel through her investigations is protected from disclosure. If discovery seeks *evidence* (facts) known to the opposing party, though gathered by that party's counsel, the information itself is not protected if properly requested, such as through an interrogatory requesting all facts known to the party

---

[23] Hickman v. Taylor, 329 U.S. 495, 512 (1947).

[24] *In re* Seagate Tech., LLC, 497 F.3d 1360, 1375 (Fed. Cir. 2007).

[25] Baker v. General Motors, Corp., 209 F.3d 1051, 1054 (8th Cir. 2000).

[26] *Id.*

[27] FED. R. CIV. P. 26(b)(3)(A)(ii).

[28] See FED. R. CIV. P. 26(b)(3)(B) ("If the court orders discovery of [work product], it must protect against disclosure of the mental impressions, conclusions, opinions, or legal theories of a party's attorney or other representative concerning the litigation.").

relating to a given issue.[29] Similarly, counsel's notes of a witness interview likely are protected from disclosure, but the identity of the witness is discoverable.[30]

3. PROPRIETARY OR OTHERWISE COMMERCIALLY SENSITIVE INFORMATION

In business disputes, it is important to safeguard your client's proprietary information, such as trade secrets.[31] There are many types of information that businesses may wish to keep private, such as:

• Customer and prospective customer lists;

• Non-patented inventions (which may qualify as trade secrets);

• Financial information;

• Marketing plans;

• Manufacturing processes;

• Research and development; and

• Tax records.

The protection of proprietary information can become especially complicated when the adverse party is a competitor of your client. Even with the protections of a confidentiality agreement or protective order, the mere fact that the adverse party may be able to conduct discovery into your client's proprietary information could put the client at a competitive disadvantage. There are forms of confidentiality agreements and protective orders that can provide some measure of protection against disclosure to the adverse party itself (as opposed to its counsel), but if the proprietary information is relevant to the issues of the case, it is difficult to fully shield that information from the adverse party.

4. PRIVATE INFORMATION

In addition to proprietary business information, courts also may protect private personal information under certain circumstances.[32] For

---

[29] See Hunter's Ridge Golf Co., Inc. v. Georgia-Pac. Corp., 233 F.R.D. 678, 681 (M.D. Fla. 2006).

[30] See, e.g., Am. Floral Servs., Inc. v. Florists' Transworld Delivery Ass'n., 107 F.R.D. 258, 260 (N.D. Ill. 1985).

[31] Many states have adopted the Uniform Trade Secrets Act. One of the elements necessary to maintain a trade secret is that reasonable efforts are taken to safeguard the trade secret. Disclosure of the trade secret in the course of litigation, without adequate safeguards in place such as a confidentiality agreement or protective order preventing the information from being disseminated, can result in forfeiture of trade secret status. See, e.g., Glaxo, Inc. v. Novopharm, Ltd., 931 F. Supp. 1280, 1300 (E.D.N.C. 1996).

[32] Constitutional principles of privacy also may protect certain personal information from discovery. See, e.g., Bd. of Trustees v. Superior Court, 119 Cal. App. 3d 516, 525 (1981).

example, you should be aware of statutes that protect from disclosure certain personal information in the absence of consent or court order. Being cautious about disclosure of private information becomes especially important when the information pertains to non-parties, such as an employer's personnel files of non-parties.[33] If you need to disclose such information in discovery, it is best to do so only pursuant to court order, and to do so only with a protective order in place, as described more fully below.

B. SAFEGUARDING PRIVILEGED AND OTHER PROTECTED INFORMATION

Depending upon the nature of the information to be protected, there are a number of approaches to safeguarding against its disclosure. At the onset, it is important to distinguish between information that should not be disclosed to the adverse party versus information that the adverse party will be entitled to see but should otherwise be protected from the prying eyes of the wider world. In those instances, a protective order can ensure that the parties do not release confidential information to third parties.

Following is a summary of tools available to counsel to safeguard privileged or otherwise confidential information.

1. CONFIDENTIALITY AGREEMENTS

Confidentiality agreements are private contracts entered into between the parties setting forth the terms of disclosure of otherwise protectable information. Confidentiality agreements are particularly useful before the commencement of litigation should the parties agree to engage in an informal exchange of information as part of an early dispute resolution process. Though they may also be used within the formal litigation process, it is better to enter into a stipulated protective order signed by the court.

Confidentiality agreements may be tailored to the needs of the parties and the particular circumstances, but they tend to share common elements, including:[34]

- Specificity as to who shall be bound (i.e., the parties, their agents, employees and any third-parties acting on their behalf, legal counsel, consultants, experts, etc.);

- That any disclosure of privileged or otherwise confidential information shall not be treated as a waiver of any privilege or other protections and may only be used for the purposes specified in the agreement;

---

[33] Whittingham v. Amherst Coll., 164 F.R.D. 124 (D. Mass. 1995).

[34] For an example of a confidentiality agreement and order, *see* Appendix.

- That all information disclosed shall be treated as confidential (or conversely, nothing shall be treated as confidential unless affirmatively designated as confidential). Documents to be treated as confidential by the parties must bear a "confidential" stamp;

- That any person to be provided access to the confidential information shall be required to read the agreement and assent to its terms;

- That certain information be limited to "attorneys' eyes only," or is subject to other restrictions that specifically identify who may, or may not, be given access to certain information;

- Enumeration of rights of the parties to enforce the terms of the agreement, often including the right to obtain injunctive relief, seek damages, and an attorney's fee shifting clause;

- Procedures for the return or destruction of the confidential information by a specified time or in relation to a specified event (such as settlement or determination the matter cannot be settled).

2. PROTECTIVE ORDERS

Once a matter is in litigation, if any party anticipates that there will be discovery into privileged or otherwise confidential information, counsel for the parties should attempt to negotiate a stipulated protective order before the start of discovery, usually as part of the Rule 26(f) meet and confer process. In the event the parties cannot agree to the terms of a protective order (or the need for one), the party requesting it may move the court for an order pursuant to Rule 26(c)(1).

Rule 26(c) grants courts broad authority on how to fashion protective orders, and outlines a number of potential provisions. Many district court local rules include standard form protective orders that can be adapted to the circumstances of the case.[35]

It is important to address issues relating to treatment of privileged or otherwise confidential information *before* commencement of formal discovery. Otherwise, the discovery process may grind to a halt when a party refuses to release information until proper protections are in place.

3. PRIVILEGE LOGS

Even when a protective order is in place, there still may be information that you properly should withhold from production, such as privileged information not covered by agreement or court order and work product.

---

[35] For an example of a standard form protective order, *see* Appendix.

When that happens, you must respond to the discovery request with a statement saying that responsive documents exist but are being withheld due to whatever privilege you are asserting. You also must sufficiently describe the documents in a way that will enable the other party to assess the validity of your claim of privilege.[36]

One way to do this is to create a privilege log.[37] Although Rule 26(b)(5)(A) governs the withholding of privileged documents and requires counsel to set forth the nature of the documents and the reasons for withholding them, the Rule does not expressly require the creation of a privilege log, but as a matter of practice, this is the manner in which to comply with the Rule.

4. REDACTIONS

There may be documents that are otherwise discoverable, but that contain within them some protected information. When that happens, it may be appropriate to redact (or black out) that information.[38] When you redact information, you need to identify the reason for the redaction, and you should include the document in your privilege log.

5. COMMON INTEREST AGREEMENTS

There are cases in which multiple plaintiffs, or multiple defendants, are represented by separate counsel. If the parties on one side or the other share common litigation interests, that is, they are not adverse to each other, communications relating to the case that takes place between these parties can be protected from disclosure.[39] For example, in a case where the plaintiff claims that several defendants acted in concert to cause the plaintiff's injuries, and the defendants have not asserted cross-claims, the defendants may share a common interest.

Although not required, when parties share a common litigation interest and wish to coordinate their efforts, it is wise for them to enter into a common interest agreement, sometime referred to as a joint defense agreement. Common interest agreements do not ensure that privilege will be applied to their communications, but it does evidence intent by the parties to treat their inter-party communications as confidential.[40]

6. FILING UNDER SEAL

A confidentiality agreement or protective order may make provision for filing confidential information under seal. Filing under seal may be

---

[36] See FED. R. CIV. P. 26(b)(5)(A).

[37] For an example of a privilege log, *see* Appendix.

[38] See FED. R. CIV. P. 5.2.

[39] See RESTATEMENT (THIRD) OF LAW GOVERNING LAWYERS § 76 (2000).

[40] For an example of a common interest agreement, *see* Appendix.

necessary, for instance, when filing motions before the court that rely on confidential documents or testimony.

Rule 5.2 allows counsel to redact confidential information or to file such documents under seal. The ability to file under seal has become more important now that the federal courts allow Internet access to specific case filings, making it easier for non-parties to search court files. Local rules typically require an attorney who wishes to file documents under seal to bring a motion and obtain a court order. Parties (and non-parties, such as the media) are then given an opportunity to challenge the request.

7. CURING INADVERTENT WAIVER, RULE 26(b)(5)(B) AND FED. R. EVID. 502

Mistakes happen. Privileged documents sometimes are unintentionally released during discovery. This is particularly true when disclosures are in the form of ESI and are voluminous. Should this happen, the disclosure does not necessarily result in waiver of the privilege. If the disclosure was inadvertent and if the holder of the privilege took reasonable care to protect its privileged information and if the holder of the privilege acted quickly to correct the error, the privilege may survive.[41] Upon notice to the recipient of the errantly disclosed documents, the recipient has an obligation to return, sequester, or destroy the information.[42]

These requirements are codified in Rule 26(b)(5)(B) and Federal Rule of Evidence 502(b). The Rules govern how inadvertently disclosed attorney-client privileged communications and work product shall be treated. Rather than wait for the problem to arise, it is better practice to simply agree during the Rule 26(f) meet and confer process that Rule 502(b) shall be incorporated into the court's pretrial order. If the case is in state court, and it is pending in a state where there is no equivalent rule, the parties should still stipulate that Rule 502(b) shall apply.

8. CONFIDENTIAL SETTLEMENT AGREEMENTS

Many settlement agreements contain confidentiality clauses. The reasons for keeping settlements confidential are varied, as is the scope of the confidentiality requirement. Sometimes the terms of the settlement are confidential; other times even the fact that a settlement exists is confidential.

A typical confidentiality clause may read as follows:

The Parties to this Agreement shall keep all terms of this Agreement confidential. No term of this Agreement, or the

---

[41] See FED. R. EVID. 502; *id.* 26(b)(5)(B).

[42] *See id.* 26(b)(5)(B).

existence of any of its contents, or any information subject to the terms of the Stipulated Protective Order issued in this Action may be disclosed to any person or entity not a party to this Agreement, except as required by court order, statute, regulation or to accountants in preparation of tax returns.

One of the many responsibilities lawyers carry is to safeguard our clients' secrets. In the litigation context, where disclosure through the discovery process puts those secrets at risk, it is nonetheless our obligation to ensure that the client's confidential information remains protected.

CHAPTER 13

DISCOVERY DISPUTES AND MISCONDUCT

■ ■ ■

> *If there is a hell to which disputatious, uncivil, vituperative lawyers go, let it be one in which the damned are eternally locked in discovery disputes with other lawyers of equally repugnant attributes.*[1]

Though the discovery rules are designed to facilitate the fair exchange of information between adverse parties, it is common for disagreements and disputes to arise over what is, and is not, discoverable. Common objections relate to the proper scope of discovery, privilege, burdensomeness (proportionality), and a host of other matters. In addition, substantive responses may be incomplete or even non-responsive.

You may also, on occasion, encounter discovery misconduct. For example, an attorney may improperly use discovery to harass or embarrass the adverse party.[2] Counsel may improperly coach a witness during a deposition or otherwise behave in a manner so as to impede the questioner's ability to take an effective deposition.[3] Information responsive to discovery may be improperly withheld. And there have been occasions when a party or its counsel have engaged in misconduct by destroying evidence that was reasonably foreseen to be relevant to the dispute.

When you run into discovery problems, you should attempt to resolve them directly with counsel. In fact, you are required to meet and confer with opposing counsel before you seek assistance from the court.

A. MOTIONS TO COMPEL AND MOTIONS FOR PROTECTIVE ORDERS

Rule 37 governs most circumstances involving disputed discovery, typically circumstances in which the party conducting the discovery contends that responses are inadequate or improper. Rule 37 allows the

---

[1] Network Computing Services v. Cisco Systems, 223 F.R.D. 392, 395 (D.S.C. 2004), *citing* Krueger v. Pelican Product, Corp., C/A No. 87–2385–A (W.D. Okla. Feb. 24, 1989).

[2] Discovery may not be used for the purpose of annoying, embarrassing or oppressing the adverse party. FED. R. CIV. P. 26(c)(1).

[3] *See* FED. R. CIV. P. 30(c)(2); Sec. Nat'l Bank of Sioux City v. Abbott Labs., 299 F.R.D. 595, 610 (N.D. Iowa 2014) (sanctions are appropriate against an attorney who coaches witness during deposition and otherwise impeded the completion of the deposition through improper and frequent interruptions).

aggrieved party to make a motion to compel disclosure, and also provides for sanctions against the non-compliant party when warranted. Rule 26(c) allows the party responding to improper discovery requests the ability to seek and obtain a protective order to prohibit or otherwise limit that discovery.

Rule 37 is the seminal rule for enforcing the parties' discovery rights.[4] The rule provides for the following:

- The right to bring a motion for an order compelling an initial Rule 26(a) disclosure;[5]

- The right to bring a motion for an order compelling a discovery response;[6]

- The right to an award of attorney's fees to the prevailing party;[7]

- The right to seek sanctions beyond an award of attorney's fees in some particularly egregious circumstances, such as failure to comply with a court order,[8] or failure to attend a deposition or serve answers to written discovery.[9]

In addition, with regard to depositions, Rule 30(d) permits an aggrieved party to terminate a deposition if opposing counsel conducts the deposition in "bad faith or in a manner that unreasonably annoys, embarrasses, or oppresses the deponent or party." Under the rule, the court also may sanction a "person who impedes, delays, or frustrates the fair examination of the deponent."[10]

1. THE MEET AND CONFER OBLIGATION

Before bringing a motion to compel or for a protective order, the aggrieved party must first attempt to meet and confer with the opposing party in an effort to resolve the dispute informally.[11] By way of example, plaintiff serves upon defendant a set of interrogatories. Defendant responds with boilerplate objections and provides little substantive

---

    [4]   *See also* FED. R. CIV. P. 26(g). Rule 26(g) requires counsel to sign all discovery requests and all discovery responses, certifying that discovery disclosures are complete and correct, and that discovery requests are not interposed for an improper purpose, nor are they unreasonable or unduly burdensome considering the needs of the case. Improper certification can lead to sanctions. *Id.*

    [5]   *Id.* 37(a).

    [6]   *Id.*

    [7]   *Id.* 37(a)(5). The court has discretion to not award fees and costs if the opposing party's position was substantially justified or "other circumstances make an award of expenses unjust." *Id.*

    [8]   *Id.* 37(b).

    [9]   *Id.* 37(d).

    [10]   *Id.* 30(d)(2).

    [11]   *Id.* 26(c)(1), 37(a)(1).

information. Before bringing a motion to compel, plaintiff must attempt to persuade defendant to withdraw its unmeritorious objections and provide fully responsive answers. The rules do not prescribe how the meet and confer process shall proceed. However, as a matter of practice plaintiff's counsel should:

- Conduct the meet and confer in writing, so there is a clear and indisputable record;[12]

- Reference applicable rules and case law;

- Explain which *specific* responses are deficient and why;

- Identify a deadline by when the opposing party must provide fully responsive answers, and advise counsel that failure to timely cure the deficiency will result in a motion to compel.

The opposing party may reply by standing by its responses, or it may agree to partially or fully supplement its responses. There also may be times when the opposing party fails to respond altogether. Depending upon the response—or lack thereof—you must then decide whether to go forward with a motion. Regardless of opposing counsel's response, note that both Rule 26 and 37 only require that "the movant has in good faith conferred or *attempted* to confer with the person or party failing to make disclosure."[13]

2. MOTION PRACTICE

Assuming the meet and confer process does not resolve the dispute, you may then seek relief from the court. Before you file your motion, you must contact the court administrator to obtain a date and time for your motion to be heard.[14] This date must provide at least 14 days' notice to the opposing party in the case of a non-dispositive motion, such as a discovery motion.[15] Local rules govern other specific motion practice requirements, but typical requirements include:

- Notice of motion (setting forth the date, time and place of the hearing);

- Motion (setting forth the nature of the motion);

- Memorandum in support of the motion;

- Affidavit(s) and exhibits in support of the motion;

---

[12] This is also referred to as a discovery deficiency letter. Some jurisdictions require an in-person meet and confer. In that case, it is still wise to follow up with a letter recapping the meeting.

[13] FED. R. CIV. P. 26(c)(1), 37(a)(1).

[14] *Id.* 6(c)(1).

[15] *Id.* Most courts require that you contact the court administrator to obtain a hearing date and time, so the notice may turn out to be more than 14 days, depending upon the court's availability.

- Certification of compliance with the meet and confer requirement.[16]

Further, though not required by all local rules, it is a good idea to provide the court with a proposed order. The proposed order should be brief and straightforward, containing language that grants you the relief you are seeking.

3. COMMON BASES FOR BRINGING A MOTION TO COMPEL

Though discovery disputes tend to be fact-specific, following are common problems that may require you to file a motion to compel:

- Failure to timely respond to discovery;[17]

- Failure to fully respond to discovery;[18]

- Failure to state objections with specificity (asserting so-called "boilerplate" objections);[19]

- Failure to specify privileged or otherwise protected information withheld from production (i.e., failure to produce a privilege log);[20]

- Failure to produce documents in the manner specified or as they are kept in the usual course of business;[21]

- Obstreperous conduct of counsel representing a witness during a deposition (often in the form of "coaching");[22]

- Failure to properly prepare a witness designated to testify on behalf of an organization.[23]

4. COMMON BASES FOR BRINGING A MOTION FOR PROTECTIVE ORDER

On the other hand, if your client needs protection from inappropriate discovery requests or conduct, you may bring a motion for a protective order

---

[16] *See* Appendix for an exemplar motion to compel. Many of the local rules include either a description of the form of the motion or an actual template to be followed. You generally can find these online. Make sure you check the local rules in order to ensure you are in compliance with local practice requirements.

[17] Generally, parties have 30 days to respond to written discovery. FED. R. CIV. P. 33(b)(2), 34(b)(2), 36(a)(3).

[18] *Id.* 33(b)(3).

[19] *Id.* 33(b)(4), 34(b)(2), 36(a)(5).

[20] *Id.* 26(b)(5).

[21] *Id.* 34(b)(2)(E).

[22] *Id.* 30(c)(2), (d)(2).

[23] *Id.* 30(b)(6).

pursuant to Rule 26(c)(1). Common bases for seeking a protective order include:

- To prevent discovery into confidential or otherwise protected information;

- To prevent discovery that is disproportionate to the size of the dispute;

- To have information placed under seal or otherwise obtain protections against public disclosure;

- To address harassing, bullying or other unprofessional conduct by counsel conducting a deposition.

5. THE IMPORTANCE OF RULE 37(a)(4)

A common (and inappropriate) tactic of litigants who do not want to answer a particular question or produce particular documents is to give a non-responsive response. For example, during a deposition, the defendant is asked if she had been drinking alcohol before the accident. Defendant responds, "I'm not much of a drinker." That answer is non-responsive to the question. If the questioner asked the question again, she may hear the objection "asked and answered," or she may get the exact same response. If the witness continues to fail to answer the question, a motion to compel may ultimately be necessary. Your tool is Rule 37(a)(4), which specifically states that "an evasive or incomplete disclosure, answer or response must be treated as a failure to disclose, answer, or respond."

This is an important rule, often overlooked by litigators, when the opposing party (or its counsel) engages in word games or simply will not answer a question or other discovery request in a straightforward manner. Unfortunately, all too often, litigants who engage in this type of behavior get away with it. When this problem arises, remind counsel, and then the court, that evasive or otherwise non-responsive responses *must* be treated as a failure to respond.

6. WAIVER OF OBJECTIONS

If you are on the receiving end of inappropriate discovery requests, your first obligation is to raise a timely objection. Failure to do so may result in a waiver of the objection, even if the information inappropriately sought is protected by a privilege.[24] For interrogatories, you must state objections within 30 days or the objections are waived.[25] Rule 34, which relates to the production of documents and things, does not contain the same waiver language that is contained in Rule 33, but some courts have

---

[24] Horace Mann Ins. Co. v. Nationwide Mut. Ins. Co., 238 F.R.D. 536, 538 (D. Conn. 2006).

[25] FED. R. CIV. P. 33(b)(3), (4) (untimely interrogatory objections waived unless good cause shown).

found there to be an implicit duty to timely object to document demands or risk waiver.[26] Perhaps most perilous of all are the time limits for responding to Rule 36 requests for admissions. If you fail to meet the 30-day limit for responding or objecting to a request for admission, you will be deemed to have admitted whatever was contained in the request.[27]

B. MISCONDUCT, REMEDIES AND SANCTIONS

In a typical discovery dispute, where the non-disclosing party can articulate a reasonable basis for its position, courts tend not to award fees or sanctions on behalf of the moving party. However, courts may use a heavy hand against a party or attorney who has acted egregiously or has displayed an ongoing pattern of resisting legitimate discovery. In such cases, courts may award attorney fees and sometimes even additional sanctions.

Rule 37(b) sanctions may apply when a party fails to make an initial disclosure,[28] fails to attend its own deposition,[29] fails to serve answers to written discovery,[30] fails to supplement written discovery,[31] or fails to produce a person for a Rule 35 examination.[32] To remedy the harm, the court may:

- Direct that certain facts be taken as established;
- Prohibit the offending party from supporting or opposing designated claims or defenses;
- Strike pleadings in whole or in part;
- Stay proceedings until the court's order compelling discovery is obeyed;
- Dismiss the action in whole or in part;
- Render a default judgment against the disobedient party; or
- Treat as contempt of court the failure to obey the court's order.[33]

Bear in mind that the court has broad discretion to formulate and impose a sanction or otherwise order remedial relief. Generally, the more blatant and prejudicial the misconduct, the more likely the court will not only

---

[26] See Hall v. Sullivan, 231 F.R.D. 468, 474 (D. Md. 2005).

[27] FED. R. CIV. P. 36(a)(3).

[28] *Id.* 37(c)(1).

[29] *Id.* 37(d)(1)(A)(i).

[30] *Id.* 37(d)(1)(ii).

[31] *Id.* 37(c)(1).

[32] *Id.* 37(b)(2)(B).

[33] *Id.* 37(b)(2)(A)(i)–(vii). Instead of, or in addition to these sanctions, the court must order the offending party, its counsel, or both, to pay attorney's fees and expenses caused by the misconduct. *Id.* 37(b)(2)(C).

compel compliance with the rules, but also impose sanctions or other remedial relief.[34]

C. TACTICAL CONSIDERATIONS

Most judges do not relish wading into discovery disputes, though courts have become more proactive with regard to managing discovery issues. Minor, relatively non-prejudicial dust-ups are generally not well received by the courts. Therefore, as a first principle, if you intend to seek relief, make sure you are able to articulate a clear, substantial harm as a result of the opposing party's discovery misconduct. Further, seeking relief from the court is much more difficult when you have unclean hands yourself.

If you are satisfied that the discovery you seek is necessary to your case, you must be prepared to articulate to the court *why* it is necessary to your case. Invariably, the court will want to know what the discovery has to do with the issues in the case. You need to be prepared to state which claims or defenses (and elements thereof) the discovery relates to and why it is relevant.[35] This seems elementary, but we have seen instances where counsel cannot answer this basic question (probably because counsel failed to think through the discovery she needed in the first place).

There also may be tactical reasons for *not* pursing an order to compel discovery. Rule 37(c)(1) prohibits a party at a hearing or at trial from using evidence not properly disclosed. So if the discovery request in question seeks information in support of the opposing party's claims or defenses, or if the adverse party fails to disclose evidence in support of its case through a Rule 26(a) disclosure requirement, then the obstreperous party should not be able to use the undisclosed evidence at a hearing or at trial. This rule is intended to deter "hide the ball" tactics during the discovery process and also is intended to prevent those who would engage in these kinds of tactics from surprising the adverse party at a hearing or at trial.[36] Before moving to compel disclosure of evidence that benefits the adverse party's case, consider first the chance of prevailing on a subsequent motion to exclude.

Finally, if you are considering seeking a protective order, do not necessarily wait for the opposing party to move to compel. A motion for a protective order filed in response to a motion to compel can look like a tactic rather than a sincere effort to limit or otherwise prohibit the disputed discovery. It may be better to object, immediately seek to meet and confer,

---

[34] An appellate court reviewing the appropriateness of a sanction order will consider the extent of prejudice resulting from the discovery abuse, whether the non-cooperating party was warned of possible sanctions and whether the court considered less drastic sanctions. *See* Toth v. Grand Trunk R.R. 306 F.3d 335, 343 (6th Cir. 2002).

[35] *See* FED. R. CIV. P. 26(b)(1) (scope of discovery).

[36] Am. Stock Exch., LLC v. Mopex, Inc., 215 F.R.D. 87, 93 (S.D.N.Y. 2002).

and then move for the protective order. Having said that, motions for protective orders tend to be the exception, rather than the rule; most discovery disputes are framed-up in the context of a motion to compel.

D. ETHICAL CONSIDERATIONS

In addition to the many requirements of the Rules relating to discovery, you also should be mindful of the rules of professional conduct. Model Rule 3.4 explicitly addresses discovery abuse, prohibiting obstruction of access to potential evidence, the filing of frivolous discovery requests, and the failure to comply with a reasonable discovery demand.[37] Though unusual, in addition to sanctions levied by the court, counsel who engages in discovery misconduct may become the subject of a disciplinary action.[38] You never want to be on the receiving end of an ethics complaint.

---

[37] MODEL RULES OF PROF'L CONDUCT R. 3.4(a), (d) (2020).

[38] *See In re* Gilly, 976 F. Supp. 2d 471 (S.D.N.Y. 2013).

CHAPTER 14

LITIGATION TECHNOLOGY: MANAGING THE LITIGATION AND THE DISCOVERY RECORD

■ ■ ■

Once upon a time, litigation files looked something like this (and many still do):

Illus. 14-1.

Though this chapter differs somewhat from the primary subjects of this book, case management is crucial to both case development and discovery. Unless you are one of the few people who have a photographic memory, if the case is even of moderate size, you need to be able to organize and manage it so that you can retrieve what you need without having to dig through reams of documents and deposition testimony.

You also must have a means by which to make subjective assessments of the evidence, such as how documents or other evidence relate one to the other. For instance, are there inconsistencies between deposition testimony and a key document? Have important terms in a draft document been dropped from the final version? What if the document is 1,000 pages?

That is why it is important to leverage the power of litigation technology. Further, because more and more evidence is in the form of ESI, it is no longer practical to rely solely on a paper file. ESI typically is produced in an electronic form (rather than printed out in hard copy) and must be uploaded to a computer and read with litigation software.

This chapter briefly surveys two types of litigation technology: (1) case management software, and (2) discovery and document management software.[1]

But first, it is important to put these tools in their proper context. Litigation technology can assist a lawyer in planning and executing case development; technology tools are not a substitute for the creative process of case development. In Chapters 2 and 3 we discussed case development as well as planning and management of the litigation. These are the creative processes upon which litigation technology can have a significant impact.

A. A BRIEF REVIEW OF CASE MANAGEMENT AND EVIDENCE MAPPING

Chapter 3 addressed litigation planning and management, and the importance of identifying, organizing, and sequencing the tasks necessary to make a case trial-ready. The overarching idea is that you must think through the steps necessary to prepare your case within the internal deadlines you create as part of your discovery plan as well as the deadlines set by the court.

Generally speaking, creating a litigation plan is a two-step process. First, you must think through all the steps (tasks) you anticipate will be necessary to make your case trial-ready, and the logical order in which those steps should be taken (recall our discussion of the Critical Path Method). Second, once you receive a pretrial order setting forth discovery cut-off dates, deadlines for motions, and a trial date, you must then attach deadlines by which each step (task) must be completed.

Recall this simplified example of a litigation plan:

Smith v. Jones, et al., Case No. 123456

Client = Smith   Updated: 2/15/20

DUE	TASK DESCRIPTION	ASSIGNED	STATUS
8/15/19	Research causes of action; Memo to all	RAK	DONE
9/1/19	Draft complaint	RAK	DONE
9/15/19	Serve S & C	JAC	DONE

---

[1]   There are a number of products out there that integrate to some degree the two types of software, but for our purposes we will treat them as if they are separate systems.

9/30/19	Draft 1st rogs, doc demands, RFAs	RAK	DONE
10/30/19	R26(f) meeting	CMR	DONE
11/21/19	File R26(f) report	RAK	DONE
11/30/19	Serve R26(a) initial disclosures	CMR	DONE
11/30/19	Serve 1st rogs, doc demands	JAC	DONE
12/30/19	P's 1st rog responses and doc demands due		15-DAY EXTENSION GRANTED (DUE 1/14/20)
1/7/20	**SCHEDULING HEARING**	CMR	DONE
1/13/20	Finalize responses to Ds' 1st rogs and doc demands	CMR/RAK	DONE
1/14/20	Serve P's responses to Ds' 1st rogs and doc demands	JAC	DONE
1/31/20	Retain liability expert Retain damages expert	CMR	DONE—ALICE DOE [Need to locate damages expert]
2/25/20	P's initial depo prep	CMR	
3/28/20	Prepare depo outlines	CMR	
3/28/20	Subpoenas and depo notices to: J Jones ABC Co. XYZ Co.	JAC	
5/31/20	Complete depos of: J Jones ABC Co. XYZ Co.	CMR	
7/15/20	Serve RFAs	RAK	
8/15/20	Serve supplemental discovery responses	RAK	
8/30/20	**DISCOVERY CUTOFF**		

10/31/20	NON-DISPOSITIVE MOTION CUTOFF		
12/31/20	LAST DAY FOR SJ MOTIONS		
2/15/21	TRIAL DOCUMENTS DUE	RAK	
3/2/21	TRIAL	CMR	

Illus. 14-2.

Similarly, as discussed in Chapter 2, it is also essential to create an evidence map. Use of an evidence map helps ensure that you obtain through discovery and your own independent investigation the evidence necessary to prove the elements of each cause of action or affirmative defense.

For easy reference, the following is Chapter 2's simplified example of an evidence map relating to an auto accident:

Elements	Supporting/Missing Evidence
1. Duty	a. Judicial notice of "reasonable care" statute b. Jury instruction on reasonable care c. [Safe driving expert?] d. Defendant to admit he had duty to not text?
2. Breach	a. Defendant to admit he was texting? b. Defendant to admit he ran a red light? c. [Safe driving expert?] d. Do text records still exist? e. Subpoena girlfriend?
3. Causation	a. Witness Smith will testify she saw defendant go through red light and hit plaintiff (Problem: witness was drunk at the time and nearly a block away) b. [Accident reconstruction expert?] c. [Medical expert to testify plaintiff's injury was caused by defendant striking plaintiff?]
4. Damages	Past wage loss: a. Pay stubs b. Job termination notice

Future wage loss:
- a. Client will testify she can't find a job with her limitations
- b. [Vocational expert?]
- c. [Statistician/economist?]

Past medical expenses:
- a. Medical bills
- b. [How do we prove they were reasonable?]

Future medical expenses:
- a. No supporting evidence
- b. [Medical expert?]

Illus. 14-3.

The examples are simplified for purposes of illustration. Many cases involve hundreds of tasks that must be managed in order to make the case trial-ready, and can involve hundreds, or even thousands, of data points, i.e., forms of evidence, that must be tracked in order to develop a compelling case. Not surprisingly, litigation-support software can help, and in some cases, may be absolutely essential.

B. CASE MANAGEMENT SOFTWARE

Case management software is a tool for managing litigation files; it is not a substitute for thoughtful planning. It cannot tell you which steps to take, and in what order, so as to properly develop a case. What case management software can do is assist with documenting the plan and related deadlines.[2] We make no specific recommendation of one product over another.

At a minimum, case management software should include the ability to create a litigation plan that includes fields for tasks, deadlines, assignment of tasks, and status reporting. It must be set up to give all team members access to it. The upside of giving every team member access is that everyone knows what everyone else is (or should be) doing. It will also allow for real-time updates. The downside is, at least for those who attempt to toil in the shadows or have a tendency to not meet deadlines, it will show up for all to see.

Consider a case in which there are 20 team members, including attorneys, paralegals and administrative assistants. Now imagine you are the lead attorney in charge of managing all facets of the case, including

---

[2] Much of the software available in the marketplace offers a number of functions, including timelines, deadline notifications, billing, the ability to create case file notes and so forth. Our focus is on the software's functionality, specifically relating to how it ensures that the litigation plan is documented in a way that you can be confident you are methodically executing the plan.

getting the case trial ready. Further, assume that the team is working out of two separate offices and several members work out of their homes. It would be impossible to stick your head in each person's office and ask, "So, what came out at the Jones deposition?" or "Are you done reviewing XYZ Company's documents?"

Back in the days before case management software that was often how it was done (and probably still is at some firms). If the lead attorney was really on the ball, there might be team meetings from time to time. Any firm that still conducts its litigation that way has placed itself at a disadvantage and, in turn, is not serving the client well.

And what about sole practitioners? Assume you have opened your own litigation firm and that your reputation quickly grows. Business is booming. You have 100 cases. How are you going to manage it all? Though you may have an administrative assistant, he can't do your thinking for you. It is *your* job to plan out the litigation—including figuring out how you are going to get the case trial ready in the time allotted to you—and determining which evidence helps, hurts or otherwise has no effect on your clients' cases. A sole practitioner can quickly become overwhelmed. That is a very good reason to invest in computerized case management and discovery software.

C. DISCOVERY AND DOCUMENT MANAGEMENT SOFTWARE

What is often referred to as litigation software is actually discovery and document management software that allows counsel to house, search, and categorize vast amounts of information. Essentially, the software functions as an *evidence map*, but allows for the creation of multiple data fields and the linkage to these fields of the evidence itself (such as deposition transcripts, written discovery responses, and documents produced in discovery). This, in turn, allows you to organize evidence according to a defined set of issues (such as the legal elements to a specific cause of action), and link the evidence to these defined issues.

Discovery software works as a relational database. A relational database is a collection of data that is stored in more than one database table in such a way that the tables can access one another and generate complex search results based on intricate search terms. This allows you to search for information within and across the databases using combinations of search criteria.

Most litigation support software programs are highly scalable because they are built on an SQL platform (SQL is an essentially unlimited size relational database) that can handle evidence in either native form (its original digital format) or in near native form (such as PDF/TIFF). For example, assume you receive one million pages of ESI documents. Once the

ESI is uploaded, many programs can search the entirety of the data for specific names, names within specific date ranges, and even names within specific date ranges but limited to specific types of documents.[3]

If you use an evidence management program, you can "issue code" evidence as you review it. That is to say, you can mark documents and excerpts of testimony as relating to particular issues in the case. In this way, you can continuously add to your evidence map and ensure you are capturing all relevant evidence, good or bad, as the case progresses. Typically, "issues" are correlated to the elements of each cause of action or affirmative defense. However, they also may include other matters, such as evidence relating to the adverse party's failure to disclose information (i.e., the absence of facts), evidence relating to specific witnesses (such as experts), subjective analysis of the strengths and weaknesses of a given witness, or any other issues that you wish to specifically identify for purposes of organizing evidence. This will help you to prepare for depositions, motions and trial.

All discovery and document management software should contain, at a minimum, the following functionality:

1. The ability to work with documents that have been imaged (such as TIFF or PDF images);

2. The ability to work with native files (such as Microsoft Word, Excel, and searchable PDF files);

3. The ability to produce and utilize full text search capabilities from documents that have been OCR'd (optical character recognition);

4. The ability to review, classify, categorize, and produce documents responsive to discovery requests in formats compatible with others' litigation support tools;

5. The ability to conduct a key word search function of all the evidence in the record;

6. The ability to conduct a multi-field Boolean search function throughout the databases (i.e., the ability to use multiple search criteria, such as a specific date + document author, or all documents contained within a date range, etc.);

7. Issue coding capacity (the ability to mark or tag evidence by defined issues that can be used for organizing and searching the data);

---

[3] Searchability of ESI is dependent upon the manner in which it is produced. It is critical to address this issue during the Rule 26(f) meet and confer process.

8.   Objective coding capacity (the ability to record objective information from the data, such as document dates, authorship, type of document);

9.   Subjective coding capacity (the ability for counsel to comment on the data, such as identifying particularly helpful or damaging evidence, or any other mental impressions that will be useful when preparing for motions or trial);

10. The ability to link the database and the evidence itself (so that you may review the summaries of the evidence but also call up for review the evidence itself);

11. Analytics capacity. This allows clustering, categorization, concept searching, email threading and near-duplicate identification (in order to weed out duplicates of the same documents). Utilizing these processes can make your review process more efficient and more accurate.[4]

Given the massive amounts of electronic data litigants access regularly, a new genre of software has emerged, called Early Case Assessment software. This software allows an attorney faced with a massive amount of electronic data from the attorney's client to review that data from a 10,000 foot level. This helps to minimize the time (and therefore the expense) required to conduct this early document review. Moreover, the more culling and filtering you can do up front, before beginning an analysis of what data (evidence) to produce, the more money you will save your clients and the more accurate and responsive your document productions will be.

There is no shortage of consulting firms that sell this technology and assist attorneys in its implementation. Try doing a Google search for litigation management consultants and pages of them will show up! If you are faced with a document-heavy case, do your research and find a product that best meets your particular needs and budget.

D. CONTROL AND BATES NUMBERING

Bates numbering is old-school—it has been around for over 100 years. But it is a useful tool when dealing with large numbers of documents. Bates numbering is a means by which every page of every document produced in discovery (or identified on a privilege log) is uniquely identified. Such numbering is essential to case management of any case of significant size.

Control numbering is similar to Bates numbering in that each and every document that is produced, received or withheld is identifiable within a discovery software system. It may or may not track with Bates numbers,

---

[4]   These advanced functions are well beyond the scope of this chapter. Suffice it to say that as litigation counsel, you should become familiar with these powerful tools in order to leverage your ability to thoroughly plumb large-scale discovery.

but now we are getting a bit too far into the weeds. Say you have 10,000 pages of documents from each of 10 sources, all in ESI form. Each of those 100,000 pages needs a unique identifier in order for the user to be able to (1) conduct a computerized search for any of those documents by a given number, and (2) to determine the source of the documents.

Regardless of how your firm internally manages its document identification, it is best to agree upon a control or Bates numbering rubric during the Rule 26(f) meet and confer process. Failure to do so can lead to a lot of confusion.

Often, the sequencing contains prefixes that identify the party from which the documents originated. Following the prefixes are sequential numbers. For example, plaintiff Acme Company might Bates stamp its document production beginning with number ACM000001, while defendant ZYX Corp. might begin its documents with number ZYX000001. Every subsequent page of every document is stamped or otherwise marked with a unique, sequential control or Bates number.

In addition to internal management of the evidence, the benefits of using a control or Bates numbering system to uniquely identify every page of every document identified in discovery is that it:

- Assists counsel with making a clear record of which specific pages of which specific documents are being referred to in depositions, motions, and at trial; and

- Ensures that the documents produced in discovery are retained in their proper sequence, that is, no pages from a given document are missing or have been added to.

E. CONCLUSION

As ESI and other forms of electronic data become even more ubiquitous, and as litigation itself becomes even more highly dependent upon computers, lawyers must use existing and emerging technologies to aid their legal practices.

This chapter touched on a few of the types of litigation technology currently available. There is more out there, such as predictive coding, optical character recognition (OCR), and bar coding of trial documents for rapid display of digitized images on monitors. The point is this: litigation counsel must keep abreast of these existing and emerging technologies in order to advance the client's interests in the most effective ways possible.

CHAPTER 15

USING THE DISCOVERY RECORD FOR DISPOSITIVE MOTIONS, PRETRIAL MOTIONS AND AT TRIAL

■ ■ ■

The close of discovery brings the case to a critical juncture. At this point, the parties should have a complete record upon which a number of decisions may be made and actions taken, including:

- Evaluating the case for settlement purposes and engaging in settlement discussions;

- Winnowing claims and defenses not supported by the evidence;

- Refining the theory of the case;

- Preparing dispositive motions;

- Preparing pretrial evidentiary motions (motions in limine); and

- Preparing for trial.

We discussed early on that one function of pretrial litigation is to evaluate risks associated with going to trial. By the close of discovery the parties should have gathered sufficient information to conduct a well-informed evaluation of the merits of their own case as well as the strengths and weaknesses in the opposing party's case. Your job at this point is to objectively analyze the case and advise the client regarding the possibility and range of a reasonable settlement.

A related goal of discovery is to narrow issues. The close of discovery presents counsel with the opportunity to assess the merits of the various claims and defenses. Those not supported by the evidence should either be voluntarily dismissed or made the subject of a summary judgment motion. Clearing out non-meritorious claims and defenses is invariably a priority of the court[1]—and a priority that counsel is wise to pay attention to—as it facilitates both settlement negotiations and a more efficient trial.

---

[1] *See* FED. R. CIV. P. 16(c)(2)(A) (a court may consider and take action to simplify issues and eliminate frivolous claims).

As you narrow the issues and engage in settlement negotiations, you also should be refining your theory of the case. Should settlement efforts fail, then the case will be resolved by way of dispositive motions or a trial will take place. Oftentimes, you must simultaneously prepare for both.

A. REVIEW THE RECORD: WHAT'S THERE; WHAT ISN'T

Throughout the course of the litigation, you should have methodically gathered and created admissible evidence that advances your theory of the case. Each element of each cause of action or affirmative defense must be supported by admissible evidence in order to avoid summary judgment[2] before trial or a motion for judgment as a matter of law during trial.[3]

On the other side of the coin, you also should have used the discovery process to reveal all of the opposing party's evidence. To the extent you have documented gaps in the evidentiary record, you may attack the opposing party's case with a dispositive motion (recall: the absence of a fact is a fact). If you have been diligent about mapping the evidence through the course of the litigation, your attack will be easier to orchestrate. As you review the record, keep the following questions in mind:

1. What *admissible* evidence is in the record to support the elements of the various claims and defenses, and what are the strengths and weaknesses of that evidence?

2. What *gaps* in the record exist, i.e., to what extent is there an *absence* of evidence necessary to support a given element of a claim or defense?

3. Where is there agreement between the parties on material facts?

Following this review, you should be able to determine which claims are viable, which are not, and which may be amenable to summary judgment. If, for example, the plaintiff has alleged three causes of action, but the third is not supported by the record or is so weak as to detract from the stronger claims, the plaintiff may make the tactical decision to dismiss the claim and focus all its energy on the stronger claims. Likewise, if the defendant asserted a multitude of affirmative defenses out of an abundance of caution, once the discovery record is complete, the defendant would be wise to advance only those defenses that are viable.

While you conduct your review of the record, you should be mindful of your theory of the case. If the evidentiary record demands it, be prepared to refine or otherwise adapt the theory of the case to the record as it exists,

---

[2] FED. R. CIV. P. 56(c)(2).

[3] *See generally id.* 50.

as opposed to what you had hoped it would be. Once you have done this, you will be in a position to make decisions about:

- Making or defending against dispositive motions;

- Preparing motions in limine and proposed evidentiary stipulations;

- Preparing outlines of your opening statement, closing argument, and witness testimony; and

- Outlining the order of proof at trial (including identifying witnesses and their specific testimony, as well as exhibits and the foundation necessary to get them into evidence).

B. DISPOSITIVE MOTIONS

Rule 56 provides litigants the pretrial possibility of prevailing on part or all of the issues in the pending case. When the record contains no material facts in dispute as to a given claim, defense, or part thereof, the court may rule as a matter of law. In order to maximize the chances of prevailing on summary judgment, a complete and clear record upon which the motion must be based is essential.

A party may file a summary judgment motion anytime during the proceedings, up until 30 days after the close of discovery.[4] That post-discovery time gives an attorney the opportunity to draft the motion papers and gather from the full discovery record the evidence necessary to support the motion. This gathering process is important, as you must prove to the court that there are no material facts in dispute if you represent the moving party, and you must prove the existence of disputed facts if you represent the opposing party.

The only "facts" you may rely on in support of or opposition to a summary judgment motion are facts for which you have admissible evidence.[5] Attorneys regularly use affidavits to present facts in support of or opposition to summary judgment motions, but remember that facts set out in a summary judgment affidavit must be facts that would be admissible at trial.[6]

Although many attorneys regularly wait until the close of discovery to move for full or partial summary judgment, if you can meet the summary judgment burden earlier in the pretrial process, you can save your client time, money, and aggravation by filing early. If you are on the receiving end of an early summary judgment motion, and if you need additional

---

[4]   FED R. CIV. P. 56(b). Local rules or the court's Rule 16 scheduling order may modify the timing of dispositive motions.

[5]   *See* FED. R. CIV. P. 56(c)(2); *see also id.* 56(c)(1)(B).

[6]   *See id.* 56(c)(4).

discovery in order to properly respond, you may ask the court to defer or deny the motion.[7] Be careful, however. A bald assertion that the motion is premature will not suffice. You must support your assertion with an affidavit or declaration containing specific reasons why facts necessary to oppose the motion are not yet available.[8]

At risk of stating the obvious, it is seldom that success in bringing or defending against summary judgment is the result of happenstance. You must plan for the eventuality of a summary judgment motion. This is one of the benefits of maintaining an evidentiary map: to continuously track the development of both the client's case as well as the adverse party's case in anticipation of dispositive motions.

C. THE USE OF RULE 37 TO PREVENT "SANDBAGGING" AND "SHAM" AFFIDAVITS

A party may not sandbag the opposing party with evidence. That is, a party may not withhold evidence that should have been disclosed in discovery, then present it for the first time in response to a dispositive motion or at trial. For example, if the plaintiff claims emotional harm but fails throughout the course of discovery to produce supporting evidence or identify supporting witnesses, you have demonstrated an *absence of evidence*, and may move for summary judgment on that claim. If, in response, plaintiff's counsel submits an affidavit signed by plaintiff setting forth the nature and cause of the alleged emotional harm, you should object. Rule 37 prohibits precisely this type of trial by ambush. If a party fails to disclose information as required by Rule 26(a) or (e), the party waives its right to use that information.[9] Although the court may excuse the non-disclosure if it is substantially justified or is harmless, if the withheld evidence will have an unfairly prejudicial effect upon the movant, the court should not permit its admission.[10]

Similarly, developing a complete discovery record will have the effect of preventing the use of "sham" affidavits. A sham affidavit is one that ostensibly creates a question of material fact by contradicting the offering party's own prior discovery responses.[11] The logic of this rule should be clear: "If a party who has been examined at length on deposition could raise an issue of fact simply by submitting an affidavit contradicting his own

---

[7]   *See id.* 56(d).

[8]   *See id.*

[9]   *Id.* 37(c)(1); *see also* Am. Stock Exch., LLC v. Mopex, Inc., 215 F.R.D. 87, 93 (S.D.N.Y. 2002).

[10]   Am. Stock Exch., LLC v. Mopex, Inc., 215 F.R.D. 87, 93 (S.D.N.Y. 2002).

[11]   *See, e.g.,* Velez v. City of Chicago, 442 F.3d 1043, 1049 (7th Cir. 2006).

prior testimony, this would greatly diminish the utility of summary judgment as a procedure for screening out sham issues of fact."[12]

In sum, the more thorough the discovery record, the greater the likelihood that the court will apply the strictures of Rule 37 and disregard post-discovery-cut-off revelations.

D. EVIDENTIARY STIPULATIONS, MOTIONS IN LIMINE, AND TRIAL BRIEFS

Trial judges do not like it when litigants waste time over evidentiary issues that can and should be resolved before trial. Further, there is nothing more boring (and irritating) to a jury than having to sit through a trial that moves at a glacial pace because counsel continuously argue over the admissibility of the evidence.

Rule 16(c)(2)(C) authorizes the court to encourage the litigants to "obtain [ ] admissions and stipulations about facts and documents to avoid unnecessary proof, and ruling in advance on the admissibility of evidence." Further, Rule 16(c)(2)(G) authorizes the court to require the parties to exchange witness and exhibit lists as well as pretrial briefs. These rules are intended to simplify trials and resolve evidentiary disputes beforehand.

1. STIPULATIONS/WITNESS AND EXHIBIT LISTS

Entering into evidentiary stipulations is one of the most practical and efficient ways of using the discovery record. By the close of discovery, you should have a pretty good idea of which witnesses possess foundation to testify to certain subjects, and which exhibits are what they are purported to be. Evidentiary stipulations allow trials to proceed more efficiently by avoiding on-the-record proof of foundation when foundation is not in dispute.

There are many kinds of evidentiary stipulations, but they tend to fall into three categories:

1. The witness or physical evidence possesses sufficient foundation (e.g., the document is authentic), but counsel reserves the right to object on other grounds, such as relevance;

2. In addition to stipulating to foundation, the parties may stipulate that the proof shall be received in evidence;

3. Illustrative exhibits, which are in aid to testimony, may be used without objection during the trial (including during opening statements).

---

[12] Perma Research & Dev. Co. v. Singer Co., 410 F.2d 572, 578 (2nd Cir. 1969).

It is best to document evidentiary stipulations and submit them to the court in advance of trial. Oftentimes, parties do this through their trial briefs; other times, by separate pleadings.

Similarly, courts usually require the parties to serve and file witness and exhibit lists. Though the parties may have identified any number of potential witnesses during the course of discovery, as well as produced innumerable documents, the court will want to know who each party actually intends to call as a witness at trial and which documents or other physical evidence the parties actually anticipate they will be offering into evidence. This not only assists the court with trial management matters, but it also alerts the litigants to that evidence the opposing party anticipates offering at trial, thus focusing counsels' trial preparation.

2. MOTIONS IN LIMINE

If you have evidentiary issues that you would like resolved before trial or for which briefing may be helpful, you may use a motion in limine. You also may use a motion in limine to seek exclusion of evidence or witnesses not properly or timely disclosed.[13] This is an efficient way to point out to the court evidentiary problems with the opposing party's case.

Even if the court denies your motion, or reserves ruling on it until it comes up at trial, the motion affords you a way to educate the judge about the issue and may make it easier to argue the matter during the trial.

3. TRIAL BRIEFS

Some judges like detailed trial briefs, others want little more than a listing of key issues and a brief summary of the applicable law. Sometimes the court wishes to receive an evidentiary summary of the case in the trial brief. If you are not sure what form the judge prefers, then ask.

Regardless of the specific components required by the court, you also should use the trial brief as an opportunity to articulate your theory of the case. If the court understands how you intend to try your case, it will more easily understand how a given proffer of evidence supports your overall theory of the case, in other words, how it is relevant to your case. Oftentimes, the first question a judge will ask in relation to an evidentiary dispute is, "Counsel, how is this relevant to the claim or defense?" If you outline your theory of the case in the trial brief, the relevance will be easier to see.

E. *DAUBERT* HEARINGS

When one party seeks to use expert testimony that the opposing party seeks to block or limit, the court may hold a preliminary hearing to

---

[13] *See* FED. R. CIV. P. 37.

determine in advance of trial the admissibility or contours of the expert's testimony.[14] This hearing, during which the court determines the preliminary question of whether a witness proffered as an expert may provide an opinion at trial, is called a *Daubert* hearing,[15]

A full vetting of the expert witness, through close analysis of the expert's report and through deposition, may lead to an order partially or fully excluding that expert's testimony. Counsel who succeeds with a *Daubert* challenge often has inflicted irreparable harm to the opposing party's case, and in some instances, will deprive the adverse party the ability to proceed with trial.

F. USING THE DISCOVERY RECORD TO PREPARE FOR TRIAL

A discussion of the nuts and bolts of trial preparation would go far beyond the scope of this book. That said, and to provide context for your pre-trial case development efforts, following is a cursory overview of how to use your discovery record to prepare for trial. It should be obvious that the more thorough, methodical, and "planful" your pre-trial preparations, the better you will be positioned to most efficiently and effectively prepare for the trial itself.

1. PREPARING FOR OPENING STATEMENTS AND CLOSING ARGUMENTS

Opening statements are supposed to apprise the jury of what the case is about, and what evidence will be presented in order to prove it. Closing argument is essentially the theory of the case, i.e., a merger of the law and the facts woven into a compelling narrative. Both are reliant on the case you have developed and the discovery record you have created. By the time you begin outlining your opening statement and closing argument, you should have completed your review of the discovery record and your evidence map should be completed as well. Through this process, you should have refined your theory of the case and narrowed your issues to those you actually intend to try.

Indeed, opening statements and closing arguments are the alter egos of your theory of the case and case development. When you present your opening statement, telling the jury that "The evidence will show . . .," you will be relying on the discovery record you have created. Similarly, closing

[14] See Rule of Evidence 104(a), which states in part, "The court must decide any preliminary question about whether a witness is qualified, a privilege exists, or evidence is admissible."

[15] The name derives from Daubert v. Merrell Dow Pharm., Inc., 509 U.S. 579 (1993). For more on *Daubert* hearings and how courts should determine the admissibility of expert testimony, see Chapter 9. *See also* Kumho Tire Co. v. Carmichael, 526 U.S. 137 (1999); Gen. Elec. Co. v. Joiner, 522 U.S. 136 (1997); Daubert v. Merrell Dow Pharm., Inc., 509 U.S. 579 (1993); as well as cases in your jurisdiction.

argument will be dependent upon the evidence presented at trial—evidence that was developed through the discovery process.

2.   OUTLINING THE ORDER OF PROOF

Once the opening statement and closing argument have been outlined, you should turn your attention to the order of proof, that is, the sequence of witnesses, exhibits and other evidence that will be presented at trial. Preparing an order of proof outline makes trial preparation a lot easier. It is highly dependent upon the body of evidence you have developed through discovery and requires that you think through *how* you will get your proof into evidence. To the extent you have created an evidence map, the map will help guide you in determining the evidence you need at trial and in what order.

3.   PREPARING DIRECT AND CROSS-EXAMINATION OUTLINES

Once you have outlined your case (opening statement, order of proof and closing argument), you can then drill down further by preparing witness examination outlines. Whether preparing outlines for friendly, neutral or hostile witnesses, it is essential to work from the discovery record in order to determine which witnesses can advance which elements of the claims or defenses. Similarly, it is important to draw from the discovery record evidence that can be used to effectively impeach, discredit or neutralize adverse witnesses.

As you review your evidence map, you can identify which witnesses you will need to call in your case-in-chief and the substance of their testimony. From there, you can outline witness testimony with confidence that you have covered what you need to cover in order to establish a record that supports your theory of the case.

G.   USING THE DISCOVERY RECORD AT TRIAL

The discovery record may be used at trial in a variety of ways and for a variety of purposes. We will not go into great detail about using the discovery record at trial, but will provide a brief overview.

1.   TO OFFER PARTY ADMISSIONS

Statements and representations made by parties through the course of discovery will be treated as party admissions. To the extent the admissions are relevant and do not otherwise contravene the Rules of Evidence, they may be offered at trial against the adverse party. Examples of party admissions that may be pulled from the discovery record and offered at trial include:

- A party's deposition testimony;
- Interrogatory responses and responses to requests for admissions;
- Documents either created or adopted by the adverse party.

2. FOR IMPEACHMENT PURPOSES

One of the most effective ways to impeach the credibility of a witness is by establishing that the witness has made inconsistent statements regarding a given matter. Through the course of discovery witnesses will make any number of statements, either written or testimonial. To the extent the witness testifies at trial in a manner inconsistent with his discovery responses, such responses can be used to impeach the witness.

Sometimes an adverse witness conveniently "forgets" things, particularly if it hurts his case or undermines his credibility. When this happens you may use the adverse witness's deposition testimony (or other documents) to keep him honest, or to show that he is not worthy of belief.

3. TO REFRESH RECOLLECTION

At times, your witnesses may have difficulty recalling events while on the stand. Even during direct examination, a friendly witness may go blank, or freeze up from a case of nerves. When that happens, consistent with Federal Rule of Evidence 612, you may inquire of the witness whether anything, such as his deposition testimony, or any other writing, would help "refresh" his recollection.

4. WHEN THE WITNESS IS UNAVAILABLE

Rules 27 and 32(a)(4) allow for the presentation at trial a witness's deposition testimony if the witness is determined to be unavailable. The deposition may be used for any purpose allowed by the Rules of Evidence. In other words, to the extent deposition testimony is offered at trial, it must be in the form of *admissible* evidence.

Objections to designated deposition testimony, as well as testimony that may be additionally designated by opposing counsel, should be dealt with before trial, preferably through a "meet and confer" process. Once designated testimony is either agreed to between the parties, or ruled upon by the court, it can then be presented to the fact finder.

H. TO SUM UP. . .

After the close of discovery, and at the stage of the litigation where dispositive motions are brought and/or trial preparation begins, there should be very little about the case that you do not know. All of the salient evidence should have been disclosed or discovered by this point. Therefore, much of the evidence you will rely upon will come from the discovery record.

Your theory of the case should have informed your case development plan, which in turn should have informed your discovery plan. Hopefully, successful execution of the plan yields the admissible evidence you need (or the establishment of the adverse party's lack of evidence) to support your case and to undermine the opposing party's case.

It begins with careful case planning. Hopefully, it ends with a successful outcome.

APPENDIX

■ ■ ■

Go to:

http://www.roencivillitigation.com

Username: Student

Password: Litigator

CASE PROBLEMS

■ ■ ■

Go to:

http://www.roencivillitigation.com

Username: Student

Password: Litigator

INDEX

References are to Pages